Through Some Eventful Years

THE BRADFORD COAT OF ARMS

THROUGH SOME EVENTFUL YEARS

BY SUSAN BRADFORD EPPES

(MRS. NICHOLAS WARE EPPES)

AUTHOR OF "THE NEGRO OF THE OLD SOUTH"

TALLAHASSEE, FLORIDA

*"Oh, wad some power
The giftie gie us,
To see oursel's
As ithers see us."*

PRESS OF
THE J. W. BURKE COMPANY
MACON, GEORGIA
1926

TABLE OF CONTENTS

ILLUSTRATIONS

THROUGH SOME EVENTFUL YEARS

PART I

Table of Contents—Continued

THE YEARS OF RECONSTRUCTION

PART II

DEDICATION

TO MY DEAR CHILDREN, WHO HAVE BEEN A JOY
AND A PLEASURE TO ME EVER SINCE THEY FIRST
OPENED THEIR EYES TO THE LIGHT; WHO
HAVE BEEN MY CONSTANT COMPANIONS
THROUGH THE PASSING YEARS, WHICH
HAVE KNOWN MANY CHANGES
AND ARE NOW MY TENDER
GUIDES AS I TRAVEL THE
WESTERN SLOPE, WHICH
LEADS TO HOME

TO THESE DEAR CHILDREN THIS BOOK IS
LOVINGLY DEDICATED

By

THEIR ADORING MOTHER

INTRODUCTION

To those who have read "The Negro of the Old South" this book needs no introduction and no apology. It really seems to be needed, the one to complete the other. To those who have not, we wish to say a few words.

The white people and the negroes of the Old South were so intimately associated that it is impossible to tell the story of the one without a large mixture of the other.

In these days, when it is quite the fashion to rail against "The Free Negroes," we, of the Old South, to whom many of them are still dear, take but little part in this. Sentiment is strong in the Southern heart and we cannot forget their faithful service in the days, or the years of war, when, but for them, our women and children, our men in camp and on the field of battle, would have starved and suffered. Ungrateful would we be if we put a ban on the entire race because some have proved themselves unworthy. In these pages we have adhered as strictly to the truth as in our former narrative—we deal not in fiction—all is fact.

Life is a mixture of sorrow and joy,
There is no bliss without alloy,
There's never a rose without its thorn,
No mortal has yet to perfection been born;
But the dear OLD FOLKS are morally sure
That all was perfect in DAYS OF YORE.

THROUGH SOME EVENTFUL YEARS

PART I

CHAPTER I

THE SOCIAL LIFE OF THE OLD SOUTH

IN the middle of the last century the South had reached the zenith of prosperity and power. Except in almost inaccessible mountain regions, or on some desolate coast plains, there was none who was poverty-stricken, or so few that they escaped mention and were so well provided for by their wealthy neighbors that they were poverty-stricken in name only.

There was a certain class in the south, corresponding to the yeomanry of England and no doubt descended from them, that occupied a position peculiarly its own. Respected by the class above them and treated with all consideration, they still did not stand on an equal social footing. They were possessed of many desirable qualities, of good habits and, for the most part, they were strictly religious and true to family ties. Occasionally one of these men could be induced to take over the management of a plantation for some wealthier neighbor and the planter, who was so fortunate as to secure the services of such a one was the envy of his contemporaries. But by far the greater part of the South was composed of men of wealth and often of distinction as well. With abundant means and leisure for study, the men and women of the Old South stood unequalled in education, accomplishments, and mental ability. Added to this they had a graciousness of manner and that true politeness, which is so sweetly expressed in a little couplet often taught to children in the primary grades,

> "Politeness is to do and say
> The kindest things, in the kindest way."

Here was a good material for Social Life, where, "In honor preferring one another," is the oil which makes the wheels go round.

The hospitality of the Old South is far-famed; and yet, there is a reason for this, which we have never heard mentioned. The original settlers of our country were not so very dissimilar. To our mind the later difference in characteristics was caused by differing circumstances. Those who settled in bleak New England suffered many hardships, and not the least among these hardships was an actual scarcity of food and this condition lasted for many years. Even when a modicum of prosperity was theirs, it was not so great that they could afford to "take no thought for the morrow." It is very difficult to be hospitable when the where-with-all is lacking, as it was, without doubt, in these early days. This close care for daily expenditures became a deepseated habit, and we know that habit becomes second nature.

In the South it was different; the climate was mild, vegetation was quick to come and it also came in great abundance; fruits ripened on every side; birds and flowers filled the soul with joy, even in the midst of the hardships, which in one way or another, came to all new settlers in the New World.

Was it any wonder that these settlers in the favored Southland held out a generous hand to all? Their very hardships and discomforts made them the more ready to help others. Lonely at times themselves, they opened their homes to others, who also knew the pangs of homesickness and longing—"the more the merrier." So it came about that crowds collected and were made welcome. Such, to our mind, was the way in which the lavish hospitality of the South was acquired. However that may be, it certainly was the case that in the mid-century days of which we write, there was nowhere on earth such a social structure as the cultured men and women of the Old South had built up.

On every plantation stood a Mansion of many rooms and comfortable furnishings, and besides this, small houses, of one or two or three rooms, were provided for the overflow from the Mansion House. Large stables and carriage houses there were also, and extra room in the "negro quarter," for the coachmen and servants of the visitors, for this was an era of "House Parties." With colored servitors, enough for every demand, with horses for both pleasure and service, and with all the luxuries of life easily obtainable, it was but little trouble to the "Lady of the Manor" to have her house full of guests and to entertain them royally.

So it came about that company came in crowds; they came mostly in carriages, they brought with them their maids and men, usually in a baggage wagon, along with all the necessary belongings of the visitors. Company in the Mansion also meant company in the Quarter, and place and food to be provided for the horses as well. Think of it!—You, who, in these latter days, groan over the thought of "company to stay."

Often these visitors were relatives, sometimes dear friends, but occasionally they were barely acquaintances, who presumed upon the well-known hospitality to make for themselves a good time without expense.

The weeks preceding and following Christmas were a round of gaiety, a party somewhere every night, and dinings were equally popular. The Old South excelled in horsemanship, and equestrian parties were an every-day sight, along the beautiful and romantic drives and bridle paths of this God-favored land. We give you a little poem which tells of a Florida Christmas of long ago:

CHRISTMAS EVE AT PINE HILL PLANTATION

Memory is a kindly friend,
  She brings us back the vanished hours,
When Time, the thief, would have us think,
  His footsteps only trod on flowers.
'Tis Christmas Eve, young hearts are gay,
  The windows glow with mellow light,
Vines twine about the polished stair
  And everywhere are roses bright.

Holly boughs, with berries red,
  Upon the walls are seen,
With the tiny, shiny Yupon, like
  Rubies 'mid the green.
Mistletoe, with berries white,
  Hangs high in the grand old hall
And the flame of many candles
  Casts a beautiful light o'er all.

To linger 'neath the mistletoe
  No youth nor maid would dare,
For Aunt Robinson watches the young folks
  From a seat on the vine-wreathed stair.
The double doors are open wide,
  Guests come crowding through the gates,
Inside, the fires burn brightly
  In the fine old brass-trimmed grates.

Mother's music fills the air,
  Perfect in time and measure,
The floors are cleared and everything
  Awaits the dancer's pleasure;
The boys all seek their partners
  When the rhythmic sounds they hear,
Each couple turn with one accord
  And dance to the tune of "The Forked Deer."

Both "North" and "South Carolina"
  Are danced with Christmas glee,
Then "Molly, Put the Kettle on
  And We'll All Take Tea;"
"Fisher's Hornpipe" speeds our steps,
  Which makes it very handy
To execute some brilliant stunts
  For "Yankee Doodle Dandy."

Then come quadrilles, as stately
  As Grandmother's minuet;
Next, like a crowd of children,
  We merrily dance the "Coquette."
Tired, we stop for supper—
  So many good things to eat—
But time is short, and most of us find
  We have little wings on our feet.

Waltzing is not in favor here,
  Yet a venturesome lad and lassie,
Are circling smoothly around the room,
  To the strains of "Tallahassee."
Mother's fingers again touch the keys,
  "Sir Roger de Coverley" rules the hour
Young and old stand up on the floor,
  Moved by the music's compelling power;
For who of us all fatigue could feel
  When Mother played the "Virginia Reel?"

  The dance is over—goodnights are said—
  Put out the lights and go to bed;
  'Tis time for Santa Claus' reindeer sled;
  'Twill soon be Christmas Morning.

With Christmas Morning came the Christmas Tree. On this tree were gifts for everyone beneath the roof-tree of the old home; generally gifts of money value, as well as tokens of friendship and love.

Sometimes sorrow came to one of these luxurious homes, for grief is no respecter of persons. In these trying hours there were no gay crowds, no feasting—

this would have been mockery—but quietly came kind, sympathetic friends, and nothing that the hand of love could do was lacking. If the shadow of death rested on one of these homes love, which never wearied, did all that was possible to comfort and console.

The social life of the South was not entirely within the home; every summer preparations began early in the season for a general flitting to "The Springs" or perhaps instead of the springs, it was the sea-side. In either case the getting ready was a work of time. Orders were sent to New York, dressmakers were called in, the home-seamstresses were put to work and such studying of styles from Godey's Ladies' Book. Trying on, careful fitting, the tucks, the frills, the shirrings, flowers appliqued on silken robes, the finest of lace-trimmed lingerie, and real lace at that, for an imitation in lace or jewels was not permissible.

After weeks of this strenuous toil, trunks were packed by maids, who were as proud of the fine clothes contained therein as if they, instead of the mistress, were to wear them. When there were children in the family this work was greatly increased, for "Mammy" never willingly allowed her "Chile" to be out-dressed by anyone's else. "A vain people, these Southerners," you say?—Well, perhaps so.

Mammy and the maids had their preparations to make, too; for they must be the very pink of neatness to be around their "white folks." A beautiful sight all this made, when the resort was at last reached. The youths and maidens, vivacious and bright, their native beauty set off by the becoming costumes; the fathers of families, dressed in the unique styles of the day, high collars, with many folds of the finest white lawn, skilfully arranged about the neck, the elaborate shirt front, the neat fitting suit of French broadcloth, the best procurable, turned-sole boots, which shone like unto a mirror; to crown all this, a high, silk beaver hat. The mothers, handsomely gowned in materials suited to their complexion and position, gracious, cordial, with a sweet dignity, and yet, withal a little anxious. The grandfathers, white-haired and stately, dressed stylishly, of course, but showing a slightly greater desire for comfort as well, for their clothes of handsomest material, do not fit quite so closely, the boots, just as shiney but easier pattern. Courtly they were and given to complimentary speeches. They liked to dance too, did these gray-haired Cavaliers, and many a flattering whisper was breathed into girlish ears, as they threaded the mazes of the dance. Sweet, harmless flattery, meaning nothing save the tribute of age to lovely youth.

And the grandmothers! We must pause for a fresh supply of words, words which are adequate to describe their charm and grace. Gowned in the handsomest of materials, with priceless lace draped about their shoulders, a cap of this same lace crowning their snowy tresses, while diamonds shone resplendent, wherever good taste allowed a diamond to shine. How sweet their voices, how winning their ways, how they beamed upon the young folks, who, in turn, smiled back at them and softened to confidence under the kindly influence Keen eyes too, these grandmothers had, for nowhere in all the world was there ever a stricter chaperonage than the Old South demanded and at "The Springs" temptation was great. There were drives through forest roads; there were horse-back rides, where one could speed up or loiter as the case required; there were long walks through shady lanes and, in the intervals of the dance, there were short strolls in the cool of evening, or they sat on the broad piazzas, while the Southern Moon looked down on happy lovers.

Like the hummingbird, flitting from flower to flower, these pleasure-seekers were not stationary, but all content one day, the next would find them preparing to depart. Someone had been telling of the delights of the White Sulphur this summer, or a party coming in from the sea-side would tempt them to the surf and rolling tide. So, Amy would collect the various belongings, Malinda would pack the trunks, Godfrey would bring the carriage to the door and another merry crowd would take the road for "green fields and pastures new," while Starling followed on with the proverbial "Big box, little box, bandbox and bundle," conveyed in a vehicle called, in those days, "A Democrat." This was nothing more nor less than a high spring wagon, roomy and comfortable and drawn by a pair of sturdy horses. Through Virginia, North Carolina, South Carolina, Georgia and Tennessee these travelers, or such as these, were a common sight during the Summer months.

Then, with the first warning of coming Winter they would turn their faces homeward again, just as anxious to get back as they had been to leave home. Back to the plantations to make ready for the festivities of the winter season, to get the children back to their studies, to enjoy, once more, the comforts of home. For they returned to homes which were kept in beautiful order during the absence of the owners, spotlessly clean, luxuriously comfortable, and were welcomed by smiling black faces and willing hands. These relieved the home-comers of every care, even removing the wraps and bonnets, as their "white folks" sank into easy chairs and listened with rapt attention to the happenings, while they were away. Memory calls up Mammy's tender touches as she divested us of travelling apparel, bathed us gently and laid us in our little bed in all its gleaming whiteness. Nothing like that, where we had been, and surely nothing like the goodnight hug Mammy gave us ere she blew out the light.

Oh, for "the days that are no more." Many and varied were the amusements of the next few months. In the early Spring there was always a tournament, followed at night by a Fancy Ball, where the successful knight, who had taken the greatest number of rings, crowned his chosen ladye faire the Queen of Love and Beauty. Would that I had an enchanted pen from fairyland, instead of this prosaic typewriter, that I might do justice to this most charming of all entertainments.

Riding out from Tallahassee, along the Thomasville Road, look to your right, where you will see a rather unusual valley with a high hill on either side. We say a rather unusual valley because it lies in a straight, unbroken stretch for quite a distance. In days gone by, these two hills were crowned by lovely woods; at the time the tournament took place the dogwood was in bloom and so numerous were these beautiful trees that the hills seemed covered with a lacy veil. Yellow jasmine gave a touch of gold and the turf beneath was white with the delicate houstonia.

Southern men were said to be "born horsemen," if they were not so born they lost no time in learning, and every Southern boy rode fearlessly and gracefully. Every gentleman owned a riding horse and great was his pride in his favorite. Petted and loved, horse and rider were almost as one and, when these well-trained men and horses appeared upon the tournament field, it was a grand sight. Each one selected some character to personate and each knight wore his ladye's colors. The characters were well-chosen; the costumes handsome and tasteful; both horses and riders were beautifully decorated.

Upon an open space next to Tallahassee, on a height which commanded a view of the entire length of this valley, carriages and other equipages of every description, filled by an eager, excited throng, collected; far down the valley an arch had been constructed and, suspended from it, was a small ivory ring; on the right hand was the judges' stand, where six judges sat in state. Far up the wooded slope on the right, hidden by the thick woods, stood the knights on their impatient steeds, reined in, awaiting the sound of the bugle and the loud voice of the Herald, as he shouts out the name of each knight. The crowd, too, is growing restless, when suddenly the clear notes of the bugle call all to attention, "The Knight of the Lone Star," shouts the Herald, and the knight comes forth, on a milk-white horse, clad from head to foot in gleaming white satin, with a large star blazing upon his breast. The blonde wearer is conscious that he is looking his best—no touch of anything but this dazzling whiteness except a bouquet of violets on his left lapel, his Ladye's Colors, his guerdon. Like a flash he rides down the valley, his lance poised and he bears off the ring, amid the clapping and shouting of the excited multitude. Proudly he rides down the course and draws rein before the judges' stand, presenting the ring on the point of his lance. And so the first score is made.

Again the bugle sounds, "Knight of the Sun, Moon and Stars," calls the Herald. Dashing down the hillside he comes and, if the beautiful severity of the first knight had called forth admiration, all thought of him is lost in the amusement afforded by this astounding figure. On his head the sun shines brightly, on his broad back is a moon, which is evidently full, and stars of every size and all degrees of brilliancy are plentifully sprinkled. With poised lance he dashes forward through the arch; but alas—the ring still hangs undisturbed. With bowed head he rides slowly up to the stand and another score was made. Many jests are made at his expense, one of the spectators asking if "the sun had suffered an eclipse?"

The winding notes of the Bugle—"Robert Bruce,"

shouts the Herald, and Robert Bruce, a veritable Scot in the plaid of his house, dashes into view, lance drawn, and bears off the ring in triumph.

"The Unknown Knight," shouts the Herald, and from the wooded depths flashes forth a most imposing figure. A large horse of midnight darkness, his flanks shining like satin. A splendidly proportioned figure, clad in gleaming armor sits on this magnificent charger; his cap is on, his visor down; every minute detail has been carried out. The Unknown Knight has spared neither time, thought, nor money on his disguise. We, who loved the history of the Middle Ages, look on entranced; on every tongue is the question, "Who can it be?" He rides like the wind. He has been planning this for weeks, but now, alas, he is to find that even one confidant is oftentimes one too many. His mother is the only sharer of his secret as she sits beside the Princess Murat in her landau. Losing her self-possession in the excitement of the moment, she stands upon the seat of the landau and screamed, at the top of her voice, "It's Phil—just Phil—nobody but Phil." We are all sorry for him, to have his dream so rudely dispelled.

There were many more contestants, but we will mention only one. After several others had shown their skill the Herald called "The Knight of the Mist." Slowly he came forth from the lacy boughs of the dogwood; he did not take the beaten path—once in the open he drew rein as if to give to all an opportunity to take in the significance of his dress. The horse he rode was a dapple-gray, slender and graceful, as beautiful in form as if he had come direct from "Araby the Blest," his rider wore a costume of gray velvet; the gray of the clouds we sometimes see at evening by the sea-shore, when water and cloud are almost indistinguishable on the sky-line. A soft felt hat of the same hue was caught up at the side with a silver buckle. Wreathed about him in graceful lines was yard after yard of gray tulle, giving the impression of wreaths of mist rising in the sunshine. Just over his heart his ladye's colors appeared; a diamond ring, from which flashed rainbow lights at every motion of the rider, was fastened by a rose-colored ribbon.

Doffing his hat to the assembled multitude, he puts spurs to his horse and fairly flew through the long valley to the arch, and bore away the ring.

This ended the first round, each knight had three chances. Again the bugle's call and the Herald's voice summoned the young chivalry of Florida to prove the claim each one had made for his "Ladye Faire." Again the Misty Knight carried off the honors. The third round was called, Robert Bruce and the Knight in Gray each had taken the ring every time—it was a tie. Once again the clear notes of the bugle called the knights to combat—this time only two took part—two rings were hung within the huge arch and "Robert Bruce of Scotland" and the "Knight of the Mist" came riding furiously abreast, with lances couched and faces set. On they came—excitement had reached its height, which one will win? Alas! for the Bruce had lost. He dropped out and the knight from fairyland bore the ring aloft upon his lance and rode slowly down the lines.

Again the twenty knights are lined up before the judge's stand. As they had been before the contest began that they might be instructed in the duty of a true knight. The judge who addressed them might have risen from the grave where he had "lain for centuries dead," so well did his robes correspond with the pictures of the past and so knightly was the language he used. Now they had come that he might address the victor and reward his valor. Beautifully he spoke and then came the ending, "Sir Knight, you have done valorously; into your keeping I now give this crown, place it upon the brow of your Ladye Faire, and proclaim to all the world that she, and she alone, is the Queen of Love and Beauty."

With words which would have sounded well from the lips of Sir Galahad himself, the knight received the crown and, bearing it on the tip of his lance, he rode down the lines looking closely into every carriage—cunning fellow, he knew just where she was. It was a blushing girl before whom he finally stopped. At his low-spoken words she bowed her head and he placed the crown upon her sunny tresses. An open barouch drawn by glossy bays drew near, and Sir Knight assisted his Queen to alight and seated her therein; Robert Bruce had found his maid of honor and she, too, was seated beside the Queen. The respective knights rode on either side and the others followed, riding two and two.

Oh, the cheers, the enthusiasm and then the hurrying off to complete some last little preparations for the fancy ball, held that night in the Hall of Representatives in Florida's Capitol. What this Ball was like we will leave to your imagination, but it is safe to say that the youth and beauty of old Tallahassee tripped "the light, fantastic toe" until "the wee sma' hours."

In those halcyon days there came to Tallahassee a very attractive young lady from Vermont; she came to take the position of governess in one of our most prominent families and she soon took part in all, or almost all, of the gayeties of our little town. At one of these tournaments, which were of yearly occurrence, she was crowned Queen; quite a small girl at the time, the writer remembers well the circumstances. This lady married one of Tallahassee's most noted physicians and they finally made their home in Jacksonville. Happening to be in this latter city two years ago, we bethought ourselves of this friend, whom we had not seen for forty years. She gave us a warm welcome; we talked of friends who were left to us here; we recalled those who had "gone on" and after awhile we asked if she remembered the day she was crowned Queen of Love and Beauty? Of course she remembered—what woman could forget? We talked it over and by this time we had other listeners. We told of the current issue of "The Floridian and Journal" in which a full description was given of the brilliant affairs; winding up with this paragraph: "If the boys of Vermont did as much execution with their guns as the Green Mountain girls do with their eyes, it is no wonder they have left such a record on the pages of history."

The dear old lady's eyes filled with tears, she laid her hand upon ours and whispered, "I am so glad you came, the weight of years seems to have rolled away. I feel almost young again." In a few weeks more she was brought back to Tallahassee to leave it no more forever. We shall always be glad we made that visit.

We have spoken of the strict chaperonage practised in the South; parents had leisure to look after their children, not only the little ones—to these "mammy" could attend; but the lads and lassies of a larger growth. In most families there was a middle-aged relative, usually a spinster, who, though possessed of many charms, had not seen fit to marry. To parents the aid such a relative could render was simply invaluable. In the household at Pine Hill this place was filled by "Aunt Robinson," as she was called by all the young people of the entire family connection. She had a history and it is well worth telling. She was the daughter of an English clergyman, refined, educated, accomplished and beautiful.

In the year 1811 Captain James Robinson was in command of a United States Man-of-War and for three years he had been aboard his ship and when his "ship-leave" reached him he was in Liverpool and, glad to have the opportunity of seeing something of "The

Mother Country," he stopped a while. Here he met and loved Maria Clement and they were married and life looked lovely to them.

A year later Captain Robinson was summoned to his ship, as war between the United States and England had been declared. Of course it was a hurried trip and Mrs. Robinson could not accompany him. Three months later, with her six weeks' old son, she sailed for Philadelphia to join her husband. As the ship she was on sailed into the harbor his ship was sailing out. They passed so close that she could see him distinctly and she held her baby up that he might see his little son.

Captain Robinson was killed in the first engagement and she was left alone in a strange land, homeless and almost penniless. She was told that her husband had sisters in Enfield, North Carolina; it took all she had to pay her way to them and when she got there she found that they, too, were in straitened circumstances and obliged to work hard to keep body and soul together and she took part in the daily work. One day the Governor's carriage drove up to the house. Her little boy, a strikingly handsome child, was playing around the door and the Governor's lady was pleased with him and asked some questions. His mother came out, was introduced and there and then began a friendship, which was lifelong. Arrangements were made for the aunts to take care of the child and Mrs. Robinson took the position of governess to the little girls of the Branch family.

She proved to be most satisfactory and Mrs. Bradford, the mistress of Pine Hill, was her oldest pupil. In the meantime, Mrs. Robinson had, with some assistance from friends, given her son a fine education, he studied medicine in Philadelphia and when, in 1832, the Branch and Bradford families came to Florida, the young doctor and his mother came with them.

Tallahassee society welcomed him warmly, and the

next year he was married to Mary, daughter of Governor William P. Duval. The young couple, accompanied by the devoted mother, settled at St. Joseph, at that time holding forth great promise. A few years later a tidal wave wrought destruction to the town and then yellow fever swept the remainder of its citizens off the face of the earth.

Dr. Robinson was buried there and his mother, with his young wife and little daughter returned to Tallahassee. After that time she made her home at Pine Hill.

As time wore on she became more cheerful and great was the assistance she rendered her whilom pupil in raising her daughters. No Spanish duenna was ever more lynx-eyed or severe than Aunt Robinson, and we strongly suspected that she had eyes in the back of her head, sometimes wondering if she had ever, ever carried on the least little bit of a flirtation, or, in all her young days, ever cast a "come hither" look at any boy. We did not dare to do any of those things. The house was large, it had been built with a view to entertaining and the rooms opened into each other in such a manner as to give to one, sitting in the wide hall, an uninterrupted view of all. Aunt Robinson's favorite seat was in this hall and if dancing was going on she sat on the broad, winding stair and we who danced below knew she saw every movement, every glance. We were pretty well guarded, you may be sure. Tall and commanding, with a figure still erect and stately, handsome, too, in spite of advancing years, always well-dressed, our chaperon was one we could not fail to respect and obey. We sometimes resented her uncompromising attitude toward youth and its failings. We did not think aunt Robinson had ever been young; we did not know, however, until long after the many trials she had endured.

There were things our parents never discussed in our

presence; one of these was money. Never had we heard it intimated that wealth made one better, or poverty made one less desirable; personality was the criterion; personality and *family* with great stress laid upon this latter qualification. So we grew up attaching no importance whatever to the prestige of wealth, nay more, we did not know it existed. Our grandfather was given to quotations, one of his favorites was this:

"Honor and fame from no condition rise,
Act well your part, there all the honor lies."

Another we often heard from his lips was:

"He who steals my purse steals trash,
'Tis his, 'twas mine, it has been slave to thousands,
But he who filches from me my good name,
Takes that which not enriches him, yet leaves me poor indeed."

Raised in such an atmosphere it is not to be wondered at that we thought little of poverty or riches. It was the custom in our home, and doubtless was in other homes as well, when we wanted the cash for any purpose to open our purses and lay them on our father's desk, they were never left empty and when we saw the purse was closed we knew we might safely take it away. Now-a-days an allowance is the thing, but money was given to us as we needed it and while we enjoyed the spending, it was a matter of little moment.

That wealth does make a difference, we learned in later years. The very first intimation we had that one was judged by the amount of money he possessed, came as a distinct shock.

It was in the Spring of 1865, on the 9th of April that General Lee surrendered the Army of Northern Virginia and this was quickly followed by the fall of the Confederacy. We will not tell you here how we grieved over "The Lost Cause." At that time we were standing

"Where the brook and river meet."

In the Old South there was no fixed time for a young girl to "enter society," in fact it was often said that Southern children entered society at birth. Mammy would bring her nursling into the parlor to see company, before the mother could leave her room; the baby was always an important member of the family. As the little one grew large, mammy grew prouder and much more strict. Her child was taught all the points of good-breeding, the polite salutation, the modest answer when spoken to, the quiet demeanor. When the child remained unnoticed was the rule, not as now, the exception. The reason for this is readily to be perceived, mammy was there, looking on, and woe be to the unlucky one who dared to be pert, or forward, or, as mammy would express it, "fergit yer manners." This goes far toward explaining the modest demeanor of those *ante-bellum* days.

There was a custom in the social regime of the Old South, which we have deeply deplored, that is the way in which New Year's Day was observed. It was "a day at home" for Southern ladies, a beautifully appointed table stood in every parlor, on this table was the richest of plum cakes, beautifully ornamented; small cakes of various kinds were also served. But alas for "tee-totalers," as those opposed to drinking, in those days, were called. A large punch bowl held the place of honor in the centre of the table. A capacious silver ladle was in this bowl, glasses of handsome pattern flanked the bowl and the guests who came in numbers helped themselves liberally. On New Year's Day the gentlemen were expected to call on all their lady friends and by the time the round had been made, you can imagine the result. A bad custom, which has passed away, yet, we hear of intoxication still. At parties, where "the flowing bowl" had flowed too freely in some directions, one of the privileges mammy claimed was to carry cups of strong, black coffee to her favorites among the sufferers, giving as her excuse, "Ain't he comin' ter see my young lady?" or perhaps, "Ain't I done hep' ter nuss him when he wus little?"

But we have not told you how we first heard of the value of money. Having just entered upon young ladyhood, we, of course, received attention, and we were at a party, for we of the South felt that we must do what we could to cheer up our returned soldiers, we heard our name and unconsciously listened. "She has one follower the less tonight, where is the Captain?" We did not turn but we recognized the voice which answered, "The Captain is evidently of the opinion that Miss ——— with a hundred thousand dollars and Miss ——— with nothing, are two distinct persons." It was the first time we had ever heard that money was considered before standing and character, but it isn't always so.

With the disastrous close of the war, social conditions in the South underwent such a change as comes to few countries. A few families tried to hold out in the same old manner, but soon these also had to go under. There was no longer the handsome incomes to meet these heavy expenditures. Life in the Southland became a life of anxiety and in many instances, of toil.

CHAPTER II

WHEN THE SERPENT ENTERED EDEN

IN the early fifties of the last century it would have been difficult to find a lovelier home than that of Doctor Edward Bradford, at Pine Hill Plantation, Leon County, Florida. It was situated amid rolling hills and green forests, with little streams here and there, and a clear, quiet stream wending its way to one of the placid lakes, which beautify this fair land. God's Country, its people claim it is, and it is worthy of the name, or rather it was worthy of the name at the period of which we write.

In the grove of towering pines stood a large and stately mansion; white and green, as a country house should be. Rose-gardens and shrubbery of many kinds, grew around the house, while away, on every side, spread smooth and velvety lawns. But do not delude yourself with the thought that this was the work of nature, it took skilled work and many hands to keep all this in beautiful order. Thorough-bred Kentucky horses grazed in the pastures, cows from Alderney and Guernsey chewed their cuds contemplatively and furnished the richest of cream and the yellowest of butter for the inmates of the mansion.

Away towards the east the cabins of the slaves could be seen; not that the owners ever spoke of them in that manner, to such they were variously known as "My People," "My black folks," "My hands," "The quarter folks," and by some they were spoken of as "My niggers," though but few used this mode of designation, for it was not liked by these dusky people themselves and was generally avoided.

At Pine Hill, (We will drop the word "Plantation," which was always made use of by the servants on this and adjoining plantations, but rarely by the owners and their intimate friends.) the cabins were kept in good order and in perfect repair, a corps of carpenters being maintained for this purpose. At the beginning of every summer the cabins and fences and out-houses were given a coat of whitewash, serving the double purpose of lending beauty and brightness to the scene and besides being a sanitary measure. These cabins were not huddled together, but there was ample space around each one for a dooryard and garden, while shade trees were everywhere in evidence.

It was a beautiful place and many were the visitors there. Guests were continually coming and going. There were evening parties, attended by the elite of the community; house parties where the guests were not only of the immediate neighborhood but often from other states as well, for in those days, though there were no automobiles, people thought nothing of starting out for distant points in their carriages, with another conveyance for baggage and servants, and prolonged visits were made. Social life in the Old South differed, in many respects from that of any other country; naturally this would be so, for surroundings were different. These large plantations were like a little world within themselves; the hospitality of the old-time Southerners is proverbial; nothing was spared to make the friends they entertained have a delightful time; individual tastes were studied and catered to; congenial souls were sought for these house-parties, which were often like wheels within wheels.

Here were assembled gay ladies of fashion, gentlemen of leisure, statesmen and earnest scientific devotees, professional men, many of them celebrated far beyond their "native heath" and most of all, the gentlemen planters; men who owned large holdings of land, who employed overseers to look after the minutiae of the plantation, while they directed. They were often aided in giving these directions by articles published in the various agricultural magazines, plentiful, both in the North and in the South.

When this set got together the listener would be sure to hear discussed scientific farming, in all its phases. In the winter the various modes of plowing, ditching, etc., the rival merits of this, that or the other fertilizer, the best method of heating cotton seed for the compost heap. Then spring would come and with its coming the topics of the hour changed to planting corn, sugar-cane and that greatest of all staples, cotton. A little later in the year the first question asked, when these enthusiastic planters met, was, "Have you finished chop ping out cotton?"

Next came that terrible enemy, the grass; if the weather was wet the grass grew apace and every hand on the place who could handle a hoe, was called into requisition. So the year went on through all its changes and the interest of these planters never waned, their ardor never cooled.

One of these agricultural magazines was edited by Solon Robinson, an Abolitionist of the most pronounced type. Many of the business men of west Florida, at that time, were from the North; particularly was this true of the brokers and commission merchants. A very popular firm was Brodie & Pettes. Mr. Pettes was a bachelor about middle-age and Mr. Brodie was a married man with quite an interesting family; both men came South with strong Abolition sentiments, which, for business reasons, they tried to conceal.

Mr. Pettes married a Tallahassee girl and Mr. and Mrs. Brodie, and the children as well, fell deeply in love with the Southern people and took very kindly indeed to being waited on by the dusky servitors, who held so strongly, the sympathy of the folks at the North. In fact it was no longer necessary to conceal their sentiments, for they had undergone "a change of heart."

In September of 1850, Mr. Brodie met his old friend, Solon Robinson on the streets of New York City; after the first greetings were exchanged the editor told the commission merchant that he had his face turned toward Florida, whither he was going in the interest of the poor down-trodden slaves, his expenses being paid by some devoted workers in the cause, who lived in Boston.

So completely had Mr. Brodie abjured abolitionism that he tried to persuade Mr. Robinson that he was simply wasting his time. "However," he said, "if you will go on such a mistaken errand, let me give you a letter of introduction to my friend, Dr. Bradford, who will receive, with true Southern hospitality, anyone I send. Go to him, spend a part of your time in Florida going over his magnificent plantations, see how all is managed; compare the happy negroes you will find there with the poor of our own section; hear them sing and dance and frolic; see how tenderly they are looked after when they are sick and take my word for it, you will almost wish you were one of the doctor's slaves yourself." Solon Robinson took the proffered letter and we will tell you what use he made of it.

Travel was slow in those days, it was October when he reached Pine Hill; there had been a storm a few days before his coming, one of the equinoctials, which sometimes sweep over this country, uprooting trees, laying low most vegetable growth and then passing swiftly by, leaving everything sweet and clean behind it and an indescribable freshness in the air.

At Pine Hill were a number of China trees. As every one knows, the "Pride of China" has weak roots, so a long row of these trees were lying on the ground; the children of the family, with their little black playmates, had been climbing the branches and riding the larger limbs for horses, but, wearying of this, they were grouped on the immense trunks and listening to the eldest of the children, a girl of twelve, with long chestnut curls, read a fairy story.

The tale was about two little girls, Rose-White and Rose-Red, who were walking in the forest and in a deep and dark place, beside a running stream, they saw a squatty dwarf, with broad shoulders and very large feet; his head was covered with thick white hair and he had a long beard, white as his hair and reaching to his feet.

The dwarf was calling loudly and seemed to be skipping about over the log on which he stood, his voice was harsh but he was very much in need of help, for when they drew nearer they saw that his beard was caught in a cleft in the log and held as if in a vise. He had been cutting some fire-wood and when he gave a mighty stroke the ax flew out of his hand and his long beard was caught, so that he could not get loose. The children were afraid of him but they were sorry for him too, so they tried to loosen the beard, but without success. At last Rose-Red remembered a pair of small scissors she had in her pocket, and drawing them forth, snipped off the ends of the beard and the clumsy dwarf was free.

Instead of thanking them he began to abuse and threaten them and they were trying to make their escape—when a horrid cry from Tinnie, one of the black playmates aforesaid, caused every one to look up. Advancing toward them came an almost exact duplicate of the dwarf. There was a wild uproar at first, with many exclamations from the irrepressible little darkeys, such as, "Lordy, dere's dem very same big feet," "He got de same hair, too," "En he beard would be jis' as long ef he hadn't plaited it an tied it up wid blue ribbins."

Attracted by the screams Mammy appeared upon the scene. "What duz you want?" she asked. "I have come to see Dr. Bradford," said the stranger. "Well," says

Mammy, "dem what cums ter see him comes to de front do'." Around the corner came Fanny, tall and slender and most imposing looking, her pink and white "kerchief" tied in a staid bow on the top of her head, her ginger-bread face drawn up in a frown.

"What is you doin' here?" she inquired, "don't you know no better den to kum 'round folks' back yards, skeering de chilluns ter def?"

"Madam," said the stranger, "I have come to call on Dr. Bradford."

"Don't go Madaming me, ef you kum ter see de Marster de place fur you ter go is de front do', das where white folks goes."

"Excuse me," said the stranger, "I have walked from Tallahassee and took what appeared to be the nearest path."

"Walked fum town, did you? Well, dat settles de whole matter, a gentleman nuver walks. Howsumever, you kin go 'roun' ter de front and de do's dey will be open, but you knock. Ab will kum ter de do' and he will 'nounce you ter de Marster."

Following the direction indicated by Fanny's long finger, he soon reached the front door. Ab was not there, but the doctor sat in an invalid chair, on the porch, a pair of crutches in reach of his hand, rendering needless the polite excuse made for not rising.

The stranger was asked to be seated while the doctor read the letter of introduction, which was duly presented. When the doctor had read it he turned the sheet and read it again.

"Mr. Robinson," he said, "as Mr. Brodie's friend, I bid you welcome; of course we know you by reputation, your paper is widely read. We shall do all in our power to convert you to our way of thinking and we hope you come to us with a desire to learn the truth."

Promising Mr. Robinson every opportunity to pursue his investigations, Doctor Bradford rang a small bell on the table beside him. This brought Ab, who was told to bring some fresh water. "But stop," said his Master, "perhaps Mr. Robinson may prefer a mint julep."

Turning to his guest, the doctor said simply, "I never take anything stronger than water myself, but we keep whiskey in the house and Morea makes a fine julep they say."

This offer was promptly accepted and Morea soon brought it in. The new-comer openly stared. To us, who knew and loved the good old woman, there was nothing repulsive in her appearance, but she was something new to him and no sooner had she disappeared through the folding doors than he asked: "What mode of torture made her like that?"

Doctor Bradford was naturally indignant. Morea was not quite four feet in height and almost square; she had a small head with deep-sunken eyes and her hands and feet resembled nothing so much as terrapin claws, yet she looked all right to us and nobody could make such dainties or tell such fairy tales as "Aunt Morea," as the children called her. The Mistress trusted her and she was the proud mother of nine strong, well-formed children. Mr. Robinson was told of this, but the sight of her seemed to fill him with horror. When supper was ready he was introduced to the family and all were as pleasant and polite as if he had been an invited guest.

At breakfast next morning he met the youngest member of the household, a little girl of four years, petted and spoiled by all, especially by her father. This child was destined to play an important part in Solon Robinson's visit to Florida.

As far as Dr. Bradford's strength would allow he accompanied his guest in rides through the three plantations, but at other times he was furnished a horse and buggy and a colored driver, that he might go where he pleased and see all he wished. The Bradford brothers entertained him in turn and he spent a week with each of the four. Captain Lester, also invited him to spend a week with him. At the end of this time he came again to Pine Hill for a farewell visit.

CHAPTER III

WHEN THE ABOLITIONIST EDITOR CAME TO GRIEF

IT was a bright, beautiful Sunday afternoon in late November; over the pine forest a solemn silence reigned. The sun was traveling westward and its slanting rays fell softly on the glistening brown pine-straw, which lay like a thick carpet beneath the trees. Lulu, the nurse of the least little one, had taken her charge to these woods, where Jim had been keeping them company, but time was passing and Jim had four miles to go before he would reach home, so he had bidden them goodbye and the baby was carefully seeking partridge berries, whose bright red attracted her, while Lulu sat on a fallen log, deep in meditation, or maybe taking a nap. Baby had strayed off quite an unusual distance from the shadow of Lulu's wing and realizing the fact she quickened her steps and returning to the log where she had left her nurse she found Mr. Robinson talking with Lulu.

As the baby came nearer she heard Mr. Robinson say: "If you will listen to me, as soon as you cross Mason and Dixon's line you will be free." Spying her little charge almost beside her, Lulu hastily snatched up the child and called back to her companion, "It's late an' I gotter take dis yere baby home, it's her supper time."

We have said that this was a spoiled child. Always when she had been bathed and made ready for bed it was customary for her father to be called to get her to sleep. At such times he sent the nurse away and, lying down beside his small daughter, he would wait to see what she would say to him. This was an hour of pure delight to them both; baby saved up all she heard but did not understand till this quiet time, when she could "ask father" and father never wearied of explaining, as far as possible, all the questions which vexed her childish brain. Seldom was this program varied, for honored indeed must be the guest who could detain him from this petted child.

On this particular Sunday night Lulu had summoned Dr. Bradford and was off, in haste, to enjoy herself "in de quarter" with the other young negroes of Pine Hill.

Baby laid her little brown head on father's arm and was quiet for a while, then she sleepily asked, "What does *free* mean?"

"You mean three," said father, "well three is two and one more."

No more was said and soon both were sound asleep. At breakfast and at dinner the baby's high chair was placed at her father's left hand, and Lulu stood behind the chair, that she might attend to the wants of her nursling.

On this Monday morning the family were assembled around the bounteous board. Mr. Robinson occupied the seat on Dr. Bradford's right hand, just opposite the baby, who was busily engaged with her bowl of mush and milk. Conversation was general around the table, the governess, for there was always a governess, talked with the school children of the coming week, the children responded and the "stranger within the gates" took quite a prominent part in the pros and cons of school life.

Suddenly the baby dropped her spoon—she had thought of something—"Father," she said, "how can Lulu be two and one more?"

"Why, she could not be, of course."

"But, father, you said last night, when I asked you what *free* meant, that it meant two and one more."

Some inkling of the truth must have come to both Lulu and Solon Robinson, for she hastily left the room while he, with a terrible scowl, turned to the waiting child.

"Hush up," he cried, "children should be seen and not heard."

"I won't hush" was the answer, "you said it yourself —you said when Lulu went across Mason and Dick's line she would be free."

The cat was out of the bag at last. A dead silence fell on the group around the table. Mother took the weeping child from the table, the governess marshalled her flock to the school-room and the master of Pine Hill Plantation was left to reckon with his guest.

Lulu was questioned first, she admitted that it was true. Mr. Robinson had tried to talk to her but she did not want him to say those things to her; she referred her master to several men on the place, who could tell him more than she could.

The investigation went on. His various hosts in the neighborhood were sent for and it developed that on each plantation the same course had been pursued.

Forgetting the generous hospitality, the kind consideration which had been shown him, he was trying, in every case to injure and undermine his entertainers.

As he listened to the testimony given by scores of negroes, whom he had sought, with more or less success, to render insubordinate, his livid face and trembling limbs spoke plainly of his cowardice and of his fears.

It was proved that at each house where he had visited he had repaid kindness with treachery. When the family retired he too, went to his apartment, but not to sleep. As soon as the household was quiet he would steal out and make his way to the negro "quarters," where the news of his coming had been spread abroad. The incendiary talks he gave them had not yet borne fruit but it had been discovered not a day too soon.

The four brothers and Captain Lester sat in judgment upon this ungrateful old sinner, and it was finally decided that two of their number should take him to St. Marks and ship him to some far Northern point on a vessel carrying cotton to market. The Captain of this vessel was a Southern man and could be depended upon to obey orders; before the vessel could have reached port a number of the agricultural magazines, of which he was editor, came in the mail; it was somewhat amusing, and also irritating, to read therein a letter, dated October 25th, telling of his arrival at Pine Hill and his reception there; he wrote at great length and while he omitted all mention of the mint julep, he did not forget to tell of "Morea, who evidently had undergone some terrible torture in her youth which had distorted and cruelly disfigured her." There was much along the same lines. Mr. Brodie was overwhelmed with mortification at the failure of his experiment and Solon Robinson lost some of his subscribers in Florida.

The situation, about this time, was very trying to the Southern people; John C. Calhoun, beloved and admired by the greater part of the country, had passed away. So true and pure was he that personally, even his worst enemies could find nothing to say to his discredit. Political enemies, he had many, but his doctrine of State's Rights was the very heart of the South. In this same year (1851) Mrs. Harriet Beecher Stowe, began the publication of her famous novel, "Uncle Tom's Cabin." It came out first as a serial.

The next year it came out in book form and was translated into many languages and the editions reached up into the hundreds of thousands. "Uncle Tom's Cabin" had but little literary merit, but it was strongly dramatic. Mrs. Stowe knew nothing whatever of the South or its people; she knew nothing of the negro or the manner in which the institution of slavery was carried on; she had never been South, but she was gifted with a vivid imagination and she had, also, a total disregard for truth. Given a vivid imagination and a disregard for truth and it is easy to be dramatic.

Mrs. Stowe's book came, too, just when the time was ripe for such a fire-brand; the abolition of negro slavery was "the burning question of the hour." Old England and New England vied with each other in this work; nothing was too bad for the Southerner, nothing too good for his slave. Brotherly love was lost sight of; Christian charity died a natural death and these apostles of abolition proclaimed "A Higher Law:"

> "A law which aimed its blows at Slavery;
> At marriage, and the home;
> A law which in its wide out-going
> Caused e'en yet full many a heart to mourn."

The dignified protests of Southern statesmen; the able editorials in Southern newspapers; the masterly arguments of DeBow's Review were treated with contempt and contumely.

Pursuing, as nearly as possible, the even tenor of her way, the South waited, to see what the outcome would be. If "our black folks" felt this unrest which pervaded the times, they gave no sign, and relations between the races, as yet, knew no change. To make our story clearer and plainer, we shall introduce, from time to time, some leaves from a child's diary.

CHAPTER IV

A FEW EXPLANATORY WORDS

THESE leaves, selected from the little girl's diary, need, perhaps, some explanation. Our aim is to use only the parts which show the trend of political events in the South, as seen through the eyes of a child. This child entered school when only four years old—she was not made to go but went of her own free will, because she so dearly loved the governess, Miss Joanna Young Scammon, of Maine.

It was a joke at first, this tiny scholar, but she was so quiet and her progress was so rapid that she became an accepted fact in the school room. In those days there were not so many fads and fancies regarding the rearing of children. It was not considered detrimental to either physical or mental health for a too-early use of the faculties with which nature had endowed them. Sunshine and out-door exercise in abundance, the children of this household had, and in every way their health was looked after, but it never once occurred to the grown-ups that a child could be mentally over-stimulated. So, at the age of seven years, we find this child a pupil at The Iamonia Female Seminary, studying History, Geography, Philosophy, Arithmetic and the usual reading and writing, besides a column of Webster's Dictionary every afternoon. A round, roly-poly, rosy little creature, she enjoyed to the full every bit of knowledge she acquired. A very child in all things, play was as sweet as study.

A very child in all things, play was as sweet as study.

Of course, there is much in this diary that is of a purely personal nature, and such we have omitted. Where there occurs allusions which tend to show the relations between the two races so prominent in the Southland, we have made use of them. Even in this household where the utmost prudence obtained in talking before children, remarks, dropped here and there, could not fail to arouse their curiosity, but this was nothing compared to the deep-seated uneasiness, which filled with apprehension the thinking element of the South.

Every Northern newspaper contained expressions, either for, or against the abolition doctrines; for all of the North did not stand for this unwarranted interference in the affairs of the South. John C. Calhoun had stated the doctrine of State's Rights so plainly that all who would could understand, but his warning voice was disregarded by the fanatical Abolitionists.

This principle, State's Rights, was embodied in the Constitution of our fathers, and with the disregard of these sacred rights came many of our present-day troubles.

So long as these doctrines remained in force, personal liberty, except to criminals, was assured; marriage laws were held sacred and divorces were rare and when these did take place, the parties to such divorces were looked upon with suspicion and mistrust. We will not try to assert that "free love" was unknown, but parties to it were not considered respectable and life was made hard for them. Business houses held to a certain code of honor and failures in business were not the every-day affair as at present and when a man wilfully defrauded his creditors he could not hold up his head and be recognized as the equal of honest men.

When the Republican Party came into power a death-blow was dealt to State's Rights and "The Higher Law" sprang into being like Athene from the brain of Zeus, fully armed and equipped, not with wisdom and justice, but casting aside all law, both human and Divine, in a mad desire to have everything their own way.

Of course, the negroes knew of the strong feeling

against the abolition movement among their "white folks." Secret though the midnight meetings were held, some news of their import was sure to get to the ears of the white people; some of the negroes were faithful and from these came the information but, strange to say, no mention of all this was made to the white children. It had always been impressed upon the negro mind that nothing but what was good and right must ever be told to the children of the family. The incidents mentioned in the diary show how little the child really knew of events transpiring around her. The real significance attending these circumstances was not felt.

CHAPTER V

LEAVES FROM A CHILD'S DIARY*

IT is March again and I am eight years old. Mother says I write well enough to keep a diary, so she has given me this book and father has sharpened a pencil for me to write with. For two whole days I have been copying in my copy-book a little verse, this is it:

"If you your ears
Would keep from jeers,
Three things keep meekly hid
Myself and I, and mine and my,
And how I do, or did."

I do not see how I can write a diary and at the same time keep this rule which I have learned. Tonight, when bed-time comes I shall ask Father; he always tells me what I want to know.

March 9th, 1854.—I forgot to put a date yesterday so today I put the day and the year. Father made it all right about that troublesome "I," he says this is for my own eyes, and maybe his too if I should show it to him. He says I must remember the rule all the time, except when I am talking to him or writing in this book. Mother is going to Live Oak today and I wish I could go too. I love grandpa so dearly, but father and mother do not want me to miss my lessons and get behind in my classes. Anyway, we are going to spend the day with him Saturday.

March 10th, 1854.—I was studying my lessons, in the Library, when mother got home last night. Often I am watching for her but my geography was hard and I did not know she had come until she was in the room. She stood in the door and did not move when I went to kiss her, she said, "Grandpa has sent you a present,

* These Leaves from the Diary are often awkwardly expressed but allowance must be made for the writer's youth. Her figures too are bad in some places and the greater part of the Diary was written on the coarse, rough paper which in the days of the war was often the only kind obtainable; so if the dates are sometimes wrong please excuse it.

guess what it is?" Now, grandpa always gives me such nice presents, sometimes he sends me beautiful picture books. Sometimes he gives me gold pieces; once he brought me a set of real steel knives and forks from Sheffield, England; once he sent me a barrel of brown sugar that my Lulu might make me plenty of candy. She makes the best candy in the world and, when she has time, she plaits it and makes splendid baskets, with high handles. Once he sent me a mother goat, with twin kids and once a pair of peafowls, which I still have and which are just the most magnificent birds you ever saw. (I wonder if I spelled magnificent right?) I have had all sorts of gifts from dear grandpa and so, when mother wanted me to guess, I just couldn't. Everybody in the room had a guess but it seemed nobody was right, for when mother stood aside there stood a little girl, something smaller than I. I drew back a little, for at first I could not believe grandpa had sent me that little girl; but he really had. I am not sure yet that I like my present but of course I will for did not grandpa think she was a nice present? I asked mother what she was for and she said she would be my maid and wait upon me, but my Lulu can do all I want done. When she had eaten some supper mother gave her to aunt Ginnie to keep until the next morning. Whatever will I do with her when another day comes?

March 13th.—Dr. Mitchell stopped at Pine Hill last night and father was busy with him and so I did not have a chance to talk with him about Frances, for that is my new maid's name. Mother says I must be very kind to her and when she gets over feeling so strange she will play with me, then, too, she says I may teach her all I learn myself, I have given her the small slate I used when I was a beginner. She is a shy child and she sits and rolls her big black eyes at me until I feel almost afraid of her. Mother says she is my Re-spon-si-bil-i-ty. Isn't that a big word? Mother told me how to spell it but when I asked the meaning she said, "It will probably take you a lifetime to learn its full meaning, but I will try to tell you what it means in regard to you and Frances."

I can't remember every word, but this is what she meant, I was to be patient with my little maid; I must not get mad with her; I must not strike her; I must not say hard things to her and if she was so bad I could not stand it I must bring her to mother to be corrected just as she corrects us. Why do I have to be so careful about Frances, mother? I asked. "Because," mother said, "Frances belongs to you." But my Lulu and Allen and Hannah belong to me too, and you have never told me all this before? "It is this way," said mother, "Frances has nobody but you, your grandpa has given you a deed of gift to her and it has been recorded in the Book of Deeds in the court house, Frances has no father and her mother does not want her, aunt Gillie, who used to take care of her is dead. She has a grandmother and grandfather, these are Uncle Kinchen and Aunt Amy. They, as you know, go everywhere with your grandpa and so they cannot take care of Frances even if they wished to do so." Well, mother is right and I will try to do my best, but I wish she did not belong to me. I am so glad when night comes and she goes home with aunt Ginnie. I go to school several hours of each day and that is a help.

We close the little diary and go on with our story. Uncle Kinchen, mentioned by the young writer, was Governor Branch's waiting-man, his valet, he would be called in France. Aunt Amy, his wife, had been maid to Mrs. Branch and the two traveled everywhere with them. The Governor went in a roomy carriage, drawn by four horses, following this could always be seen a carry-all with a pair of sleek Kentucky mules, and on the driver's seat sat uncle Kinchen and aunt Amy.

This old couple showed plainly that old age was upon them. Kinchen, as a youth of twenty, had carried his little Master, in his arms, on rainy days, to the "Old Field School," which he attended. This school was near Elk's Marsh and it was a frolic for both master and man when the rain came down. Now uncle Kinchen was treated with respect and affection by the entire family and oftentimes the grandchildren would gather around him while he told them wonderful stories of the many great deeds their grandfather had accomplished, to all of which they listened with delight. Aunt Amy was almost as old; she had waited upon her mistress from her babyhood and she too, had much to tell to these same grandchildren. In their opinion it was hard to find anyone more entertaining than these old people.

Riding behind the "Democrat" came Starling, who also traveled with Governor Branch. To him really fell all tasks requiring strength and dexterity and he rather resented the secondary position he occupied. Starling rode a small Spanish mule and he was frequently admonished to be careful of his mount. Often along the journey the Governor would ride "Janet," for that was the mule's name, and Starling would ride on the box beside Uncle Godfrey, the coachman.

This mule had a history which we may as well give here. In the year 1822, John Branch made his first visit to Florida, he came as United States District Judge. Pensacola was his headquarters and the Spanish residents of thc city interested him deeply. He made many friends among them and some of these friendships lasted through life. Governor Branch was an athlete, fond of all exercises of that nature and especially fond of horseback riding. He had ridden an Arabian from North Carolina to Florida and, speaking one day to a Spanish friend of the easy gait of the Arabian, the Spaniard said, "You will never know the full delight of such exercise until you ride a Spanish mule." Governor Branch made some polite reply and thought nothing more about it. Fourteen years later, coming to Florida to live, he again visited Pensacola and renewed the pleasant acquaintances he had made. The conversation turned on horseback riding and the Spaniard, who had spoken of the mule so many years before, said, "Governor, I have a steed for you now, and when you have tried her you will never care for an ordinary horse again."

True to his word he sent this mule to Tallahassee and she proved to be the very finest riding animal the governor had ever tried. He never willingly rode anything else and "Janet" made the trip from Florida to Carolina with as much regularity as the governor himself. Once, in Philadelphia, a broad-brimmed Quaker, of a rotund figure, accosted him on the street, "Are you the old gentleman who rides a mule?" he asked, so you see Janet's fame had spread.

These journeys were leisurely ones for oftentimes they stopped to visit along the way and never, while he lived, was the home of John C. Calhoun passed by. To the end of his days Governor Branch looked out for the comfort and welfare of all his faithful servants and dying, they were provided for in his will.

THE CHILD'S DIARY CONTINUED

April 1st, 1854.—This is "All Fools Day" but nobody feels like fun, even sis Mag has not played any tricks and Buddy hasn't a word to say. Father got a letter this morning saying that dear, sweet sister is very sick in Savannah. Mother is not well enough to go but father is going in a few minutes and will bring her home as soon as she is able to travel. He is going in the carriage as far as Oglethorpe, in Georgia, and then take the train. Mother is so sad and her beautiful blue eyes have lost their light. What if sister should die as sister Sarah did.

April 15th.—God is good to us for sister and father are at home again. Sister is pale and weak, but she smiles as sweetly as ever and she says now that she is at home she will soon be well. Everybody wants to wait on her at once.

May 4th.—Sister is so much better, she goes to the table now and we are so glad. I can hardly stay away from her long enough to go to school.

May 11th.—Sister is worse, three doctors are here, not counting father and Buddy; all the servants are so distressed; aunt Dinah cries and prays all the time. Will God hear our prayers?

May 18th.—Sister died last night—there is nothing more in the world to say.

June 20th.—It looks as if our world would never come right again. Miss Brewer whom we love so well, is going away to her home in New York and she is not coming back, because she is going to be married. Mother says she has been a great comfort to her in these days of trial. She will not go until the 1st of August. We go to school ten months and have holiday in September and October; sometimes we have August and September, and begin school in October. We go somewhere every summer. If we have to go before school is out, the governess goes too.

August 22nd, 1854.—We will have to say goodbye to dear Miss Brewer tomorrow, she is going back to her home in Brooklyn and next winter she will marry Mr. Albro. He came here to see her, when she first left Mr. Wolfe, and the Iamonia Female Seminary, to teach in our family. Her younger sister, Miss Addie, is almost as sweet as she is; I am so sorry they are going to leave us; everybody is sorry.

August 30th, 1854.—I was afraid the days would be lonely without school and lessons, but we are getting on quite well; we miss sister dreadfully but mother and father tell us such beautiful things about the Heaven she has gone to, that I would like to go there, too. We gather flowers every morning and take them to her, to her and the other loved ones who are there.

Oct. 1st, 1854.—We spent the month of September at the sea-side. Mother is never well now and she is so white and thin and when she wants to go over the house to see if all is right, father takes her up in his arms and carries her as if she was a baby, for he is strong though he is lame.

Oct. 15th, 1854.—Aunt Eliza Bailey came today to spend the winter with us. Her only daughter, Teresa Leigh Reid, died the week after sister did and they brought her home and buried her under the myrtles. Mother and aunt Eliza both feel so sad, as indeed, we all do.

Oct. 21st, 1854.—We are going to have Miss Julia Parkman Young for our governess. I have only seen her once; she is from New York city and she is very nice looking and quiet. I wonder why all our teachers come from the North? They are all very pleasant and so are the three governesses Dr. Holland has had to teach at Minerva Hall, since I have been going to school. Their governess goes everywhere with the girls but after school time our governess does whatever she pleases.

October 2nd, 1854.—School opened yesterday. Miss Young is our governess. She is a little pretty and she has pretty clothes, but whenever she thinks nobody sees her, she cries. Her eyes are big and brown, a light brown, her hair is like her eyes. Uncle John who makes fun of everybody, says she does not look as if she could say boo to a goose, but there is no sense in that, for all the geese stay at the Horse-shoe with aunt Pendar.

October 5th.—This is Friday night. I have studied hard and tried to have good lessons. I do not have much time to play for I have to teach Frances some every day. She learns well most of the time and mother says she is a credit to her teacher. I hope it suits mother.

December 21st, 1854.—Guess what has happened—aunt Eliza Bailey has a dear little son and he is named Edward Bradford for father. Aunt Eliza calls father "Brother Doctor," and she says he is the very best man in all the world. I think she is right. I just love that baby to distraction.

December 22nd.—I have a Christmas present three days before Christmas. It is a baby, aunt Dinah gave it to me, she says the rabbits brought it to her and she thought right away "I'll gie dis chile ter Susie." Wasn't it kind of aunt Dinah? It is a beautiful baby and of course she really wanted it for herself. Aunt Dinah says she will take care of it for me and I can have it to play with whenever I want it. Mother says Lulu can make me a trunk full of clothes for my baby and I can keep the trunk in my doll house and when I want the baby to play with, we can get her and give her a bath in the blue tub, she has given me, and dress her in the clothes from the trunk. Her name is Lavinia and she is too little and soft yet to play with. When I asked mother if the baby was really mine, just as Frances is, she said, "She is yours, and so are Dinah and Henry and all their children except Nellie and Bethiah, that is, they will be yours some day, they are left to you, in your father's will." I do not know what that means and company came in so mother could not stop to tell me.

Jan. 1st, 1855.—Miss Young feels so bad that she wants to give up teaching and go to her grandmother in New York. I am sorry, for I love her in spite of the tears, she says I must not say "crying," she says she is weeping, but she does not tell me why.

Jan. 10th, 1855.—Aunt Robinson has come back from Texas, just in time, mother says. She taught mother when she was a little girl, and she has offered to teach us until mother can find a suitable governess. Father and mother are pleased for they think she is the best of teachers. She is an English woman and very strict. I went to school to her when I was quite small. I have promised mother that I will be good and study hard.

Always I have wanted an express package to come addressed to me, well this morning it came. It was a very nice package, indeed, books for the most part, which is just what I like best. It was from our dear Miss Brewer who is now Mrs. Albro, and her sweet young sister, Miss Addie. There was something for each member of the family. My gifts were a string of pink and silver beads for my biggest dolly, "Julia Parkman Young," a drawing book with four pencils and a beautiful book called "Mrs. Nancy Bradford's Diary." Miss Brewer thought I would like that especially because I, too, have an aunt named Mrs. Nancy Bradford and she has a husband and house full of sons. This Mrs. Bradford lived in the days of the Revolution and she was very patriotic but very unhappy for all her people were in the army, helping General Washington. I hope our dear little aunt Nancy will never have to send her sons to war.

There was a book for Frances in the box but I am afraid she is ungrateful; the book is a Primer, bound in dark yellow, about the color of Frances herself, it has pretty pictures, too, but it made her angry, for she is just on the last lesson in McGuffey's Second Reader and this is the second time, so she will be ready for the Third Reader next Monday; she is quite scornful of the pretty little Primer but she shall write a nice letter of thanks, never-the-less. Father says if he had known

I wanted an express package so badly he would have seen to it that one came; he is always so kind.

There is something wrong somewhere. This morning everything seemed lovely but just after breakfast uncle Tom and uncle Richard came and in a few minutes Captain Lester came, too, next came Dr. Holland and Mr. Berrien Manning. They did not come as usual to the house, but stopped under the big trees at the front of the flower-garden to talk. How I did wish I could know what they were talking about. It was nothing mother said, but I believe it was something about those Abolitionists.

March 8th, 1855.—Another birthday, nine years old. I have a lot of nice presents. My folks are so good to me. This has been a long winter, for the first time in my life grandpa did not come to Florida, all this winter I seem to have been looking for something and I know it is grandpa. Next to father I love him better than anybody in the world. Frances is learning fast.

April 24th, 1855.—We are going to Tennessee. Mother's health is bad and she has not seen aunt Margaret for years. I have never seen her. Aunt Margaret is Mrs. General Daniel Donelson. She is a little younger than mother and she has a large family of boys and girls. Uncle Daniel was a general in the Mexican War and General Andrew Jackson was his uncle.

May 29th, 1855.—We have been here in Tennessee for some weeks. Father did not come with us as he expected to do. At the last something happened which made it necessary for him to stay at home. When I asked mother what it was, she did not tell me, but Fannie told me, one night when I was getting ready for bed, that some white men, who had no business on the place, had come in the night and were hidden away on the place. Fannie said they were some of the "Abolition crew." I asked more questions but she would tell me no more and she told me to keep my mouth shut; so I do not really know anything about it. I do not even know what she meant by "Abolition crew." I hope it is nothing that will hurt father.

June 2nd, 1855.—I have had a splendid time here with my kinsfolk, aunt Margaret is tall and stately and beautiful and she has the jolliest children, and when we get to playing we almost take the roof off the house. We went to the "Hermitage," where President Jackson lived, but what I liked better was going to see grandma Saunders, who lives on a mountain side and has a cold, cold, cave with a stream of ice water running through it.

We are going home next week.

June 6th.—I have found out a little more about that "Abolition crew" Fannie talked about; last night I fell asleep on the sofa in the front room at aunt Margaret's and nobody found me and when I woke mother and uncle Daniel were talking. He said, "These abolitionists are everywhere through the South. Sooner or later they will make trouble for us. Dr. Bradford writes that those on Horse-shoe were made to leave and will be severely dealt with if they return." I sat up and called out, "Oh, uncle Daniel, please tell me all about it?" Mother called Fannie to put me to bed, so I haven't heard any more.

THE STORY RESUMED:

The early Spring of 1855 found Dr. Bradford preparing to take his family to Tennessee and Kentucky. Under the sorrows and trials of the past year Mrs. Bradford had faded as some delicate flower and to divert her he had planned a visit to her sister, Mrs. Donelson, of Davidson County. Mrs. Donelson was the third daughter of Governor John Branch, of North Carolina, who was, at the time of her marriage, Secretary of the Navy in President Jackson's Cabinet. Daniel S. Donelson was the nephew of Mrs. Andrew Jackson; he was a handsome blonde giant, splendidly proportioned with a brain to equal his brawn. He was a graduate of West Point and moreover a classmate of Jefferson Davis, the South's beloved President and of Robert Edward Lee, whose name ranks with "The Immortals."

Like his classmates he took a prominent part in the War with Mexico and, at the period of which we write, he was living on his fine stock farm some sixteen miles from Nashville and, with his beautiful wife and eleven splendid children to help him, the doors of hospitality were ever held open. The brothers-in-law were devoted friends and great pleasure was anticipated by all concerned.

The leaves from our little girl's diary tell of some mysterious happenings, which she could not quite understand though she suspected the Abolitionists; looked upon, evidently as a kind of bug-a-boo or a first cousin to the devil. As the time approached for them to leave home, troubles of this nature came thick and fast. Dr. Bradford soon found he could not leave home and Governor Branch, Mrs. Bradford's father, offered to accompany the family to the home of the Donelsons in Tennessee. Anxious to get his wife where she would have a change, Dr. Bradford accepted the offer gratefully, and the first of May found them en route for Nashville.

In the meantime Dr. Bradford, with his valued manager, Mr. Manning, and the other slave-holding neighbors found they had on their hands the worst abolition tangle they had yet met with. Three miles from Pine Hill Plantation, near the little village of Centreville, was a large saw-mill owned by Mr. Columbus Williams, who, though he owned valuable property in Florida, did not live here. He had hired, to run his mill a mechanic from New England; there were negro laborers of course, but this mechanic was in charge. The young man attended service at Pisgah Church, near his place of business. He was not looked upon as a dangerous character and yet he was, for first one negro and then another came with tales of what had been said by this man, and finally it was discovered that he was giving parties at night, in the big mill buildings and inviting the young negro men and girls to be present. Uncle Henry and Aunt Dinah, Uncle Randal and Aunt Julianne came to complain that their daughters had been coaxed off to these gatherings and many other parents of young negroes in the neighborhood came with the same story.

The gay mechanic at the Williams Mill had invited to help him at these parties, other mechanics from his own section of country, who were working at the railroad shop in Tallahassee. It was proved that they were not taking any active part in abolition work but only following these very questionable methods in search of amusement. Notice was served upon them that this must stop and they were told most emphatically what would happen if another gathering of like nature should be held. Also a patrol of responsible negroes was appointed on each plantation with orders to severely whip any white man found lurking around "The Quarter."

One night Dr. Bradford was aroused by a call at his window, "Marse Ned, come out here." He was out in a moment. Held by two pair of strong, black hands was the mechanic aforesaid, stripped to his skin and covered with bleeding welts from a cow-hide, that most efficient of whips. Frightened and angry he was, but the hands which held him knew no mercy and they would gladly have whipped him again but Dr. Bradford interposed.

"You contemptible cur; how dare you set foot on my place after you were forbidden?" said the Doctor. "You have been well whipped but it is nothing compared to what will happen to you if you should come again. If you attempt to revenge yourself on my boys I shall know who did it and you shall suffer for it; if the torch is applied I shall know whose hand did it and nothing will be too bad for you. Now boys, turn him loose; if you ever find him here again flog him twice as hard."

Two or three such instances occurred on different plantations around and every time one whipping was enough to put a stop to it, but the doctor's trip to Tennessee was spoiled. That winter the first mulatto child ever born on Pine Hill Plantation, opened his eyes to the light; Dr. Bradford promptly summoned the Rev. McDaniel and had the baby christened with its father's surname which name he bears to this day.*

The gay and festive New Englander was furious but he could not help himself. During the summer he made arrangements to marry a young widow with three little daughters, owning a small plantation and a few negroes. He thought he was ruined, but strange to say the widow did not care and the wedding took place. All this was very disagreeable, to say the least of it.

The close of the season found the Bradfords at home again and with them came two lovely daughters of General and Mrs. Donelson, Sarah and Emily; they helped to brighten up the home which had known so much sorrow. Aunt Robinson, as the children called her, was to be their governess for the winter. There was much company that winter and spring.

THE DIARY RESUMED:

July 7th, 1855.—Home again, and I am glad, but I miss Sister Mag. Father says "she is the darling of

* In the summer of 1865 Emeline and her son left Pine Hill Plantation and went in search of the boy's father. She had been expected to be welcomed with open arms, but not so. They were greeted with harsh and abusive language and ordered off the premises. In his home there was no place for Hagar and Ishmæl.

Sue's heart." I know I love her and I hope she will soon come home. She is traveling in the North with Aunt Eliza. It is so good to see father once more, and the first quiet time for a talk, I mean to ask him about those men.

July 10th, 1855.—After school was out yesterday, mother said as my reports were so good, I might have Lavinia to play with. She is seven months old now, and she is beautiful. Her brown skin is so smooth and fine, her hair is black and curly, and she has dimples in both cheeks. I love dimples. She has two little white teeth, and she smiles and plays all the time she is awake. Aunt Dinah brought her to the house. Lulu filled the little blue tub with warm water. At first I wanted cold water like I am always bathed in, but aunt Dinah said she had never been washed in cold water, and she might cry. You see, I am part grandpa's and he thinks it is unhealthy to bathe in warm water. When we go to Live Oak he has the bath tub in the bath house, which he built in the rose garden, filled to the brim wath water from the ram, and lets me play in it as much as I wish. None of the other children can do this because, he says, none of the other mothers would let him manage. I love cold water. Lulu helped me bathe Lavinia, while aunt Dinah looked on and laughed. The baby splashed the water everywhere with her plump brown hands. Her hands are so fat, she looks like you had tied strings around her wrists.

September 15th, 1855.—Our school closed today for a two weeks' holiday, which we will spend at Newport. Mother is still feeling badly and she likes the sulphur water. Aunt Nannie Meginniss is going too, so I will have her children to play with; that is fine, for I love Eliza Lane better than I can tell and Dannie is a dear, good little boy.

September 29th.—We have had a delightful stay at this place but we are going home tomorrow. I have enjoyed listening to Captain West and Aunt Robinson talk about the many voyages she has made in his boat going to and from St. Marks to New Orleans.

October 6th, 1855.—School once more—Aunt Robinson "at the helm" as Captain West says. Mrs. Woods, who taught my older sisters when they were too small to be sent off to boarding school, is here on a visit. Something funny has happened. Mrs. Woods came in one morning and handed father a book, she said she bought it to read on the journey down and she was going to give it to him. He thanked her and took the book, his face flushed, he said "This is Uncle Tom's Cabin." "Yes," she answered, "it is now in its hundredth edition, but I read in the newspapers that it was not allowed to be sold in the South so I brought this copy for you to read."

He read it carefully and then he read parts of it over. When he had finished the book Mrs. Woods came in and she asked, "Well, Doctor, what do you think of aunt Harriet Stowe's production?"

Father looked her in the face and then he laid the volume on the library fire and watched it burn.

"There, Mrs. Woods," he said, "that is the best place for it."

I wanted to read that book myself but it must have been a bad book for Father, who loves books, to have treated it that way.

November 4th.—This is Grandpa's birthday and he will be here tonight. I am so glad. Mother says I may go up the road to meet him if Father will go too. I know he will. Mother has a birthday feast ready for him and the long table is set with the prettiest things. Aunt Morea is scolding Bill and aunt Ginnie has cooked her very best sweet wafers, for, she says, "Ole Marster don't git no sech sweet wafers nowheres else, he say so his-self." Everybody is glad Grandpa is coming.

November 10th.—Last night I was telling Brother

Junius how we rejoiced to see grandpa and how all the older ones among the house servants came after breakfast to shake hands with him and ask after his health, and how he had a present for each; some of them had presents he had brought them from North Carolina and to the others he gave some money, and then I said, "Everybody loves Grandpa." But Brother Junius said that was not so. I asked him why, he said that and this was his answer, "I do not love him—in fact I have a deepseated grudge against him. When your sister and I were going to be married your father and your mother opposed it; well, they had a right—but grandparents have no right to meddle and I dislike the governor and always will."

I love Brother Junius and always will as he said about Grandpa, but I think it is ugly for him to talk that way. And why did Father and Mother object? I have never heard of it, but I will ask Father tonight what he meant.

November 16th.—Last night was the first opportunity I had to ask Father, he said, "I am sorry you have heard anything about this. Mr. Taylor should not have told you but, as he did, I will tell you this much, it is all over, your Sister Sarah has gone to a better land, you must forget it but I will have to explain your grandfather's position. He did not do anything wrong but a man rarely ever forgives interference in his love affairs. There is nothing wrong with your grandfather; he is a splendid man." So, I am satisfied, though I do not quite understand.

December 10th.—There is trouble in the air but I cannot find out just what it is. The grown folks keep very quiet when we children are around and if they are talking when we come into the room they stop right away; I wonder what it is? When I asked father, he said, "Some day I will tell you." When he says that I wait.

December 20th.—I know a little bit now. It is something Uncle Kinchen found out and told Grandpa. It is about those same Abolitionists and it must be serious, for the grown-up folks all look troubled. When Grandpa told what uncle Kinchen had found out, he said: "Kinchen is trustworthy and absolutely faithful. You know how often he and Amy have accompanied me to Northern cities, they have frequently been approached by Abolition agents, but their talk had no effect on them whatever.

"Since the publication of Uncle Tom's Cabin these agents have grown bolder and there have been instances where they have carried off negroes, who were unwilling to leave their owners. Fearing this, I made out manumission papers for Amy and Kinchen and had them recorded at Halifax court house, for it was my intention to take them with me to Boston, which is, as you all know, the very hot-bed of Abolitionism. Before leaving home I gave them these papers and explained their meaning, telling them that henceforth they were as free as I myself am.

"We went to Boston and just as was expected, the Abolitionists swarmed around the old couple, like yellow jackets around a sugar kettle, but, when they found that they were really free they lost interest and let them be.

"We stayed several weeks. I had business there and when business was disposed of I paid a long-promised visit to General Green. When we were again at home I was very busy and did not take much notice of little things, but one day something peculiar in Kinchen's face made me observe him closely. I also took a good look at Amy and she, too, seemed to have something on her mind, so I questioned Kinchen as to the trouble.

" 'Marster,' said he, 'it's dese here Free Stiffikites, what you gin ter me an' Amy, we ain't got no use fer dem. Ef 't gits out mongst de plantations 'round erbout dat we is free niggers, we won't ever hav' no 'spectability nur standin' in dis kummubity,"

This made us laugh and then Fannie and Bill brought in the bedroom candles and we said "good night" and went to bed. I did not sleep well. I dreamed the Abolitionists were after me and they like the Devil as uncle Aleck describes him, with horns and cloven feet. When I told father this he said "That is the fruit cake you ate last night," Perhaps it was.

Dec. 23rd.—Almost Christmas—preparations are well under way and all the family will dine with us on Christmas day. The next day we go to Live Oak; the next day we spend with Uncle Richard and Aunt Nancy; the next day we go to Uncle Tom's; the next day we spend in town with Aunt Sue and Uncle Arvah and then we go to Walnut Hill, to Uncle William and Aunt Mary.

Isn't it great to have so many kinsfolk? We always have a Christmas tree at our house and it has presents for everyone; not just one present, but lots.

January 8th.—This is Aunt Sue's birthday and she and her three dear little boys spent the day with us. They have only been gone a little while. Aunt Sue says her mother wanted to name her for General Jackson because she was born on the anniversary of the battle of New Orleans. I am so glad, so glad she did not, for I am named for aunt Sue and how I would hate to be named Andrew Jackson. The baby came too, but she is so little.

January 24th.—Uncle Bailey is here. He came last night and brought Aunt Eliza and Eddie. He is going to leave them with us for a good long while. The people of Jefferson have had some trouble with the Abolitionists. Why can't they stay at the North and let our people alone? Uncle Bailey was once a general in the army and afterward he was Captain of Regulators in Jefferson County. I love to listen while he tells of the stirring scenes in which he has taken part. Last night, when he was telling how ugly these men from the North had talked to the negroes in Jefferson, brother Junius said, "General, did you know what to do with them?" Uncle Bailey's blue eyes looked like they had sparks in them but all he said was, "I did." I shall not ask what it was.

February 9th.—John Robinson's Circus is coming to Tallahassee. I hope we can go. The posters are pasted all over town. Frances is begging to go.

March 4th.—We went to that circus and we took the measles, the black measles, which the doctors say is the very worst kind. People are dying with it in every direction for, as Father says, a circus is like a magnet and draws from all sides. There have been three deaths on Pine Hill Plantation and five on the Horse-shoe. Aunt Ginnie and Frances are both very ill and there are many more cases. All in the house had it "lightly" except our little Mattie. Father and Mother and Brother Junius sat up with her for a week and now Father and Mother are sitting up with Aunt Ginnie, who is so sick and all of us love her as well as if she was one of the white family.

March 9th, 1857.—This is terrible. Aunt Ginnie is dead. Isaac and Jane died in the night and Mother thinks my Lulu may die. Uncle Tony is wild with grief and Mother is almost as bad. They have sent to town for a coffin for Aunt Ginnie and they have dressed her in a pretty white dress with a white silk kerchief around her neck. She does not look like her dear self. We will all miss Aunt Ginnie.

March 18th.—Mother says death has taken his toll from us for none have died since that dreadful night Aunt Ginnie and the others died. Lulu is getting well and so are all the rest.

March 25th.—My birthday came and went and nobody thought of it, not even I, myself. There was so much else to think of and so much else to do. This is the year 1857 and I am eleven years old. There has been so much trouble that we have not been to Live Oak in a long time. Grandpa has been often to see us though and he says we must spend this next summer with him at Enfield. Father and Mother have consented and I know we will feel better to go to him and try to forget. So, we are planning to go in July. Father does not think he can leave home before that time.

April 6th, 1857.—We are trying to get back to our studies again. Sister Mag is practising her music once more and Sister Mart has never stopped hers She loves her music so dearly. Mattie is well again and she is so dear.

CHAPTER VI

A SUMMER IN NORTH CAROLINA

THE heated term of 1856 was spent at the sea-side. That winter Aunt Robinson again taught the children; you may be sure they learned, too, for a stricter teacher or one more thorough never lived.

This brings us to the Spring of 1857 with preparations going on for a visit to Enfield, the home of Governor Branch, in Halifax County, North Carolina. On the Aucilla River some trouble had developed but it was soon put down. The papers told us of similar troubles in Louisiana and Mississippi, also along the coast country of South Carolina but it seemed to have blown over.

We had no means of knowing how all this had affected the negroes. It was something we could not talk to them about. "Uncle Tom's Cabin" had reached its hundred and thirtieth edition; it had been translated into almost every language; it was the most popular book in all the world and yet it was a tissue of lies from beginning to end. What could we poor Southerners do? "Whom the Lord loveth He chasteneth, and scourgeth every son whom He receives."

Mrs. Stowe had gone to England, where she was entertained by royalty and from thence she made similar visits to every court in Europe. By means of "The Underground Railway" many slaves were enticed from their homes. These, for the most part, were never heard of again, but now and then one of intelligence and imagination, like Fred Douglass, would flash like a meteor across the Abolition skies. The tales he told, as false as those told by "Aunt Harriet" herself, were sent broadcast to the world. None questioned their truth and like all big lies they grew with the telling.

Sitting on Governor Branch's porch one summer morning we saw a man approaching the house, bearing in his hand a case which suggested a piano tuner, and such he proved to be and, when the piano had received the finishing touches, we were invited in to hear some music. The man proved to be a fine performer with a taste for classical music. After playing awhile, he sang some selections from different operas and then turning on the piano stool, he said, "How would you like to hear one of the very latest?" Of course we wanted to hear it, and after a plaintive prelude he sang:

"I went to New York City a month or two ago,
A huntin' fur dat lady Aunt Harriet Beecher Stowe,
I seed de Abolitions, dey sed she's gone away,
Dey tole me in de city dere warn't no place ter stay.
Oh, Oh, Oh, Aunt Harriet Beecher Stowe,
How could you leab de country an' serve pore Niggah so?"

"I cudn't git no wurk, I cudn't git no dinner
An' den I wished dis fugitive wus back in Old Virginner.
Oh, Oh, Oh, Aunt Harriet Beecher Stowe,
How could you leab de country an' serve pore Niggah So?"

After the lapse of so many years this is all we can resuscitate but it is enough. "You would not dare to sing that song in New York City?" some one questioned.

"Oh, yes," he said. "There is not a spot in the South more Southern than New York City, itself."

He told us then of the strong anti-abolition sentiment in New York and the friends the South had there. It was pleasant to listen to and we hoped it might be true.

During this visit to Enfield we took many short trips to other places; to Schocco Springs; to Old Point Comfort; to the White Sulphur Springs in Virginia; to various other points of interest. Then there were the many little excursions to nearby places, such as visiting the innumerable relatives; going to Weller's vineyard where were found such grapes as grew nowhere else in such perfection, as in the Old North State. We will let the little girl tell of some of these pleasures.

We did not find that the ghosts of Abolitionism were laid in North Carolina, on the contrary the subject was not tabooed as with us in Florida. Nearer the base it seemed to be and was often the subject of general conversation, yet even so but little could be known of the sentiment among the negroes. There had been at times, both in North and South Carolina, uprisings of a more or less serious nature.

THE DIARY RESUMED:

May 29th, 1857.—We are really going to North Carolina and Father is going with us this time. It is almost too good to be true. There is one cloud in my sky. Mother says we must take Frances with us that she may see her mother and grandmother. Now, Frances is very bad and nobody likes her very much, I have grown fond of her. Mother says we always love the child who gives us the most trouble and all the family laugh at me about "my objectionable little maid," as they call her but she will not be any trouble after we get to Enfield, for Aunt Amy and Ann will have her all the time with them.

Aunt Robinson says we must keep on at school until the Friday before we leave. I am glad of that but it is hard to think of your lessons when so many pleasant thoughts are coming to your mind. She is going with us and Sister Mag says she is thankful the lessons are not to be continued all summer. But Sister Mag is a grown young lady now and does not study any more; she sings and plays a great deal and I love to hear her, she has such a sweet voice.

June 5th, 1857.—Our black folks are all sorry we are going away, I hope Aunt Dinah will take good care of Lavinia. I have given her the trunkful of clothes for they will be too small for her by the time we get back. I am wondering, too, what will become of me without my Lulu, I do miss my black Mammy dreadfully when we go traveling, but she has little children who need her even more than I do.

June 20th, 1857.—We have had beautiful weather until today, it is raining hard and the wind is blowing like a storm.

June 30th, 1857.—The rainy season is certainly with us. It has rained nearly every day for ten days and tomorrow we start for Enfield. The roads through Georgia are never very good in wet weather because there are so many little streams everywhere.

This visit to North Carolina was always looked forward to as a great event; there were no railroads at that time south of Albany, Georgia, and travel to the railroad terminus was in carriages. Naturally it was slow, two days were spent on the road and if there was any delay, two nights as well.

Southern Georgia, at that time was an almost unbroken forest of stately and beautiful pines. The turpentine operator had not laid his destructive hand upon them and only one saw-mill showed up on the way to Albany. Houses were few and far between and if the weather permitted, camping out was preferred to seeking accommodations in the homes of the settlers, for these homes were of the crudest designs and finish. The floors were "puncheon" the chimneys "stick and dirt." There was seldom room enough for the family themselves, but so kind and hospitable were these Georgians that the traveler seldom, or never asked in vain. It was the country *par excellence,* for children. We have sometimes counted as many as eight in one home, like steps, each a little smaller than the next until the baby was reached.

We have often wondered, and we wish some scientific investigator would find out, and tell us, why so many of these South Georgia families were blondes, of the fairest type too, and "lint-white locks" were the prevailing style. We loved to ride through this land of pines; the air was delicious, the wiregrass was studded with flowers of every hue and from the clear, limpid waters of the Ocklocknee to the rolling waves of the muddy Flint, streams were abundant and sometimes so deep as to be dangerous.

CHAPTER VII

LEAVES FROM THE DIARY

ENFIELD, North Carolina, July 16th, 1857.—We have been here more than a week and this is the first time I have thought of you, my diary. Before we left home I let Brother Junius read a few pages of these records and he says I write correctly but I do not tell of events in a way to make them clear to those, who, in future years may read them. "But Brother Junius," I said, "I am not writing for the future, but for myself, and I understand."

"Yes," he answered, "you think so, but it may be as I say, so I want you to write out fully all that you think is of sufficient importance to put in your diary; most especially do I ask this of you for this summer. You know Mattie is all my world and everything you write, all the pleasures you share, all the adventures you meet up with, and the new acquaintances you make will be of interest to me."

So I have promised to do my best. We left home on the 1st of July. The clouds were black, and before we reached Duncansville the rain was pouring down; we reached the river in safety but the road was under water all the way. The rain had come to be just a mist by this time and the river was so high it was impossible to ford it as we usually did. An old man had a flat-boat there and said he could take us over. Father said it looked doubtful but there was no other way to get across. There were two baggage wagons, three carriages and a double buggy and it took five trips across to get us all to the other side. The ferry-man was old and thin, his hair was long and white and blew about in the wind. He wore neither hat nor shoes and as he poled us across he sang:

"Jesus wept, and well He might,
To see the sinner take his flight."

Brother Junius thought this was poor comfort and Aunt Robinson looked severe and said he was a wicked old man. Once on the other side we made better time but there was rain all the way. Not a hard, washing down-pour, as it had been, but enough to be disagreeable. That night we had to seek shelter and we were fortunate in finding a clean, new house. Only one room, to be sure, and there were fourteen white people in our party, but Mrs. Morgan was most accommodating and she was well-paid for her trouble.

Next morning we made a very early start and reached Albany that night. We thought our troubles were at an end when we boarded the train, but not so, a few miles from Macon there had been a wash-out and the train turned on its side and frightened us half to death. The smoky little lights all went out and the lanterns of the trainmen were the only lights to be seen. Frances took that time to be just as bad as she could be and that is pretty trying. Now she is almost as old as I am and dear little Mattie, who is five years younger, was as good as gold. We were delayed several hours and so we missed the train we should have gone on. We stayed at the Lanier House and mother let Fannie take us walking around the city. It was rather wet but pleasant in spite of that. Father and mother could not go with us because they had company. I do believe they know people wherever they go.

When we left Macon we thought we would get to Enfield the next morning, but it was an awful spell of weather and we made many stops, we were six days on the road and when we reached grandpa's we found him almost wild with grief, because Dr. Holland, who was on the opposite side of the river when we were considering whether to risk the old ferry-man or not, had reached Enfield the day before and had told it that he was sure, if we attempted to cross we were drowned. Everything was in readiness for us and a few hours' rest made us all new again. It is delightful here and all the kinsfolk are just fine. I do love kinsfolk.

September 6th, 1857.—Little Diary, I am afraid you stand a poor showing here, where there is so much going on, but I can write when I get back to Florida and use my eyes and ears while I am skipping around in this exciting fashion. We are at Shocco Springs, in Warren County, North Carolina. It is a lovely place; there are five hundred people here, the manager says. There are more than usual because there is to be a tournament next week and after that a fancy ball. It will be fine and we children are looking forward to it all as eagerly as the grown people. Mrs. Brownlee's pretty niece, Miss Winslow, is going as a shepherdess and she has borrowed my brown leghorn hat to wear.

There are a number of nice children here, Cora and Valentine Jordan, from Charleston; the Stanford boys from Petersburg, and a lot of others, including those of our party, Theora, Eliza and John Branch, of Enfield; my little step-uncles, who are no older than I am, and Mattie and I. The grown people talk of nothing but the ball and we follow suit.

September 10th.—Well, the tournament is over! The knights were not as prettily dressed as those in Tallahassee, but the riding was good and they had the ball but I have been a bad girl and the worst of it is I still think I was right. Of course mother is right but I cannot see it yet. It was this way, the girls I play with had agreed that we would wear white dresses to the ball. I did not think mother would care and I did not have a chance to ask her, for she was visiting Uncle Washington Branch and Aunt Julia. The morning of the tournament I put on a rose-colored lawn and was on my way out of the room when mother called me back.

"Susie," she said, "take off that dress and put on the white one with the white ribbons."

"Oh, mother," I said, "please let me wear this, I want to wear that pretty white dress to the ball tonight."

She made me change my dress and I cried and was ugly about it. I know that was wrong and I will not say one word but I was unhappy all day. That night all the girls had on white dresses but me. My dress was a gold-colored silk tissue, trimmed with lace and grandma talked to me and told me my dress was far handsomer than any little girl there had on, but grandma does not understand. I do not care to have prettier or nicer things than others have, I only want to be like the rest.

The Fairchild children in Mrs. Sherwood's books always tried to remember all the bad things they did and prayed about them constantly. Maybe this is not the way I ought to feel but I shall try to forget this trouble and I shall be such a good child that mother will forget, too.

September 12th.—We are at Enfield once more. This morning grandpa called me to get my bonnet and go to ride with him. When I was little I rode on a pillow in front of him but now I am so big I ride on a horse by myself. I rode Betsy Trotwood this morning. We went to the apple orchard. The apples had ripened up amazingly while we were gone. We rode down by the spring, where I had never been before and we stopped under a tree loaded with beautiful red apples and grandpa said, "These are queer apples, examine them and see if you can find out why they are queer?"

I looked and at least a dozen apples had my name on them in white on the red skin. It was so wonderful and I could hardly believe grandpa had written on these apples with a piece of tallow and then covered the place with a strip of cloth. I was so pleased and I am just as proud as can be. Haven't I got the dearest grandpa? Father is going to New York tomorrow. He will take Sister Mag and Sister Mart and Cousin Lizzie and Miss Hennie Winchester who is Grandma's niece. I want to go with him but Mother thinks I would be in the way. She says when I am eighteen she will take me to New York herself and buy me all the things a young lady should have. I wish I was going now though, for Father is taking them to Niagara and Saratoga and they will stop quite a while in New York City and see all the sights. We are going to Old Point Comfort.

September 15th.—I am glad I did not beg to go with father and the girls. Old Point Comfort is a most interesting place. Fortress Monroe, with its moat is not like anything I ever saw before, the general commanding is an old friend of Grandpa's and he lets us look over the fort and see so many things. The officers' quarters are inside the fort, the men are drilled nearby and they have a splendid band.

We are stopping at the Hygeia Hotel, the ball-room is very large and every night the band plays and the enormous room is filled with dancers. There are no children here, so we do not dance but sit quietly by Mother and Grandma and look on.

Professor DeBow, of DeBow's Review is here. Grandpa says he is a very brilliant man. Last night at supper-table the conversation turned on abolitionism. The people here do not avoid it as we do in Florida. Professor DeBow said, "The entire North is saturated with this unfortunate 'ism; here and there you find a nugget of pure gold, which cannot be contaminated but they are few. I see in the future, as an outgrowth of this movement a disregard for the sanctity of the marriage relation, a setting aside of the command to honor thy father and thy mother" while the Golden Rule sinks into oblivion. Even the field of Poesy is invaded by this spirit, a late poem from the pen of one of the North's favorite poets reads like this:

'Dusky daughters of a down-trod race,' etc.

"Take my word for it, there is trouble ahead—God grant that our united efforts may avert it."

I have tried to write this word for word just as the great man spoke it.

September 20th.—Father has come back from New York. They did not stay as long as we expected. I am so glad to see him but sorry to leave Old Point Comfort. We have had a fine time here. Grandma has taught me to swim and I have been out to the rip-raps. (I hope that is spelled right) it is a kind of lighthouse but not like the one at St. Marks; they say it is built up from the bottom with stones and the waves lash around it all day long.

September 22nd.—We came over to Portsmouth yesterday on a large steamer. We reached here in the afternoon and as soon as the hotel people recognized Grandpa they sent large trays filled with delicious things to eat as a compliment to him. I forgot to tell that the people everywhere know Grandpa and show him so much attention.

We had hardly finished eating when a waiter came with a letter, on a tray. It was an invitation to our party to visit the man-of-war "Pennsylvania". We went and had a glorious time. The Stars and Stripes were flying and the band playing when the small boat we were in drew up to the vessel's side. At a word from the captain, they began to play, "All hail to the Chief." Father says that is because Grandpa was once Secretary of the Navy.

The Captain had his men show us all over the vessel we drank some water, which had been in the casks for twenty years, we saw the shining weapons which hung ready for use and we felt very proud of this great ship. The captain invited us to come aboard after supper and have a dance and the young ladies in the party would have liked it but Grandpa did not accept.

I am writing this on the train for Enfield and must stop to see the Roanoke River.

September 30th.—We have seen many places this summer; we have met many new kinspeople and now we must think of going home. Mother has sent Fannie on ahead to Charleston, S. C., to see her kin there for a few days and we will stop for her on our way home. Ann is waiting on Mother until we leave. I am sorry to say goodbye to all these dear ones and most especially Grandpa, but it will be nice to get home again.

October 12th.—We have passed Charleston and Fanny is with us once more. We are taking Frances back, too. I asked her this morning if she had a good time in Enfield?

She said, "No, I didn't, I ain't done nothing all this time but nuss Mammy's baby an' I fair hates him, I'm glad der ain't no babies at home."

"Don't you love your little brother?" I asked.

"No, I don't love him one bit, I hates young niggers."

Mother told her that was an ugly way to talk but she just rolled her big black eyes and pouted. She is not amiable.

October 22nd, 1857.—It is so pleasant to be at home again and see everybody, that I have neglected my diary. Mother had her carriage out and took us around the neighborhood; it was such fun to tell Cousin Rob about our trip. I did want him to go with us just the worst in the world. Buddy has been very busy all the summer, there has been so much sickness and still is.

Father took me to the Horse-shoe and we saw dear little Lorah and aunt Pendar and the ducks and geese. Everybody seems to be well on both plantations except uncle Alick, who will never be well again and aunt Polly, who has "Bin tricked by de Kunjer-man and is full of lizards and snakes." That is what she says is the matter with her. Anyway she does not do one thing but sit in her house with Lilah to wait on her. Her legs are bound around with strips of cloth and she talks about the reptiles running up and down her limbs all the time. I asked father what was the matter with her and he said "varicose veins," so I shall not believe in the snakes.

My Lulu and her children are well and I am so glad to have her again. Robert has kept well while we were away. Robert, you know, is Fanny's only child. He is ten years old and very small for his age. Mother told Fanny, when we were planning to go away for the summer, that she would like to have her go too, but if she felt bad about leaving her child she would take one of the younger maids who had no children. Fannie did not want to be left behind. She spoke up without hesitation:

"Miss Patsey, I know Lulu will take good care of him, just as good as I could myself, and I don't want to gie my place to none 'o dese gals."

That settled the matter and Brother Junius, who spends one day in the week at Pine Hill, when we are away, promised to write a letter to her for Robert and tell her how he gets along. This he did and now she is at home and nothing has happened to him. Each of us brought Robert a present but I think Fanny must have bought him one in every town we visited, she had such an armful, toys, candy, new clothes, a cap, a hat, fancy shoes for Sundays and a small umbrella; he was almost wild with joy.

October 25th, 1857.—Mother told us at the breakfast table this morning that a new governess was coming next week. She was born in England, was educated at The Patapasco Institute in Maryland and comes with the highest recommendation from Mother's old friend, Mrs. Heywood.

Both pianos have been tuned, the school room is being put in apple-pie order, the flowers around the door have been worked and trimmed and I will be glad to get to work once more. Mattie will go to school this winter, her little head of golden curls will look sweet bending over the desk.

November 1st, 1857.—School begins today. Mother wanted Miss Damer to wait until tomorrow but she said "no." We had a big dancing party last night with a frolic for Hallowe'en and Mother was afraid Miss Damer would be tired but she said she was not. She dances beautifully and sings gloriously. She is pretty, too, with quantities of chestnut curls. In front, just above her forehead is the funniest roll of wirelike hair. It is as stiff as wire when you touch it and just the color of her curls, she says it is a "family mark."

I told her how I loved to hear her sing and she said she had studied music for the stage but her people would not hear of it. We have all new books as mother had written to Miss Damer to buy in Baltimore the books that were used at Patapasco, so we have Woodbridges & Willard's High School Geography, Willard's Universal History, Boyd's Rhetoric, Brewer's Science of Things Familiar, Davies' Algebra, Scholar's Companion, Ollendorf's French, Ware's Elements of Character. The last is not one of the books used at Patapsco but is one father selected; perhaps some of the others were, too.

We read alternately in the Sixth McGuffey and the Sixth Towns Readers; we also write compositions every two weeks and recite alternate weeks. I know what is coming because Miss Damer has programmes which she has tacked up on the school room wall. I began with Frances' lessons as soon as we got home; she had not forgotten and she is learning nicely now; she is never bad about her books and she studies often when I have not told her to. Mother says that speaks well for both of us.

November 5th, 1857.—Today ends our first week at school. Such a delightful surprise; cousins Theora and Eliza have come from North Carolina to go to school here and cousins Anne and Alice have come, too, also cousin Jennie Whitaker. We will have a large school for sister Mart and Mattie also attend and we have three of the neighborhood children.

Our school room is large and airy with plenty of light but there are trees around it which prevents the sun from shining in too bright. We have a large blackboard on an easel with a musical score, as well as other things. We all study music and a music-master comes out from Tallahassee. That gives Miss Damer time to play and sing for us—that is, when she feels like it.

Her name is Letitia Hannah Damer, and we are all wild about her. She is not like anyone we ever saw before. I forgot to say we opened school on Tuesday and Miss Damer would teach Saturday to make the week, she has such a nice way of making us study.

November 7th, 1857.—This is Monday night, all went well in school. Miss Damer explains things to us and makes our lessons so interesting. We are studying Smith's Grammar, too. We had studied Murray's Grammar to aunt Robinson—it is a big, leather-covered book with a rule for everything. Smith's is a small book and easy.

November 21st, 1857.—Monday night again. Miss Damer makes us study for an hour after supper, so I have very little time to write in my diary. Lessons grow more interesting every day.

Miss Damer does not want me to teach Frances; she says it takes time which should be devoted to other things and father and mother agree with her. I have told Frances and she is sorry, but she promises that she will read some in her third reader every day and try to remember what she has learned. When vacation comes I can teach her as I did before.

December 12th, 1857.—We are all excited over the largest Christmas tree we have ever had. So far it is only planned but we are making gifts and sister Mag bought me a pair of large wooden needles and some white Shetland wool to knit a nubia for mother. It has to be three yards long, maybe I'll have to sit up nights to get it done.

December 22nd, 1857.—The tree is up and we are making decorations. Miss Damer took us for a walk in the woods to select the tree and Peter and Mack, who are carpenters, brought it to the house and nailed it securely to the bottom of a large tub; this was filled with earth and planted over with the soft green moss which grows beside the stream. There are also some partridge berries planted in it. The tree is a beautifully shaped short-leaved pine.

Miss Damer knows so many things to do to make it pretty. We have dozens and dozens of colored wax tapers and we have picked the prettiest pine cones and, after dampening them slightly, we rubbed them with sifted flour. We then fastened them with fine wire to the branches of the tree and, warming the end of each candle to make it stick, we put each on a pine cone for a candle-stick.

When the decorations are done Miss Damer is going to shut us out while she and Sister Mag and Mother and Brother Junius put the presents on. All the kinsfolk are coming to dine here and there will be presents for everybody. We do not put the Christmas gifts for the servants on the tree, but give them Christmas morning, when they all assemble in the back yard.

Dec. 28th, 1857.—Oh, the fun we have had. A dance Christmas eve; the beautiful tree, with the splendid fruit it bore, the dinner which mother takes so much pride in (she is just the best housekeeper in the world) ; the merry games Christmas night; the games the grown people join us in; the visiting around the family circle. Oh! it is too jolly for words.

There is one thing, however, I do not quite like, we will not see Miss Damer until the two weeks holiday is over. She is very attractive and Mrs. Call and Mrs. Gamble and Aunt Sue (Mrs. Hopkins) are entertaining her at their different homes. I know she will enjoy it and we must not be selfish. Mother's nubia got done and she likes it and wears it.

January 15th, 1858.—A New Year and two weeks have passed without an entry here. It takes a little time to settle down to study after a holiday, then, too, we have been hearing so much of Miss Damer's visit to town. She has organized a Shakespeare Club, of which she is the President, and the young ladies and gentlemen of Tallahassee have gone wild over it. Miss Damer is a splendid reader. She added elocution to our course of study after the first month. The Club meets twice a month and she is to go in on Friday afternoon previous. Mother offered to send her but Mr. Wilk Call and Mr. Villepigue and Dr. Shine are all contending for the honor of coming for her and bringing her home Sunday evening.

February 4th, 1858.—I never did love my studies as well. I love them all except algebra. I never did like arithmetic and this is as bad. I am stupid where figures are concerned. We have such long lessons that we are well on in our books and have finished Brewer's Science and have taken Johnston's Chemistry in its place. Along with that we are reading Chemistry of Common Life. One does not really enjoy the good things to eat though when the eating and drinking is reduced to a science.

March 2nd, 1858.—Compositions are such fun. Miss Damer selects our subjects for us and we write absolutely what we please. On Wednesday we hand them in to her and she corrects mistakes and explains to us why the corrections were mistakes. Then she sends out invitations to the neighbors, for Friday afternoon and she reads the compositions aloud. We have a house full and they all say that we are improving rapidly. We finished Rhetoric today and we take up Kames' Elements of Criticism.

We have gone through Willard's Universal History and we have in its place a very entertaining history of England, with many illustrations. We were looking these over when cousin Alice exclaimed, "Oh, girls, look here; this picture of King George is exactly like Miss Damer." We looked and all could see the likeness, even the roll of rough hair above the forehead, the profile was exact. Miss Damer came in and we held up the picture for her to see the likeness. She merely glanced at it and said, "Yes, I know, I am his granddaughter." Her voice was sad and she immediately rang the bell for us to get to our places.

I felt bad and after school I asked mother what it meant? She said, "I cannot tell you anything more than that, you must not ask Miss Damer any questions, there is a mystery. She told me when she came. She has not done anything wrong, she has only been unfortunate." And with that I had to be content.

April 6th, 1858.—Such a delightful happening today —too good to be true. "All's well that ends well," they say, and this did not end well. The last lesson in old Davies' Algebra was recited just before noon and I walked to the open window and pitched the book as far as I could send it into the tangle of sweetbriar, just beyond. The weather is very warm for April and the sun was like July, but Miss Damer made me go and pick up that book and bring it to her.

Nothing on earth is quite so thorny as the sweetbriar. I wear low-necked, short-sleeved dresses, and my face, my hands and my arms are torn and bleeding.

I feel ashamed for father to see me, for this is a "bad mark" indeed. We will study geometry now. I think I shall like it better than algebra.

May 1st, 1858.—Our new drawing books came from New York last night; ever since we started to school we have been taking a simple course in drawing but these new books are much more difficult. It is the course taught at the Marietta Military Academy and they are recommended by cousin Johnnie Bradford, who graduated from that institute. There are three large books and Father ordered, to come along with them sheets of bristol board; also thin drawing books the size of the large ones so we can copy conveniently, and dozens of pencils. Miss Damer says if I will try my best she will let me copy The Temple of Time as a birthday gift for Father.

May 7th, 1858.—We have been through the grammar twice and stood a good examination on it, so we are to put it aside and take up botany in its stead. The botany we will study is by Mrs. Lincoln Phelps, who was Miss Damer's teacher. I know I shall love botany for Father is a fine botanist and he has taught me to analyze flowers and to recognize many plants by their leaves. Brother Junius says I do not write about anything but my lessons but I do not think of much else. When your whole mind is on your studies there is not room for other things.

We take long walks in search of specimens and we are to have herbariums, in which to arrange and classify these specimens, after they have been properly pressed. Miss Damer goes twice a month to the Shakespeare Club and it must be a fine amusement for all who belong to it take such a deep interest. We miss her when she is away, she gets letters sometimes, which trouble her, but Mother says I must not ask questions.

Mother is teaching Frances to embroider and Lulu

is teaching her to hemstitch and roll and whip; she is also learning to make tatting and to crochet. I'm afraid she will get ahead of me she will be so smart.

May 29th.—Cousin Lize is the best musician in the school, except Sister Mart, who is a wonderful performer and never tires of the piano. I love music but my broken arm hurts me so when I have practised even a little while. I enjoy hearing the other girls play and I love Sister Mag's songs and Miss Damer's music is splendid.

June 5th, 1858.—Sister Mag has a number of new songs and I always sit beside her when she is learning them, even if I have to study out of hours to get my lessons; last night, I sang one of these songs with her, she said I sang it all right. It is a patriotic song; there is a colored picture of The Star-Spangled Banner on the cover and the tune is fine, also the words.

Today I went to ride with Father and we were talking of Sister Mag and I offered to sing the pretty new song for him. When I sang

> "Oh, perish the heart and the hand
> That would mar our motto of
> Many in one,"

Father said, "Take care, my baby, you may be calling down condemnation on your own." Of course I wanted to know what he meant, for "E Pluribus Unum" had seemed a beautiful sentiment to me. Then Father, explained what he meant, for the first time I heard of the strong, deep feeling of dislike and mistrust, which existed between the North and the South. For the first time the much dreaded Abolitionists took a tangible form.

I asked many questions and Father answered patiently and when we reached home he called me to the library and gave me a book by John C. Calhoun to read.

He said I could come to him if there was anything I did not understand.

The doctrine of State's Rights is very clear, perhaps it is clearer because I have so often heard it discussed by Father and the various gentlemen, who talk with him in the library. I study my lessons in there, and I sometimes stop to listen. I have learned more of the history of Virginia from the conversations between Father and Mr. Lane, who teaches in the Military School in Tallahassee, than I ever found in the books.

June 27th, 1858.—I have read a great deal in the two volumes of the Writings of John C. Calhoun and Father has told me still more. I have found out something else, Mother does not approve of slavery—she would be glad not to own a single slave, you see they are called slaves in these books I have been reading. She says her reason for this is that the white people are the real slaves. She thinks as time goes on it will become more so and she wishes to see them all freed and sent to Liberia. I do not want to give up my Lulu, nor do I want her to be sent to Liberia.

July 1st, 1858.—Uncle Tony has had another stroke of paralysis; this time it is much worse than before. He is Lulu's father, and Mother has excused her from all duties in the house, that she may take care of him. Lulu's house is just outside the back yard, it has one large room and two smaller ones; uncle Tony stays in the large room where he can have all the company he wants. He likes everybody to come to see him, that is, he did, but now, since this last stroke he cannot speak, though he understands all that is said to him. Mother has his meals cooked and sent to him and Lulu eats from our table just as she always has done. Mother says a fire this warm weather would make him uncomfortable.

July 20th.—We are studying hard. Miss Damer invites all in the neighborhood to come every other Friday afternoon to hear us examined. Father has requested the pleasure of examining us on "Elements of Character." I am so glad I really learned the lessons as we went along, for now I am not afraid. Father says if he could be sure his baby would live according to the rules laid down in that book he would be satisfied and happy. I shall take care of my book as long as I live and read it over now and then.

July 30th, 1858.—Dr. English and Charley came last night to spend the next two months with us. Charley is a dear little boy and I try to like the doctor but he is a very fine mathematician and he does not take it into account that we are going to school. He wants us to engage in all sorts of abstruse problems, such as distances between stars, the movements of the sun and the earth, and every sort of calculation, which astronomy calls for. I do not like figures and it hurts my eyes to look long at the heavens and I do get so sleepy, Miss Damer says she does not intend to allow it this summer.

August 1st, 1858.—Cousin Nolan is here on a visit; he is cousin Jack Whitaker's son and they live in Louisiana. Cousin Nolan has been at college until four weeks ago and his eyes are so bad that he cannot go back. He is to stay in Florida for a year and see if his eyes will not improve. He cannot use them at all and has to wear a bandage all day; at night he sits in the dark. He is something of a nuisance for he sits in the school room door, or sprawls on the floor and makes fun of our recitations and compositions. Brother Junius tells him he is sure he could not do as well himself, and then he laughs. He is full of fun and very good natured. He is twenty years old. Father says big boys always love to tease girls younger than themselves and he is suffering so we must be kind to him.

August 25th, 1858.—This is Father's birthday and my picture of The Temple of Time was ready for him.

He was pleased and surprised. It is prettily framed and is hanging on the Library wall.

August 26th.—Miss Damer has such an odd plan for the month of September. School should end the last Friday in August, but she wants school to continue through September and then another term would begin in October. We have been at home all the summer. All the family have kept well and our house is cool and airy. We have been quite comfortable. Her idea is to change the hours devoted to study in this way, instead of riding horseback from dawn to seven o'clock, we are to give up the rides and go instead to the school room and study and recite until we are called to breakfast at half past eight. At nine we return to our studies and at twelve o'clock we will be through for the day, except for music.

At first Mother and Father were not willing, but when Miss Damer explained to them that in this way we would finish some of the books and also advance in others, thus enabling us to finish the prescribed course in the succeeding ten months, they gave their consent. Some of the girls refused to do this as they wished to have some time for visiting, but there are eight of us in all to follow this new plan.

September 18th.—Such a strange thing has happened. It seems that Mother has known, ever since Miss Damer came to live with us, that there was some mystery where she was concerned but we did not know what. This morning a gentleman came and asked to see Miss Sandys. Mother knew whom he meant and sent to the school room for Miss Damer. He proved to be a barrister from London, who came to represent her guardian and brought papers with him to prove his identity. These same papers told that she was the granddaughter of King George of England and she had inherited a large fortune, her name was Letitia Hannah Sandys and she had to go immediately to London. She was overjoyed for she had been looking forward to this fortune and the call to England. We were distressed beyond measure. We love her and she is the best teacher we ever had.

The gray-eyed Englishman gave us a talk, while he was waiting for Miss Damer. First he asked why we loved her so well. This was easily explained and then he asked if we would like to hear something of her history. Of course we would, so he began by telling us of Prince George, of England, who loved the beautiful and attractive Mrs. Maria Fitz Herbert. She would not listen to him at first but finally he persuaded her to marry him. At this time he was Prince of Wales. The marriage ceremony was performed by a clergyman of the Church of England. It was in every respect, a legal marriage, but the laws of Great Britain forbid one of royal blood marrying a subject. This, Mrs. Fitz Herbert did not know. When George the Fourth ascended the throne, he put aside his forbidden wife and married Caroline of Brunswick. It was a most unhappy union, and after years of misery Queen Caroline left him and he recalled his first wife. This lady was Miss Damer's grandmother. Her mother married a young army officer named Sandys.

For some reason, (he did not tell us why), he left the British army and came to America under the assumed name of Damer. His wife had died and left two small children; our Miss Damer was the oldest. Her guardian in England looked after her education and paid all her expenses. When she came to Florida her guardian knew just where she was and who she was with. Now she was heir to a large fortune and he had been sent to escort her to England. We might rest assured, he said, that all would be well with her.

My heart aches at the thought of giving her up. It is like a romance.

Mrs. White-Spunner, of Belfast, Ireland, who, in 1857-58, as Miss Letitia Hannah Damer, taught the children at Pine Hill Plantation

THE STORY GOES ON

Again we close the diary to explain Miss Damer. Mrs. Bradford knew her history before employing her to teach her children but it was to be kept a secret and her pupils only knew that she was in some way a descendant of King George the Fourth. Her face was so exactly like the pictures of the King that one could not doubt. She was remarkably bright in mind and beautiful in person, despite the likeness mentioned. Her voice would have made her fortune on the stage and we believe she was intended by nature for an actress, so eloquently did she render Shakespeare at the Club meetings. Though no one knew it, she was being carefully looked after by her guardians in England. Her father had been an officer in the British army but for some cause, to us unknown, he had lost his position and under an assumed name, had taken refuge in America. Two little motherless children accompanied him and they settled in Baltimore, where he married again.

We have told you how closely she was kept at the Patapsco Institute and, when she left Patapsco to come to Florida, her guardians knew just where and to whom she was going.

When she was sent for by Mrs. Bradford to see a stranger her first thought was of news from England and yet she was so frightened that she could not, at first, control herself.

"I have been so happy here," she cried, pale as death she sat like a statue, while this dignified Englishman explained his errand. There were papers to be read and signed; pictures to be compared and arrangements to be made. We had never met an Englishman of this type before and the interest felt was deep.

He was tall and rather spare, he wore the inevitable "mutton chops," but even that could not destroy the highly intellectual expression, and the steel gray eyes bespoke one who could be trusted. He had his orders not to lose sight of her after finding her. We suppose they felt that she might not wish to go but they need not have had a fear, after the first few minutes she was simply wild with delight; she was like a child.

All the family were pressed into service to help her, while Fanny, the maid, folded and packed, all the rest were looking around to see what could be added to contribute to her comfort. The hour of departure came all too quickly and many were left behind to regret our loss. There was never a young lady in Tallahassee, who was more admired and sought after, yet she had no money. We had almost said she had no clothes, for the first thing Mrs. Bradford did, the morning after her arrival, was to put a seamstress to work to mend up such garments as she had, and materials were ordered to make more.

The young lady herself told it among her friends, when she had become well acquainted, "I arrived in Tallahassee on the mid-day train and was met at the depot by a trim, dignified maid and a coachman of equal dignity, with a message from Mrs. Bradford, to the effect that a headache had prevented her from meeting me herself, so she had sent a thoroughly trustworthy maid. I was told to 'bring one trunk with me and the wagon would come in that afternoon for the rest of my baggage.' Oh, how I laughed! I had only one small trunk and that was not half full."

It seems an allowance was placed in the hands of her father, for her use but it had never reached her. Her expenses at school were paid directly from England.

She made us many promises to write, but it was months before we heard from her, she was in the midst of change and excitement and happy in the spending of a great fortune.

Later on came the news of her marriage to the Rev. White-Spunner and her removal to a castle in Ireland.

Letters came more frequently, accompanied by pressing invitations to visit her in her Irish home; but in the meantime the War Between the States had resulted in the conquest of the South and the Southern people were left poverty-stricken indeed. No longer was there money for travel and we considered ourselves fortunate if we could supply our daily needs. To do this, required steady and unceasing effort, with no time for pleasure except that which comes from the consciousness of "duty done."

CHAPTER VIII

WEDDING BELLS

OF course Miss Damer's departure broke up the school at Pine Hill. The Branch cousins went to relatives in Tennessee and were put at school in Nashville; the Bradford cousins, to the dismay of their uncles, who tried to take the place of the father they had lost, turned out in society as young ladies, at the age of fourteen and sixteen. The children of the household were again placed in Aunt Robinson's care and study went steadily on. At least it did with the writer of the diary and the little niece, Mattie Taylor.

The two older girls were now in society and were having a gay time. In those days entertainments were not at all as they are now; a crowd of ladies by themselves was unknown, whether the party was a dining, an afternoon affair or a regular party at night, there were, as nearly as possible, an equal number of ladies and gentlemen. Those were the days when Sir Knight, even if he did not deserve it, aspired to be a Sir Galahad. Courtesy toward all women was the order of the day, no doubltful remarks, no double-entendres, no satires on womanhood were heard. The man who indulged in such would have been speedily banished from polite society and all knew this, consequently such innuendoes were not in evidence to offend good taste and propriety. A gay winter was added to by the presence of the Misses Donelson from Tennessee and a number of young Georgians, graduates of the preceding spring from The University of Georgia, at Athens. Before the season was fairly over three weddings were announced. The Bradford neighborhood was all excitement and activity, for, to prepare for such events means a world of work. We again read from the pages of the diary:

June 1st, 1859.—For two months now there has been nothing but

> "Buying and planning and sewing,
> With dressmakers coming and going,"

for Sister Mag is to be married on the 15th of this month to Mr. Amos Whitehead. I felt very bad about it at first but she is so happy that I try to be, too. They were playmates when they were children and sweethearts then, but they had not seen each other for years. They met and the childish love blazed up at their first meeting as grown folks and "the course of true love" seems to be running smoothly, for everybody is pleased. The families have been friends for generations. That is, everybody is pleased except a young gentleman who thought he held first place in her heart until Mr. Whitehead came.

I have been so busy thinking of all this, and getting acquainted with my brother, who is to be, that I have not written one word of dear Cousin Mag's wedding, which took place two weeks ago. She is a beautiful young lady and she wore the loveliest dress. All of us went to the wedding. There were ten bridesmaids and as many groomsmen; they quite filled the back parlor and made such a pretty picture.

I had my first real trouble with Frances in connection with the wedding. For each bridesmaid there was a basket, made of cake, iced and ornamented, with a high handle wrapped with satin ribbon. In one basket was a ring and in another a three cent piece, the bridesmaid who got the ring would be the next bride and the girl who drew the three cent piece would never marry. Sister Mart brought her basket to me and I thought I would give it to little Eddie Bailey, who is staying with us for a few weeks. He was in bed asleep when we got home, so I asked Mother where she thought I had better put it. She wrapped it carefully and put it in the library and next morning I told Eddie I had something for him and, lo and behold, it was gone.

I have tried so hard to raise Frances with good principles. She knows every one of the Commandments and they have been explained to her. I have told her that when she wants anything she must come and tell me and if I can give it to her she shall have it. So far as I then knew she had never taken anything, so I did not think of her when I missed the basket, but when a search was made we found Frances under the bed in the front room with the remains of the basket in her hand and crumbs scattered about the floor. It was such a disappointment to me for I wanted her, above all things, to be honest.

Mother gave a big dining the day after Cousin Mag was married and I heard the funniest thing. Gentlemen, nowadays, wear the tightest clothes, that is the young ones and the fashionable ones. Father does not dress in this ridiculous fashion, neither does Grandpa nor my uncles, but most people do. Brother Junius says I must not say "pants"—he says "pantaloons" and so I must too, I suppose. Well, these pantaloons fit a little tighter than the skin and the coats are just as tight, the vests are splendid garments, made of flowered satin, usually white, and they are fitted to the figure like a lady's dress. Take it altogether they are very peculiar looking and I have often wondered how they got in and out of these tight garments; now I have found out.

One of the ladies at the dining is a very bright woman, she is always saying something which, as Father says, "brings down the house." She speaks rather slowly and her voice is soft and low, like Annie Laurie's

I imagine, and this makes her funny speeches more effective.

"We were a little late getting to the wedding last night," she said, "in fact we came near missing the ceremony, and it was all due to the fit of my husband's clothes; he ordered two suits for this occasion and in order to wear both he had to wear the satin suit on the ride out, thinking to change when we reached Greenwood; but we were late getting off and it grew dark, or nearly so, when we got to the Honeysuckle Swamp.

"My husband was in despair, he had brought Reddick, his valet, along on the box with Abner, for he was sure to need help with those new clothes. It was almost time for the ceremony; he could not appear in satin clothes when he had velvet ones, which had been made especially for the happy event. There was nothing to do but seek the swamp and, by the light of the carriage lantern, make his toilet.

"Talk about a woman's vanity—I had dressed hours before and waited for him. The velvet suit was brought forth and Reddick undertook the task of getting his master into it. Groans and exclamations issued from the thicket, at last I could distinguish words, 'shake me Reddick, shake hard,' came in agonized tones, then 'Reddick, I believe they are splitting in the back.' 'No, Master, dey aint split, dat is jis de strop what's done gin way.'

"At last the difficult task was accomplished and my husband again seated himself by my side, mopping his red face and mourning over the discomforts of following the fashion."

"Isn't it a good thing for you that your husband did not come today?" asked one of the company.

"Why, no," she said, "he must know it was funny."

The gentlemen who are fat look like stuffed sausages and those who are thin look like match stems. I wonder why they wear such uncomfortable clothes? Father looks so much better.

I cannot spare any more time on these things for I like to hear all the plans for Sister Mag's wedding and it will come so soon now. We will not have to give her up for she will live at Mossview, once Dr. Whitehead's home, on Lake Jackson. It is only seven miles from Pine Hill and I can ride horseback to see her.

June 3rd, 1859.—Sister Mag is having perfectly beautiful dresses and everybody we know is making something pretty for her. I never saw such delicate, lacy creations, as cousin Nannie calls them. One dress is a pink and white pineapple silk. Of course, with the immense hoops we wear now, dresses have to be made very, very wide, it takes many yards of material. This dress is striped Bayedere and has two deep flounces embroidered by hand in a pattern of roses and ferns and was imported from Paris.

Another is of maize-colored silk tissue, trimmed with innumerable rows of very narrow black velvet, with "angel sleeves" and a low-necked bertha of black silk lace. Another is of white crepe lisse over rose satin and another is of pale gray silk with lace to match and garlands of roses, a pale pink, that makes Sister Mag's dainty coloring even prettier. They are real French flowers. But I cannot tell of all these fine things so must stop.

June 7th, 1859.—The wedding presents are coming in every day now, it is very interesting, such beautiful silver and jewels. I like Mr. Whitehead very much indeed. He is just a little older than sister Mag. Everybody makes jokes at them but they do not mind it. He has four brothers and they have all been to see us, (they are old friends, you know).

Last night the gentlemen in the library were having a serious talk regarding the latest news from the abolition movement and all seemed to look for trouble and agreed that they could see nothing ahead for our country but for the South to be, or to have, a government of her own; I did not hear how this was to be done.

June 14th, 1859.—Lots of pretty things have come for the bride. I helped unpack them while Cousin Sarah wrote the names and addresses of the senders. She said Sister Mag would have to write a note of thanks to each giver and she must know what the gift was. She hardly looks at them so somebody must keep a record. There are two gifts, however, which gave her great pleasure, a splendid set of pearls from Father and a magnificent cross of diamonds on a handsome chain, the gift of the groom. I begged Sister Mag into sitting down and letting me put the pearls on her, she had to put in the ear-rings but I clasped the necklace about her neck, pinned in the brooch, put the bracelets on her pretty arms and arranged her hair high on her head and put the tiara in the most becoming position. Oh, she did look so sweet! She has golden-brown hair that curls wherever it gets loose, merry gray eyes and a complexion like a baby, such a clear pink and white.

Everybody says Sister Mart is beautiful but she is a different style, her eyes are very dark, her hair is black and she is not fair though she has a lovely color, a brunette beauty. I am the "ugly duckling" of the band, nothing in particular, just a mixture of everything, brown eyes, straight golden-brown hair, with a complexion much darker than any of my sisters, but "handsome is as handsome does," they tell me for my comfort and I hope I may be better looking some day. Tomorrow I am going to help with the decorations, we want everything to be as pretty as possible for dear sister.

June 17th, 1859.—Such busy days! The wedding is over and Sister Mag was beautiful in her dress of silk brocade and the long veil and orange blossoms. The house was crowded, there was music and dancing and feasting, and—yes—drinking, too—such quantities of champagne. Basket after basket was opened and emptied and no wonder some grew lightheaded. Father and Uncle Richard never drink but so many do.

If ever I get married there shall not be one drop of intoxicating liquor to make people lose their wits.

The next morning the bridal party (twenty or more) left for Bath, Georgia, where most of brother Amos's relations live. (I have promised to say Brother Amos and the sooner I get used to it the better). It would have been lonely after they left but we have several of the kinsfolk staying with us and when they leave we are going to the mountains for the summer.

June 25th, 1859.—Cousin Nannie has been teaching me to make French rolls. She took lessons in New York at a French cooking school and she offered to teach me to make several dishes which are new to me. Mother is a fine housekeeper and I love to follow her around, when I have time and learn what to do but Mother does not cook. She has a good cook and she only goes in the kitchen once a day, just to see if all is clean and neat. She directs and orders the meals but Cousin Nannie can cook and she is going to teach me.

July 4th, 1859.—This is Father's day to give the annual barbecue to all the Bradford black folks—all come from Live Oak Plantation, too. They number several hundred all told and vast preparation has to be made. We do not go to the barbecue for Father says we would spoil their pleasure. No white folks must go, they must feel free to enjoy themselves in their own way, but early this morning Father took me to see the pits, which were ready for the meat to be barbecued. It was a wonderful sight.

Ever so many deep pits had been dug and all night fires had been burning in these pits, fires made of oakwood (for pine would spoil the taste). Over these pits of glowing coals green hickory saplings had been placed and the cooks for the day were busily engaged in putting into the pits whole beeves, many of them; whole hogs, I dare not say how many. It takes a lot to feed so many strong, healthy appetites. Later in the day bread would be baked, potatoes roasted, coffee made; already jugs of milk and watermelons without number had been sunk in the cool depths of a nearby stream; for this is on Lake Iamonia on Horse-shoe Plantation. Every available boat had been collected from all points and fishing tackle spoke of the sport to be enjoyed.

Next year Uncle Tom will have them all with him, the brothers take it turn about. When Uncle Henry died his wife withdrew from this arrangement and Uncle Henry's negroes were so distressed and disappointed, but the other brothers said "Let them come on, we will bear the expense," and so it has been ever since.

This crowd of faithful, cheerful servitors enjoy their holiday to the full and talk about it for weeks. Men, women and children go, even the house-servants are excused if they wish to be.

July 19th, 1859.—All our company have gone and yet Mother is not ready to leave home. I do not know why this is but I am enjoying learning to keep house and cook. Adeline is a fine cook both for meats and pastry and cakes and she likes to show me how each thing should be done. Aunt Morea, too, is teaching me to make sweet wafers and jumbles and little hearts of sponge cake; these are her specialties. Next week I shall make some sweet potato rolls which Father likes best of all.

August 1st, 1859.—I know now why we did not leave home early in the summer. Father and Mother have been at Cousin Sarah's for two days and this morning they sent Jordan in the carriage for Mattie and me, to go to them. When we got there Cousin Sarah had the dearest little red-headed baby I ever saw, lying in her arms and it is hers and Buddy's. Mother says she thinks it is time for me to stop saying Buddy and call him Cousin William. I do not like to do this but if Mother says so it must be the right thing to do. I couldn't love them better if they were really and truly mv brother and sister.

Mother says we will wait a few days longer and then we will make a start for the mountains of Tennessee. We will leave Frances at home this time, aunt Dinah will take care of her. Fanny and Ike go with us. We will go in private conveyance to Albany and take the train there. It is very pleasant at home but I love to travel and see interesting things, but I am afraid I have little or no taste for everything interests me.

August 15th, 1859.—Here we are at Montvale Springs—the loveliest place in the world, I do believe. It is a valley of green grass, with clear cold streams of water, swirling and boiling and bubbling over the rocks; rushing headlong over some miniature precipice then broadening out into placid pools. All around this beautiful valley giant mountains raise their wooded crests to the sky. Look where you please, there is only one outlet and that is between high walls of rock through which the light of Heaven seems to filter down like golden dust. Never before have I seen so glorious a sight.

The hotel is very large, not a fine building but comfortable; in a semi-circle on each side with a broad lawn between, are cottages which are rented to families who wish more of privacy than hotel life can give. These cottages are all occupied so we have rooms on the second floor of the east wing, cool and pleasant. Brother Amos and Sister Mag joined us in Atlanta and we will be together the rest of the summer. They brought with them a little niece, about my age and we will have a fine time together, I know. Her name is Mamie Whitehead.

The dining hall is the longest I ever saw, instead of small tables there are three long tables running the length of the big room. These are well filled and we are waited on by white servants—something new to me. The fare is fine and such appetites as everybody has in this bracing air. Tonight a boy sat at our side of the table just next to Mother and he ate *nine* rusks—will he be alive in the morning?

We have been here thirty-six hours and except for some old acquaintances of Mother's, to whom she introduced us, we do not know a soul. Fannie nurses Mattie and so she knows a number of little girls of her own age. The nurses get together to talk and their charges do likewise but Mamie and I are both of us a bit shy and feel strange in this big crowd. When I was little like Mattie I did not mind strangers. Tomorrow we are going to set out on a tour of investigation, perhaps we may find some playmates, too.

August 16th, 1859.—We have found some very nice girls. We went early to the spring, this morning, for mother wishes us to drink freely of these mineral waters. There we met Sallie McWhorter, Josephine Cassel, Susie Phinizy and Gertrude and Sallie Lanier. We have planned a walk up the mountain side after breakfast and I have stolen these few minutes because I am so pleased to meet these girls and fear I may forget their names.

August 17th, 1859.—We had a splendid time. There is a variety store at the foot of the mountain where we bought quite a lot of goodies to take with us, some other girls came along and three boys, Sidney and Clifford Lanier and Westmoreland Spotswood. I like the Lanier children best of all. They are as jolly as my Tennessee cousins, that is, all but Sidney, he has been ill and is here for his health.

Clifford, his brother, is much smaller and full of fun. Mr. Lanier, their uncle, keeps the hotel and the grandfather and grandmother are here, too. The Lanier House, in Macon, belongs to them and it has the reputation of being the best hotel in the whole country. We have stopped there several times when we visited in Macon.

The Lanier family occupy one wing of this vast hotel. In this wing are all the business offices and apartments, butler's pantry, kitchen, the supply pantry or store room, the chef's sleeping quarters, etc. The wing extends a long way and here, too, are the apartments devoted to the Lanier family. There are windows on both sides and the loveliest view and, to me, it is the most attractive part of the house. I speedily made friends with the grandmother and, when she found that I was interested in housekeeping and cooking, she went with me to the kitchen and let me see how the French chef prepared his matchless cookery. After I had eaten one of his delicious rusks, hot from the oven with a generous slice of fresh country butter, I did not wonder so much at the boy who ate nine.

August 18th, 1859.—We tried another mountain climb today but I have been lame for several weeks and my ankle is still weak, so I begged Mamie to go back to the hotel. She was very much interested in some specimens of rock she was finding, so I tried to go on. It was quite painful and Gertrude and Sidney offered to stay with me until the rest of the party came back. Sidney said he was not strong yet, in spite of all the goodies his grandmother insisted on his eating. He is older than the others; he is fifteen and he has been kept steadily at school. He knows a great deal more than Westmoreland Spotswood, though he is a nice boy too, and so polite to everybody. Gertrude is a bright girl, too, and we had a pleasant hour while we waited for our friends. Father says as I cannot walk far he will get a conveyance of some kind and we will take rides over these roads and see the sights.

August 19th.—No walks or rides today. There is to be a horse-race, real Kentucky horses, and there are many entries. There is a magnificent race track here, with a grand stand that will accommodate a great many people. Perhaps it isn't exactly ladylike, but I do love horse racing. Mother says it was handed down to me from her side of the house; that may be so for Father does not care for races, nor cards, nor drink, he does not use profane language on any occasion; he does not even smoke. I know he is the very best man in all the world. Sidney Lanier thinks Father is splendid. He told his grandmother so. I must stop now and dress for the races. Every one must look their best when they sit on the grand stand.

August 20th, 1859.—I had a delightful time. The races were most exciting and the excitement was at its height when a Tennessee mare took the first prize—won the race with all those beautiful Kentuckians competing. All the Tennessee people shouted themselves hoarse and their hands must have been blistered, they clapped so hard and so long. However, Kentucky will have an opportunity to redeem her reputation, for these races are to take place every two weeks throughout the season. I wore my new blue silk to the races and Mamie wore a pink brocade. Mattie was the sweetest thing—she had on a green silk dress, trimmed with white. She is a perfect blonde, with curls of pale gold and she looked like a flower. The Lanier girls sat with us and they had on very pretty dresses of barege with satin bands, and Sallie McWhorter wore a shot silk.

The grand stand was crowded and when those hosts of enthusiastic people cheered and clapped I was really afraid it would fall for it shook perceptibly.

August 22nd, 1859.—Yesterday Colonel Strother Jones, a fine old gentleman from Virginia, who is fond of children, called us all into the big ball room at eleven o'clock (the band plays there every day at that hour) and told us he did not think we were having a good show at Montvale. He said the grown people had the dancing all to themselves and he did not think that was fair, so, in a few minutes he had a set formed and we were dancing merrily to "Money Musk," then the band played one tune after another and we danced until we were tired out.

Some of the children had never tried dancing before. We knew how, because our people do not object to dancing and we dance very often at home. Mother is a beautiful dancer and she is a fine musician, too.

Col. Jones is so kind to children and he teaches those who do not know how to dance, how to keep time with the music and the steps they must take. He is about sixty years old, very tall and spare and he is bald but he is just as good and kind as can be.

August 26th, 1859.—Today there was a court held in the ball room and it was most entertaining. I had never been in a real court room and the terms used were not familiar but Judge Hilton, of Tallahassee, is one of our party and he has kindly explained what I could not understand. Judge Steinaway presided and, lo and behold the prisoner at the bar was Colonel Strother Jones. Mrs. Taylor, a pretty and attractive grass widow was suing him for breach of promise. Her lawyers were Colonel Bulloch, of Alabama; Colonel Cassel, of Nashville and Colonel Wainwright, of Georgia. The defense had employed Judge Hilton, of Tallahassee; Judge Caruthers, of Tennessee and Colonel Hill, of Georgia. We are told that these lawyers are justly celebrated and everything will be carried out in strict accordance with law and custom. A number of witnesses have been called and court, after a short recess, will convene to try this case.

Five o'clock P. M.—The trial takes time. The case will come up again tomorrow. Mrs. Taylor weeps copiously in a lace-trimmed handkerchief and Colonel

Jones mops his heated brow with a red China silk bandanna, with a pattern of diamonds in white. Said handkerchief having been purchased in Knoxville for this occasion.

August 27th, 1859.—The trial goes on. Some eloquent speeches have been made on both sides. Judge Caruthers expounded the law governing such cases and Judge Hilton made a touching plea on behalf of his client. Colonel Hill was even more eloquent and the jury was evidently deeply impressed, but Colonel Bulloch fairly tore their eloquence to fragments as he plead for the youth and innocence of his beautiful client, of the depravity of the man who would trifle with her young affections, etc., etc., etc. The jury was visibly moved. Next came Cassel and he, too, dwelt on the character of the man who could deceive so fair a victim. Before these speeches were made the different witnesses had testified and I never imagined anything so ridiculous as it. The court room was filled with laughter and the court was forced to have some ejections made before order could be restored. When all the counsel had spoken the judge delivered his charge to the jury and they retired. It did not take them long, however, to decide upon a verdict. The defendant was guilty. The judge pronounced sentence upon our friend and what do you suppose it was? Colonel Jones was to present Mrs. Taylor with the prettiest basket of grapes to be bought in Knoxville and the judge, the counsel, the jurymen and the witnesses must be treated generously to *champagne*.

Listening to it all, it was hard to believe that all this, which seemed so serious, was in jest; that this court, which had been called; with the dignified judge, the able lawyers on both sides, the witnesses, who held up their hands so solemnly; the courteous defendant and the beautifully gowned woman, who was the prosecutor, were all playing parts—just a mimicry of real law. I shall never forget this *mimic court* while I live.

August 30th, 1859.—Tomorrow is our last day at Montvale. It has been very pleasant. I have learned to make rusk from the French chef. I have made quite a number of friends whom I shall be sorry to leave, and I have learned to love old Mr. and Mrs. Lanier and their grandchildren. I shall miss Sidney, for we had so many pleasant hours together. He is an ambitious boy, he is looking forward to a time when Sidney Lanier will mean something. He writes verses, pretty ones, too, but, though he read some of them to me, he will not give me even one.

"Wait," he said, "until I write a book and you shall have them all."

It has been fine to know these nice boys and girls and I have enjoyed it, but Mamie goes with us and we are going to Hendersonville, where we will see Aunt Margaret and Uncle Daniel and the house full of merry cousins. I can hardly wait to get there. I only got two rides through this mountain land. Father got sick and that put a stop to the excursions he had planned.

This country is grand but Florida is better. Ike, who has been with us all the time here at Montvale, is anxious to go home but I heard him tell Fannie last night, "When de preacher tells me dat de jedgment day kin be expected jist any day, I gwine ter tak' a ticket fur dese mountains and git back here jis' as quick as I kin."

"Why?" asked Fannie.

"It's dis-a-way," said Ike, "I heard ole man Mose preaching on de jedgment day an' he say before de end kums de Devil got ter paw down all de mountains an' hills an' dis here yearth is got ter be jis' as level as a table. Now, it gwine tak' a long time ter level all dis but de Devil won't hav' much work ter do in Florida. He'll git dem folks fust an' I ain't agwine ter be dere ter de demonstration."

Ike likes to use big words but Fannie has very little respect for his learning.

September 1st, 1859.—We had a lovely ride over from Montvale to Knoxville. Mamie and I persuaded mother to let us ride on top the stage that we might see better. It was the grandest ride I ever had. There is only one gap you can go through to get out of this enchanted valley. On each side the mountains tower above us, in some places there is a sheer precipice on either hand, so high that you see only a glimmer of blue sky and the scattering rays of light, catching on mica and crystals resemble a network of jewels.

Finally we reached a place where one side was sloping and wooded and here the driver stopped the stage and invited us to get out and take a drink from the Iodine Spring. Already we had discovered its proximity, for iodine has what my black Mammy calls "a loud smell." The taste was even worse than the odor but the driver assured us the water was a cure for many ills, notably goitre and every day somebody carried away jugs and carboys of the healing fluid.

When we reached the hotel in Knoxville only the bridal suite was vacant so we had the best rooms in the house. Mr. Hilton had to seek a lodging elsewhere. Next morning, just as the sun was rising across the mountains Mr. Hilton sent a note asking us to go with him to see the finest catawba vineyard in Tennessee. The rest of the party were too sleepy to accept, but Mamie and I hurried into some clothes and went with him. Never before had I seen such a sight, the southern slope of the mountain was literally covered with the staked vines, fairly loaded with the rich, dark clusters. The proprietor showed us around. He said the grapes were just ready to be harvested, work would begin the next day; they are shipped in many directions and I do not wonder they meet with ready sale. In Florida we have scuppernongs and the Spanish grape, Isabella, but these are not at all like our grapes, they are thick and meaty as well as juicy and the color is so rich and red. After breakfast Mr. Hilton took us around the city and we hated to stop for dinner. I keep forgetting to say "Judge" Hilton, and Father says "every man likes his title." I must not forget.

When I get home, my dear little diary, I shall ask brother Junius if my present style is pleasing him? I am trying to write like Frederieka Bremer, I read her travels last winter. Tomorrow we are going to Chattanooga for a few days.

Sept. 5th, 1859.—We are having a charming time, two days on Lookout Mountain. I could stay there a month, but sister Mag is in a hurry to get to Nashville. We went in a boat around Moccasin Bend. We have visited coal mines; we have gone into the icy depths of a cave, that to me is wonderful; we saw the sun rise and set on Lookout Mountain; we went through the City of Rocks and climbed up on the Elephant's Back; we drank water from the spring on the mountain top, where you have to lie flat on the rock and catch the water in a little cup as it trickles down.

None of these things can we do in Florida. We have seen a good many Indians, too, they come to the hotels with large flat baskets, apparently woven of some kind of grass, filled with delicious ripe grapes. We always buy some and they like to sell to you but they will not talk nor do they smile or look the least bit pleasant.

September 8th, 1859.—Hendersonville again and oh, how good it is to see the dear kinsfolk once more. Dannie, who was a fat baby, as white as milk, when I saw him last, is a fat little boy now and just as sweet as he can be. He talks so brokenly that his sisters tease him by calling him a "Dutchman." Everybody else looks natural and I had to go to the kitchen and see

Aunt Purdy, to the dairy and see Charity and on and on until all the servants had been spoken to. Then we went to the pasture to kiss Lady Lyle and her twin colts; all this before I took my hat off. I love to be here.

CHAPTER IX

HOME TO FLORIDA

FROM these scattered leaves of the diary we get an insight into the life of this child, who is fast ceasing to be a child since this is the thirteenth summer of her life. We leave her full of delightful anticipations of the days to come, but Dr. Bradford was taken dangerously ill and for a time his life was despaired of. Three weeks later the doctors advised that he be taken home to Florida as soon as possible. There were rumors of trouble ahead but this was kept from him, as, in his condition, no excitement must be risked. As usual in the South mention of such news was carefully avoided.

On the 4th of October the Bradford family reached home. Home-coming to the Southerners of that day was a joyful and carefree event. Trusted servants had been in charge during the owners' absence. The house was kept clean and well-aired, the grounds shared the same care and there was "no crumple in the rose-leaf" of satisfaction and comfort.

Smiling black faces greeted the family as they drove up to the door, willing hands made light work of unpacking and straightening, welcome fairly filled the air. Dr. Bradford had stood the journey home better than we had hoped, it was heart trouble and his physician thought that in the peace and quiet of his own home he might improve. This coveted peace and quiet, however, was not to be his.

On October 16th, 1859, John Brown's famous "raid" on Harper's Ferry shook the United States to the remotest point. Back and forth over the wires the dreadful news flashed, filling the South with terror and apprehension and the North with unholy joy that the first blow had been struck for Negro freedom.

For years this had been suspended, like the sword of Damocles, over the heads of the Southern people, and now that the blow had fallen, consternation covered the land. For the first time in the history of Pine Hill plantation, the doors of the mansion were locked when the day was done and the servants had departed to their own houses. Always hitherto Lulu had taken the key of the mistress's room, that she might come in without disturbing the occupants; Fannie carried the keys to the rooms upstairs and went in and out as duty called her; Aunt Morea had a key to the dining room and she and Bill made everything as it should be before Adeline had the breakfast in readiness. That night the horror-struck family knew not what was best to do.

So far not one word of this news had passed between ourselves and the servants, and now the question arose shall we hurt their feelings by locking the doors and thus letting them see that we feel suspicious, or shall we put ourselves entirely at their mercy by leaving the doors unlocked? This was a momentous question and was solved in this manner: There was a barrel-bolt on the inside of every door, before we retired for the night these bolts, that is, those on the outer doors, were shot into place. Aunt Robinson had a habit of waking at daylight and she offered to unfasten the doors and keep watch until the rest of us were awake. This she did and the servants were none the wiser, but nobody in the house slept soundly that night and the excitement of the horrible news had brought to Dr. Bradford another heart attack.

Fast and furious came telegrams and newspapers, filled with all the details of the raid, the capture of the incendiaries, the plans they had made to murder and burn the white people, which would have succeeded but for the love of the slaves for their owners. They were not willing to engage in this nefarious warfare. It was no longer possible to ignore all this in the daily intercourse with our black folks. They are a talkative race and while it behooved us to be careful, it was better to talk it over, in a measure, with them. Their view of the subject was very sensible in the main, and so impressed were we by this, that fear ceased and when the trial of John Brown and his associates went on and they were convicted and hung, confidence was fully restored and apparently everything moved as smoothly as before.

We are sure that in few instances was there bad feeling of any kind between the races; evidently it would take something more than this to fan the flames of race-hatred in the South.

On the 5th of November Miss Cornelia Platt came to Pine Hill as governess. She was from Rhinebeck, New York, a tall, dignified lady of thirty or forty, a fine musician and a good mathematician, but otherwise lacking in every requisite for a teacher. She had no love for children, no patience with them and the gift of imparting knowledge was not hers. She had three pupils, Sue Bradford, a girl of thirteen; Mattie Taylor and Lucy Branch, nine and ten years old. The oldest of her pupils had been trained under good teachers; she studied hard and gave no trouble, but the two younger ones were insubordinate and the governess scrapped openly with them. This they resented and begged to have Miss Platt sent away. Of course no notice was taken of this, but Miss Platt was doing more to bring this about than they could.

One night the mail was received rather late (it was brought from the Tallahassee post office by whichever one of the neighbors had business in town that day) and Lucy was sent to carry a letter to Miss Platt, who was in her room up stairs. The child was gone so long that Mrs. Bradford sent to see what had become of her, the messenger met her on the stair with the letter still in her hand. She raced past and called out, "Aunt Patsy, come quick, Miss Platt has got Robert in her lap and she is kissing him and crying over him and telling him how sorry she is for him."

Mrs. Bradford went to Miss Platt's room and found her just as Lucy had described. Robert was sent away and Mrs. Bradford gave Miss Platt a kind but serious talk. She could make allowances for her because of the section of country she had come from, but "when you are in Rome you must do as Rome does," she told her and, receiving a promise that she would be more particular in future, she delivered the letter, said good-night and departed. Back in the library she told the children that Miss Platt did not know any better and they must never mention it again to anyone.

A few nights later Jordan, the carriage-driver, had a sick horse and was on his way to "de Gret House" for medicine, when he met Miss Platt. He asked if he could do anything for her and she answered, "Yes you can, I am on my way to the quarter to have a talk with the people there, we have arranged a meeting in the Gopher-Hill House (a vacant house some distance off) and will be glad to have you join us." Jordan explained that one of his horses was very sick and he could not leave and, touching his hat respectfully passed on. Not to "de Gret House," however, but back to his own dwelling, he woke his wife, Adeline, and asked if she knew of this meeting.

"No, I didn't know of dis one ternight, but she ben havin' 'em pretty reglar, she don't ax me no more 'cause I done tole her what I thinks er her an' her doings," replied Adeline.

"Well," said her husband, "you git right up an' go, tell her you had a change of heart an' den you listens good an' tell me all she says," and Jordan was off at a run to get the needed medicine. The next morning after Adeline had cooked the breakfast and her white folks had partaken of it, Dr. and Mrs. Bradford had a full account of the night's proceedings. Miss Platt was summoned from the school room and told of the discovery, she did not seem surprised, she admitted that she had accepted the position with this object in view. She thanked Mrs. Bradford for the many kindnesses shown her by the entire family but did not seem to feel the slightest shame at the traitorous part she had played.

Mrs. Bradford did not lose sight of her until her trunk was packed and Miss Cornelia Platt, under a suitable escort, departed, to be put on the train at Tallahassee, a ticket for New York in her hand-bag and the conductor's promise to pass her safely across Mason and Dixon's line. Never again was there a Northern governess at Pine Hill Plantation.

Right here let us tell you why governesses from the North were so universally employed. It was not that we had to go North to find educated women, but it was due to the fact that the Southern people, except for a very small proportion were in more than comfortable circumstances. An old maid relative was looked upon as a gift direct from Heaven, a blessed boon to add to the comfort and pleasure of home. These women could not be spared and moreover there was a prejudice in the South against a lady going out to work. Governesses were needed; they must be had. It was easy to get one from the North and they were, for the most part, satisfactory, hence the great number of Northern ladies who taught in Southern homes.

When the War Between the States was ended; when General Lee's army surrendered, the wealth of the South disappeared. Her people were stripped of all their possessions save the land on which they lived and, in most instances, there was nothing on that land. The men of the South came home to blackened hearthstones; to almost starving families. No houses, no barns, no fences and a living to make. The women of the South endured privations, sufferings, indignities and insults which, when repeated in the case of the Belgian women, in the recent world war made the *whole world weep*.

Yet to us no hand of mercy was extended. The fortunes of the South scattered to the four winds of Heaven; her man-power depleted; her homes destroyed; her sons and daughters heart-broken over the many losses they had sustained; crushed and bleeding at every pore, her conquerors laid upon her the heaviest burden ever placed upon a helpless people when she was turned over to the tender mercies of "the Carpetbagger" and the work of terror, "Reconstruction." That word, as we hear it used now, differs greatly in meaning from Reconstruction in the sixties. Now it is to relieve suffering; to build up the waste places; to heal the ravages of war. Then it meant wrong and cruelty and insult, persisted in for long years until the conquered South was ground down into the dust. Military law was the only law and an appeal to those in power was worse than useless. Let us cut the word reconstruction out of our language that we may possibly forget it.

We have tried to make it clear why the children of the South were not taught by the women of their own land; these rarely or never left the protection of their homes. In these latter days the women in all sections go to their work with almost the same regularity that the men do. A great many of them are justly proud of the ability to be self-supporting, and in many instances, they are taking care of a family as well. There are no abler business women to be found in any section than in the South. Sixty years have made many changes.

Christmas at Pine Hill was celebrated as usual, if anything the merry-making was greater both in the "Gret House" and in the "Quarter" for the master had regained his health and that was joy enough in itself. The negroes were as light-hearted and pleasant as before the outburst in Virginia, seemingly it had not affected them to any great extent; confidence was entirely restored. Not only did they play as usual but, when the work of the New Year began, they were the same cheerful laborers. The momentous year of 1860 apparently held no threat for the future. We now go back and read again from the Diary.

CHAPTER X

LEAVES FROM THE DIARY

OCTOBER 18th, 1859.—The horrible, horrible time that has come to us; our world seems turned topsy-turvy. We feel that we can trust none of the dear black folks who, before this, we had relied on at every turn. I am afraid to say a word for fear it will prove to be just what should have been left unsaid.

When the mail comes in we crowd about the mail-bag as though something could be told by looking at the outside and, when it is opened, some one must read the news aloud, the news from Virginia, for we are impatient. What will become of us? Will our Father in Heaven let us be destroyed? Will the people we have always loved put the torch to our homes and murder us when we seek to escape? This is what John Brown was urging them to do.

I cannot see that there has been any change; Lulu is just as good and kind as ever; the rest are more quiet but they do not seem disturbed or ill natured. Frances said to me last night, "Do you understand what all this is about?" I told her I did not; I told her we would know more after a few days. She laughed, a crazy kind of laugh, and said: "Yes, you will; you white folks will know a heap you ain't never knowed before," and then she ran out of the room. I did not tell this, for I am sure she has heard something I have not and if I keep quiet she may tell me more.

The newspapers from Richmond and from New York come daily and they give the details of proceedings in Virginia. It is more exciting than anything I have ever read either in history or fiction.

October 28th, 1859.—Governor Wise and the Court

in Virginia have condemned John Brown to death and he is to be hanged on the 2nd of December. The New York paper says he is a fanatic and believes he is right in trying to incite insurrection among the slaves of the South. I am sorry for any man who has a nature so depraved that murder and arson seem right to him.

Judge Baltzell thinks the negroes will rise up on that day and apply the torch as Brown urged them to do, but Father does not think so, neither does Brother Junius.

November 7th, 1859.—Well, in spite of Ossawatimie Brown and all the trouble his diabolical efforts have called up we have another governess from the North. She is not like anyone we have had before. I do not believe she has ever taught school in her life. She has no idea of discipline or order in arranging studies; she is a good music-teacher and when I asked if she liked to teach music, she said she had never taught anything else until now.

November 19th, 1859.—Mattie and Lucy do not like Miss Platt; she does not like them either and lets them see it. There is something strange about her; she does not care to sit with us at night and rarely speaks except to answer a question. I went to her room yesterday to carry her some oranges, to keep in her room, so that she could eat them whenever she wished and when I knocked at her door she had to unlock it, *in the daytime*—just think!

November 26th, 1859.—Sister Mart is a young lady now and does not go to school any more. I study music with Miss Platt and Sister Mart is carrying on her music with an extra fine teacher in Tallahassee. We both study French under a language master, who is a native Frenchman. There are some rumors that he is an abolitionist and a watch has been put upon his movements. Isn't it dreadful to have to suspect every stranger?

December 2nd, 1859.—This is the day John Brown is to be hung. We are not going to school today for

Miss Platt is sick in bed with a headache. When Fanny took her breakfast upstairs to her she would not open the door, just said she did not wish any. I took her dinner to her but she answered me through the half-opened door that she was too ill to eat. I asked if I could send the doctor to her but she did not want him; said she often had such attacks and she would be well in the morning; said she did not wish to be disturbed at supper time.

December 15th, 1859.—Miss Platt has gone—last night a letter came in the mail for her. It was a little late but the children had not gone to bed so Lucy carried it upstairs and she came back so excited. Robert, who is Fannie's little boy, eleven years old he is now, was in Miss Platt's room; she was holding him in her lap and kissing him and crying over him. Mother went upstairs to see about this and it was just as Lucy said. Mother talked to her and explained that in our country we did not do things like this and advised her to refrain from all such in the future.

Mother told us not to mention this to anybody. Well we did not, but Miss Platt was caught trying to persuade the negroes to rise up and follow in John Brown's footsteps, put the torch to the home of every white man and murder the people wholesale, sparing none. Jordan and Adeline had found it out and told it. I am so glad our black folks love us and are our friends. Mother says it is so near Christmas she will not try to get another governess until after the holidays.

December 26th, 1859.—We had a very happy Christmas; just as good as if John Brown had never stirred up so much that was terrible. The scene on the back porch was just as merry; the presents were as joyfully received, the drinks as eagerly quaffed and the good wishes, which, with the negroes, correspond to toasts, were as heartily spoken. I do not believe it will be easy to turn our dear black folks against us though no doubt the abolitionists will keep on trying.

Inside the house we had a lovely time; the day was bright and beautiful. Father is well again; Uncle Richard and Aunt Nancy and all the boys took dinner with us; Cousin Bettie is at school in New York City; she is studying music under Francis H. Brown, the composer. Cousin Rob and I had such a good time. Christmas night we spent the evening at Dr. Holland's. I forgot to say that Sister Mag and Brother Amos, Cousin Sarah and Cousin William and sweet little Nannie, their pretty baby and Brother Junius, of course, were with us Christmas day. We all went together to Greenwood, we always have a delightful time when we go there and this Christmas Cousin Mag and Dr. Betton were there, too. Dr. Holland does not allow dancing but we played games and had music, both vocal and instrumental, and everything good you could think of to eat. It was a set supper, for this is the way we do things in our neighborhood; all the house-keepers vie with each other in entertaining and not one surpasses Mother, if I do say it myself.

January 8th, 1860.—This is Aunt Sue's birthday; and she is spending the day with us. She brought the boys and Teresa and little Mary Eliza, who is a darling. Cousin Henry Whitaker is here, Aunt Sue and Mother love him dearly; but he hurt Aunt Sue's feelings today. He is a great tease and sometimes he is not as careful as he should be not to give offense. Since all this trouble between the North and South, there is a tendency to say disagreeable things and you often hear of "Yankees" and always in derision. Everybody does not do this but you do hear it sometimes. Cousin Henry lives in North Carolina and we do not see him often, Aunt Sue called her children to speak to him and as he shook hands with the dear little boys he said: "Well, Sue, what are you going to make of these little Yankees?"

Uncle Arvah is a New Yorker by birth and it was a thrust at him and Aunt Sue was angry and hurt; the children did not know what was meant. It is a pity to "stir up strife."

March 24th, 1860.—I have a splendid piece of news to record here, my diary: Sister Mag has a baby boy and he is the first grandson in the house and my nephew. I feel as if I could not love him enough for he is to be named for Father. He is very small and very red, but he is a dear in spite of that and I know he will be lots of fun.

March 26th, 1860.—The baby is not to have Father's full name after all; he is to be named for both of his grandfathers and that makes him James Edward Whitehead. Maybe I won't love him so well, but I think I will, for he is Sister Mag's own dear little son and I shall love him for that, even if I am disappointed. When Brother Junius looked at him he said, "another soldier to fight for the flag," but I hope he will never have the opportunity to fight. War and bloodshed seem very terrible to me.

Lucy Brodie is making us a visit, she does not think much of babies. Her father was my father's commission merchant once and the Brodie family lived in Tallahassee but they went back to New York when Lucy was quite young and she does not remember her Florida home. She is thirteen years old now and deeply interested in all she sees. The negroes are something new to her every time she looks at one and she often remarks on their queer looks and ways. Yesterday when Lulu had braided her hair and dressed her, even putting on her shoes, she said, "When I get back home I am going to think of this and wish I had one of my very own to carry about with me."

I do not believe Lucy has been kept at school as steadily as I have been, for the books she studied last term are like those I studied three years ago. Lucy has been visiting at Woodstock and Goodwood and she says she has enjoyed it all. She would like to stay longer and she has promised to come again.

April 12th, 1860.—We are going to have a May Party at Greenwood. Florence Holland will be our Queen. She is the prettiest of all our girls. I am Maid of Honor and we have ever so many different ones in it. It will be pleasant no doubt, but I have been so happy all the winter and spring, having Grandpa and Grandma in Florida, that I really begrudge the time given to anything else. They do not stay at Live Oak any more. Grandpa gave Live Oak to Uncle William (his youngest son) and he lives at Waverly. The house is not the splendid mansion that he left but it is pretty and comfortable and it sits in the midst of the most magnificent grove of oaks in Leon County.

Henry and Dan (my step uncles) and Johnnie Branch came with Grandpa and we have the best times. We each have a horse and Grandpa lets us ride whenever we like. He is not nervous and isn't always looking out for us to get hurt, which is very gratifying, for we think we are big enough and old enough to take care of ourselves.

April 22nd, 1860.—Grandpa has consented to stay until after the May Party and we feel so complimented that he should honor us with his presence. Now I am going to practice my part in good earnest for I do not want to fail when he is coming to look on.

May 3rd, 1860.—The May Party was a complete success; everyone who came said it was. Our Queen was beautiful and the flower girls were, too. All the party looked their best and there was a large crowd from Tallahassee and from Thomasville. Grandpa was pleased and said so many pretty things about the whole affair.

On the morning of the 2nd Grandpa and Grandma set out for North Carolina, taking the boys with them.

I had hoped we could go to visit them this coming summer but Father says planters in the South will have to stay at home for awhile. The sky is clear now but the storm may come at any time.

May 16th, 1860.—Now that the frolicking is over and there is plenty of time to read the papers, I find much to trouble and alarm. This is a Presidential year and already there are indications of a hot fight. Brother Junius is an Old Line Whig and Father and Buddy are Democrats. They almost quarrel over their different views. Everett and Bell are the Whig candidates, while Breckinridge and Lane are ours. General Lane is our cousin and we feel an interest in his success, but there are others in the race also and nobody can tell how it will be decided.

Lincoln and Hamlin are the Black Republican candidates. This seems to be a new political party and, as near as I can come at it, they have two objects in view, the freeing of the Negroes and the downfall of the South. I am only a child but reading the papers, that is the way it seems to be.

The Convention was held in Charleston, South Carolina, and there was great excitement, the Democrats were not satisfied at putting out a good strong ticket but brought out another, Stephen A. Douglass and Herschel V. Johnston. I cannot remember which name comes first. Father regrets deeply that they should have done this, for, he says, it will weaken the chances of the Democrats.

Mattie is so cute; because her father is a Whig she says she is a Whig too, she shakes her golden curls and turns up her pretty little nose when Cousin Rob and I sing Democratic songs, one especially, sung to the tune of "Benny Havens, Oh:"

> "Hark from the tomb a doleful sound,
> We hear a mournful yell,
> Old fogies shout discordant notes
> For Everett and Bell."

This to Mattie is like shaking a red rag at a bull, isn't it too funny? I mean to read the papers every day and keep up with the news.

Half an hour later. Just as I was closing my diary Father, who was lying on the couch in the library where I was writing, said: "What is my baby writing? It has brought a real grown-up frown to her face." I gave him the book to read, he did not say a word for awhile and then he said, "You are getting to be quite a politician. I didn't know you felt such an interest," and then he talked to me for some minutes concerning the campaign, which was even now upon us and he told me to come to him whenever there was anything I could not understand. He thought well of the plan of reading the newspapers. He said it was the duty of men and women to keep themselves informed in all matters concerning the welfare of the country.

July 4th, 1860.—We went to Tallahassee to attend a celebration of our country's birthday. Brother Amos belongs to the Governor's Guards, most of the younger men and boys about grown belong to it too. They have handsome blue uniforms and a brass band to play for them to march. It is a cavalry company and all have fine horses; it is needless to say they make a splendid appearance. The color-bearer carried a large silk flag and I was so proud of The Star-spangled Banner. Francis Scott Key, who wrote that beautiful song, was a friend of Grandpa's and sent him one of the very first copies ever printed; it is bound in Mother's music book, and she is so proud of it. Today when the company paraded the band played Hail Columbia first but the crowd clamored for The Star-spangled Banner, showing which they loved best. After the parade there was a picnic dinner and a dance on a platform built for the occasion.

All are tired but me, I am so excited over the day's proceedings that I cannot sleep, so I am writing it up.

Some fine speeches were made and politics were left in the background for once. We came home in the cool of the evening and as we rode along the quiet country road we woke the echoes with one patriotic song after another. When I studied English History it seemed to me that our history was not near so interesting as it was and Scotch History was more entertaining than either English or French. Will there ever come a time when the history of the United States of America will fill one or more big volumes?

CHAPTER XI

POLITICS IN EIGHTEEN HUNDRED AND SIXTY

OUR young friend of the diary is not going to school this summer; the days are long and hot and the political fight which is on is much hotter than the weather.

Two years before this time Mr. Hopkins, the "Uncle Arvah" of the diary, had brought from his old home, Ithica, New York, a nephew who wished to come South and engage in business. Mr. Hopkins was *par excellence,* the merchant prince of Tallahassee; his income was large and his heart was ever open to the call of any who wished assistance. He carried a stock of goods which in richness and elegance surpassed anything ever seen in Tallahassee before or since. His home "Goodwood" was a model of beauty and comfort and was the centre of all social activities. Mrs. Hopkins was the youngest daughter of Governor John Branch and had been a belle in Washington society. She had a delightful voice and was an accomplished performer on the piano, the harp and the guitar. Her husband had a splendid baritone voice and the music they made was worth going far to hear.

This young nephew they brought south was fresh from the typical small farm of the North. He had a part to play in the life of that farm and the change, to him, was great. He entered the store of A. Hopkins & Co., and under the tutelage of his accomplished relatives he took on a polish which was more than "skin deep." Polite, accommodating, always on the lookout for an opportunity to serve, he soon became a general favorite. You will hear more of him later on.

Storm clouds hung heavy over our land and yet we did not realize to what we were drifting. The year of Eighteen Hundred and Sixty was a most momentous year—it held in its grasp the fate of the Nation—it behooved the people of this great country to gather their wits about them, to move slowly and with caution, to bear, with patience the recriminations which continually passed between the two sections. To hold fast to that Constitution, which, at its first conception, had threatened to be drawn up in blood of the people, who it seemed at first, were unable to agree to the provisions of this, the greatest political document ever known to the world. Now an insistant voice from the Northland, ever increasing in volume, sought to set aside this Constitution; to install in its place a "Higher Law."

The advocates of this higher law did not seem, themselves to know just what it was they were insisting upon. Freedom for the negro came first; freedom from matrimonial bonds; then freedom from the constraint laid by the Holy Bible upon the passions of human-kind. The Commandments were relegated to the background; the rights secured by the Constitution to all citizens of this great and growing nation, were set aside and a wholesale system of stealing was inaugurated in the effort to bring about negro freedom.

These slaves had been bought and paid for by the Southern planters; often these slaves had been bought from Northern owners, who felt no qualms of conscience in accepting from his Southern brother the full value of the aforesaid slaves. The stealing of his property naturally roused the ire of the owner. It is our belief that if the United States had offered a fair price for these slaves and fixed the time for freeing them in such a manner as to make it gradual, in this way each slave as he reached the age of twenty-five to be automatically free, nine-tenths of the Southern slave-holders would have been glad to accept. The life of the master, and more especially the mistress of slaves was not an enviable position. It entailed great responsibilty; it brought with it many cares; there was a certain pleasure accompanying the cares, to be sure. It was a pleasure to look around on a well-ordered plantation, on healthy, happy laborers whom we loved and who returned that love; to see little children, with their engaging ways and to pet them as we would so many playful kittens, only with a deeper feeling; for white children are not the only children who are interesting.

Naturally the Southerner did not relish the idea of having his property stolen. This campaign of 1860 came on a people heated almost to the boiling point by Harriet Beecher Stowe and other writers of that ilk. At the North a fanatical determination to carry their point; at the South an equally firm determination to stand up for State's Rights and to abide by the Constitution of our fathers.

It was like two brothers who held different views and each, feeling he was right, held fast his determination. Rapidly the months passed. At the Democratic Convention in Charleston, South Carolina, the ultra Southern ticket was nomiated, Breckinridge and Lane were the candidates. In Richmond, Va., another Convention was held; this did not accomplish much and still another was held in Baltimore. The Democratic party after its usual manner failed to agree and the result was two, or perhaps you might say three tickets in the field. The pity of it! For now defeat stared them in the face. The Republican party nominated as their candidates Abraham Lincoln and Hannibal Hamlin and though, at first their chances were slim enough, the stubborn stand made by the Democratic party, virtually gave to the "black Republicans" the victory.

Never before, not even in the days of "Tippecanoe and Tyler too" was there so much excitement and unrepressed ill-feeling. Breckinridge and Lane were the most popular of the candidates put forward by the

Democrats. Stephen A. Douglass and Herschel V. Johnston, former Governor of Georgia, were more conservative and were not so enthusiastically greeted in the running. John Bell, of Tennessee, was not, strictly speaking, a Whig, Edward Everett, of Massachusetts, was his mate on the ticket. There were some Old Line Whigs, who were not satisfied with these, but nevertheless they voted the ticket when the election took place.

At the North the excitement was great also. The conservative element saw danger ahead; the Northern Democrats had an intense jealousy of their Southern brethren; the Republicans (the black Republicans) were true to their name and harped continually on the one string of negro freedom. Lincoln at first, expressed himself freely as being opposed to this, but later he found it more expedient to lull conscience to sleep and adopt the views of those who had brought him into the limelight.

So the situation rested. The straight-out Democrats stood for State's Rights and the Constitution of our fathers, the negro meant little or nothing to them. The conservative Democrats were more prudent; they saw probable loss in the event of a split in the Union, none of them really believed war would be the outcome. This loss, in their minds would, in the event of secession, confine slavery to strictly southern territory and thus it could never spread. The Whigs, too, were conservative and slow. To them, secession was obnoxious and they fought it bitterly to the end. Not, however, after it was *un fait accompli* then with one accord every true son of the South, casting politics to the winds, cast in his fortunes with his state and later with the Confederacy, and the result was the finest body of soldiery the sun ever shone upon. But all this came later.

The die was cast, the election was over and the black Republicans would come into power the succeeding March. South Carolina spoke up at once to express her sentiments. She hoisted the banner of a palmetto with a coiled rattlesnake and the motto: "Don't tread on me," and we who knew South Carolina fully recognized the fact that she was dangerous.

Florida was wild to follow South Carolina's lead; Mississippi was just as ready and the other states had the question under discussion. The Legislature of South Carolina was in session when Lincoln was declared elected and they promptly called a convention to discuss the situation.

CHAPTER XII

FLORIDA SECEDES

ON the 20th of December, South Carolina withdrew from the Union and became a *sovereign power*. The Legislature of Florida met in November and they, too, called a convention. This convention was presided over by Judge John McGeehee of Madison County, it was a representative body of men, for Florida had placed there some of her best and wisest citizens. It was a time for deep and earnest thought, a time to put all else aside and

"Meet the stern needs of the hour."

Those who stood within the walls of the old Capitol in Tallahassee, who listened to the eloquent prayers for God's guidance, with which each day's deliberations were begun; who looked into the thoughtful faces of this fine body of men and listened to them as each point in the situation was thoroughly entered into, can never forget. Nor can they fail to recognize the depth of feeling portrayed in the action taken.

On the 10th of January, 1861, Florida, too, severed the bonds which held her and stood forth free and independent for the first time in her history.

The storm had burst over the honorable, law-abiding people of the South but even yet we did not realize the force of that storm. The Constitution gave to every state the right to withdraw from the Union, into which they had voluntarily entered and we were exercising that right. Some pessimistic folk spoke of war but by far the greater part looked forward to a peaceful passing.

In a short time seven states had seceded and proceded to form a Southern Confederacy, with Jefferson Davis as president and the Capital at Montgomery, Alabama. No braver, truer, better man ever lived than our President. He had proved his mettle upon many a battlefield, he had proved his ability as a statesman in the councils of the nation. He had shown his constructive diplomatic knowledge as Secretary of War for the United States. There could be but one opinion regarding Jefferson Davis and his people adored him.

North Carolina, Virginia, Arkansas and Tennessee were still hesitating, when Lincoln made his first call for a certain quota of troops from those states to fight against the South. That settled the question. One after another these four states seceded and

> "The single star of the Bonnie Blue Flag
> Had grown to be eleven."

The South was not, in any sense of the word, prepared for war. An agricultural country, there were but few factories of any kind and absolutely none for the manufacture of war supplies. A few factories for the manufacture of cotton cloth of rather rough texture were scattered here and there through Georgia and northern Alabama. The various railroads had small shops barely sufficient to supply their daily needs; nowhere were there any facilities for turning out fire arms nor for the manufacture of gun powder.

CHAPTER XIII

LEAVES FROM THE DIARY

DECEMBER 8th, 1860.—Miss Sadie Talbot, our new governess, arrived today. She and her sister are Southern girls from Easton, Maryland.

They are tall blondes and very pretty, I think. They have the little touch in their speech which most Marylanders whom I have known have had, and it sounds real sweet from them though it sounds affected in a great big man like Mr. Burton. These young ladies were educated at Poughkeepsie, New York, but they are real Southerners, though they are not in favor of secession; but they are quite young and full of fun.

The legislature met in Tallahassee in November and Governor Perry advised that they call a convention to meet January 3rd, to consider whether Florida shall follow South Carolina's example or not; so I suppose we will soon know our fate. Florida is a big state in area but her people are comparatively few and the settlements are far apart. Florida is a young state, too; she is only one year older than I am, so she must be almost a child still. The question is, can she stand alone? I hear all the *pros* and *cons* of this movement from both the Secession and the Union side, so I am afraid I am sometimes a little mixed as to politics. Anyway Christmas is much more interesting so I will think about that. I like Miss Sadie, (she says we must call her Miss Sadie and it is best for her sister is Miss Talbot).

December 28th, 1860.—We had a fine Christmas. I cannot see that our black folks ever think of John Brown's raid and if they do it evidently does not interest them much. We are trying to forget it and perhaps the clouds may pass away.

There is trouble at Live Oak. Miss Lottie Church,

from somewhere in New England, came in October to teach Lucy and Horton Branch and Uncle William and Aunt Mary liked her very much, the children did, too. She said it was the easiest work she ever had to do, for the children are small and must not be closely confined and Miss Church had a carriage and horses and a good driver to take them out riding every plesant day. She could take them riding in the country or she could go in town and she laughed and said it was the first time she had ever had a carriage at her commnd. She was pretty and vivacious and she was often asked out in the evenings and there was a way provided for her to go when she wished, for it is in the country and she must have an escort, though she thought that entirely superfluous. Yesterday Mr. R. Barnwell Rhett, the editor of the Charleston Mercury, and Mr. Colcock, both of them from South Carolina and both aunt Mary's brothers-in-law came on a flying visit to Live Oak. At the dinner table politics naturally was the sole topic of conversation and these gentlemen expressed their views as plainly as the King's English would allow. Miss Church was furious. She forgot that these gentlemen knew nothing of her political faith nor of the land of her nativity and she burst forth in such a wild tirade of invective and abuse that everybody was astonished—to say the least of it. The carriage in which she had taken so many pleasant rides was ordered to be at the door in time to catch the first train out of Tallahassee and that was the last we knew of Miss Lottie Church. I am so glad we have Southern teachers in this neighborhood. Hattie Lester came home on a visit for Christmas; I am going to miss her dreadfully when she goes.

CHAPTER XIV

WAR AND SORROW

IT is true that the South was not prepared for war but she had within her borders some of the very finest materials on earth. Her men had been accustomed, from babyhood, to ride, to hunt, to fish. To test their skill in marksmanship, to ride at tournament and, with lance and eye, win the right to crown the Queen of Love and Beauty. All this contributed to make good soldiers and, besides these, in the mountains of the South are found some of the finest men anywhere. When President Davis made his first call for troops there was no hesitation. Volunteers came pouring in, planters from the big plantations, lawyers from their offices, merchants from their stores, mechanics from their shops, school boys who had closed their books and offered themselves to their country and, besides these, came the mountaineers, of whom we have spoken. Men of splendid physique and indomitable courage, tall and straight, active and sinewy; eye and hand trained to do good work and quick work as well. They came in crowds and they came singly as the case might be, but whether it was one or fifty, they called forth admiration, even if their uniforms were of butternut jeans and their caps of coon-skin. These mountaineers were not slave-holders.

It is often said, even to this day that the South fought to retain her slaves, but such was not the truth. Thousands of the soldiers, who enlisted in the Confederate army had never owned a slave; they fought for liberty of opinion and action, for principle and for HOME.

We leave the Confederacy marshalling the soldiery of the South and return to Pine Hill Plantation. Dr. Bradford was lame it is true, but he was an ardent

Secessionist and took part in all the proceedings. When the convention was called in Tallahassee he repaired to the Capital to inform himself.

January 1st, 1861.—A New Year has come to us now. This is dear Grandmother's birthday and, though she went to Heaven years ago, her children still meet on her anniversary and talk of her and of the days of their childhood. I like it and I never will forget when Father's and Mother's birthdays come. As we sat around the long table today the conversation turned on the convention, so soon to meet in Tallahassee. Father said he considered this the most momentous year in the history of the South. He is for Secession and he does not think that war will necessarily follow. Brother Junius is a strong Union man and he thinks we will certainly have war; he says we will have war in any event. If the South secedes the North will fight to keep us, and if we do not secede all our property rights will be taken from us and we will be obliged to fight to hold our own. He says he is in for the fight but he wants to fight in the Union not out of it. Father thinks it is more honorable to take an open and decided stand and let all the world know what we are doing. Everyone at table who expressed an opinion was firmly set against the Republican party. Mother says she wants the negroes freed but she wants the United States Government to make laws which will free them gradually. All agree on one point, if the negroes are freed our lands will be worthless. I wonder how it would feel to be poor and work like the people Hannah Moore writes about?

January 2nd, 1861.—Uncle Richard and Uncle Tom spent the morning with Father, the three brothers are going to Tallahassee tomorrow to the opening of the Secession Convention. They are so deeply interested.

January 3rd, 1861.—I would not write this morning because I wanted to put down in my diary the first news of the convention. Tonight father has told me what they did; it was simply to organize and then they adjourned. Some of the delegates had not arrived and this will give them the opportunity to get to Tallahassee and present their credentials. Father says the Capitol was full of men from all over the State and they look very serious.

January 4th, 1861.—I can hardly keep my mind on my books I am thinking so much of the probable action of the convention. I know Father must have been glad when the school bell rang this morning, it seems impossible for me to refrain from asking him questions, which, of course, must be troublesome.

January 5th, 1861.—This is Saturday and Mother lets Lulu make candy on Saturday and if she, my black mammy, will let us, we help with it. She says we "do not help but hinder;" maybe she is right. Cousin Rob is spending the day here and Lulu has promised to teach us how to make the candy baskets, which we love to have her make for us. Cousin Rob does not care about the convention, he is going to school in town but comes home Friday after school and goes back Monday morning. He is calling me now to play Graces, so will say goodbye for this time, little diary.

January 6th, 1861.—This morning we went to Mount Zion to hear Mr. Blake preach. It is a treat to listen to his sermons, he uses such beautiful language and he explains the passages of Scripture he reads, so clearly that it really stays in our minds and we remember. All ministers do not do this. Today he spoke so earnestly of the representatives of the people of Florida, now in convention assembled in Tallahassee. He spoke of the heavy responsibility resting on them; of the high compliment paid them by the people of Florida, in trusting them with an issue of such paramount importance. He said we, none of us knew which way was best; we must trust in God and do good. We must remember that our strength cometh from on high and the way to gain that strength is to pray to the Lord, for He has said "knock and it shall be opened unto you. Ask and ye shall receive." Of course I cannot tell it as he spoke it, but it made every one feel solemn and as if some share of the responsibility rested on each one of us.

Mr. Blake took dinner with us and Eddie came with him. He is just the shyest little boy. When the company were all gone Father told me to ask Lulu to get me ready to go with him to town next morning. He said he was going to show me what a convention was like. I was so happy at the thought of going and my heart fell when Mother said: "Surely, Dr. Bradford, you are not going to take the child away from school?" (Mother does not like us to miss any time) but Father said, "Yes, I am going to take her with me in the morning, this is history in the making, she will learn more than she can get out of books and what she hears in this way she will never forget." I am so glad. I am so excited I cannot hold my pencil steady but I must write this down.

January 7th, 1861.—I am so glad it is not raining today. I am really going and, little diary, I will tell you all about the day when we get home.

8:30 p. m. We have just finished supper. Mother would not let me write until we had eaten, now she says I can only have one hour because I am going again tomorrow and must have a good sleep.

The convention was assembling in the hall of representatives when we entered the Capitol, and soon everybody was in place and Dr. DuBose made a very fine prayer. I like Dr. DuBose and perhaps I ought not to write this about him, but nobody will see my diary and really I do not mean any harm, but he has such a convincing way of praying; like he was determined the Lord should grant all he asks. It is very comforting.

After the preliminaries were disposed of a communication from the Governor was read and the first thing I knew Aunt Mary, who was sitting next caught me by the hand and said, "Look, there is the ambassador from South Carolina." A small man very erect and slender was being introduced by Mr. Villepigue as Mr. Leonidas Spratt of South Carolina. Mr. Spratt bowed gravely and looking around upon the audience with a pair of brilliant, beautiful eyes, he began somewhat in this manner, though I probably will not get it quite right.

He said he felt some delicacy in appearing before this convention, coming as he did from a foreign power, but the heart of South Carolina was filled with love and sympathy for Florida, who now was standing where Carolina had so lately stood. Then he read aloud a communication from his state, recounting the grievances, which had led her to sever the ties which bound her to the Union. You never heard such cheers and shouts as rent the air, and it lasted so long. When quiet was restored Mr. Villepigue introduced Colonel Bulloch, of Alabama, and I found that he was the same Col. Bulloch who had taken part in the mock trial in the ball room at Montvale Springs. He made a fine address but a short one. Said his own state was now deliberating as to what course she should pursue and had sent him to assure Florida of her cordial good-will. He sat down amid cheers for "Bulloch and Alabama."

Mr. Edmund Ruffin, of Virginia, was introduced and said he came to tell us that Virginia was with her Southern sisters in feeling and, if the worse came to the worst, she would be with them, heart and soul. He is a splendid looking man, quite old and yet he is perfectly erect and only his snow-white hair shows his age. He reminds me very much of dear Grandpa, who is taking such a warm interest in these proceedings, though he is so far away. I believe it will break his heart if North Carolina does not secede.

When the speaking was over and a few resolutions had been passed the convention adjourned and we came home. We left a noisy crowd behind us. As far as we could hear there were cheers for South Carolina; cheers for Mississippi; cheers for Alabama and for Florida. Never before have I seen such excitement. It even throws the horse races in the shade. What will tomorrow bring?

January 8th, 1861.—We are at home again after a day filled to overflowing with excitement and interest. We were in such a hurry to get to town that the convention had not assembled when we reached the Capitol. There were groups of men talking earnestly and there were other men running hither and thither with papers in their hands. Father has a great many friends and I stood quietly beside him while he and they discussed the situation. The ambassador from South Carolina had evidently made an impression on his audience of yesterday and somebody had been busy last night, for in every direction could be seen Palmetto cockades, fastened with a blue ribbon; there were hundreds of them. When at last the hall of representatives was opened and Father and I took our seats, Judge Gwynn came in and pinned a cockade on Father and one on me. Oh, I was so proud.

Judge McGeehee is Father's friend and he shook hands with us as he entered the hall.

The members of the convention took their seats and Mr. Blake, our dear Mr. Blake, whom we love so well, opened the day's session with prayer; such a beautiful prayer. I had never seen a convention until Father brought me here and it is strange to me. I wish I could tell all I heard today but the language the members used is not familiar to me and some of the things they talk about are just as new. Then, too, I am just a little girl. A message was read on the floor of the convention, from Governor Brown of Georgia, to Governor Milton. As near as I can remember it was this way: "Georgia will certainly secede. Has Florida occupied the fort?"

Mr. Sanderson was very interesting. He recounted the rights which the states retained when they delegated other rights to the general government in the Constitution. He made it so perfectly clear that all and every state had the right to withdraw from the Union, if her rights and liberty were threatened. He said the Committee on Ordinances had carefully examined into the question and they could find no reason why Florida should not exercise her right to withdraw from a compact, which now threatened her with such dire disaster. I cannot understand all the work assigned to the different committees; perhaps I am not old enough; people grow wiser as they grow older; so aunt Robinson says. I am going again tomorrow. My palmetto cockade lies on the table beside me.

January 9th, 1861.—There has been a hot time in the convention today; the nearer they get to a final decision the hotter it gets. Colonel Ward made a most eloquent address to the convention. He told them that he was a Union man but it was in this way: in his opinion the South had done more to establish that Union than any other section; it was a Southern man who wrote the Declaration of Independence, it was a Southern man who led the American army, it was Southern men who framed the Constitution, a Southern man wrote our National Anthem and, in so doing had immortalized the Star-spangled Banner and he proposed to hold on to that which we had done so much to bring about. He was willing to fight, if fight we must, but he wanted to fight in the Union and under that flag which was doubly ours. The heartiest applause greeted him as he sat down. It was plain to see that his audience was tremendously affected but the next speaker tore his fine argument to shreds. So it went on all day, some committee business would interrupt now and then but the most of the time was spent in debate for or against secession.

Our old friend, Mr. Burgess says: "If Mrs. Harriet Beecher Stowe had died before she wrote 'Uncle Tom's Cabin,' this would never have happened." He says, "she has kindled a fire which all the waters of the earth cannot extinguish." Isn't it strange how much harm a pack of lies can do?

January 10th, 1861.—It is night and I am very tired but there is much to tell. The Ordinance of Secession was voted on today. Bishop Rutledge made the opening prayer and it was very impressive. He pleaded so earnestly for God's guidance for these members, in whose hands lay the future of Florida. These men feel their responsibility I am sure, their faces are so serious and yet so alert. Not one word escapes them and when an amendment is needed they are so careful to make it plain to all. I heard something today about a flag which had been presented to Florida but I have not seen it as yet.

After the committees were disposed of the Ordinance of Secession was voted on. The vote was 62 for and 7 against. The ordinance was declared adopted at 22 minutes after 12 o'clock. It was resolved that at one o'clock on the next day, January 11th, the Ordinance of Secession should be signed on the east portico of the Capitol. The convention then adjourned until the afternoon session.

Mississippi seceded last night and it seems we will have plenty of company. The Union men in the hall looked very sad. They have worked hard for their side, but they had only a few followers.

January 11th, 1861.—We did not try to be early this morning, as the big event of the day did not take place until one o'clock. Capitol Square was so crowded you could see nothing but heads and the Capitol itself was full of people looking from the windows, which looked out on the east portico. Somehow Father and I had seats on the portico itself, close up to the wall where we were not in the way and yet we could both see and hear.

There was a table already there with a large inkstand and several pens, nothing more. A subdued murmur came from the assembled citizens but there was none of the noise and excitement which had prevailed on other days; all seemed impressed with the solemnity of the occasion for oh, it is solemn! I did not realize how solemn until Mr. Sanderson read the Constitution and I understood just why it was necessary for Florida to secede.

As the old town clock struck one, the Convention, headed by President McGehee, walked out on the portico. In a few moments they were grouped about the table on which some one had spread the parchment on which the Ordinance of Secession was written. It was impossible for me to tell in what order it was signed, the heads were clustered so closely around the table, but presently I heard Col. Ward's familiar voice. There was a little break in the crowd and I saw him quite plainly. He dipped his pen in the ink and, holding it aloft he said, in the saddest of tones, "When I die I want it inscribed upon my tombstone that I was the last man to give up the ship." Then he wrote slowly across the sheet before him, "George T. Ward."

The stillness could almost be felt. One by one they came forward and after a while Col. Owens, a Baptist minister, who is lame, came up to sign and in a loud voice he sid: "Unlike my friend, Colonel Ward, I want it inscribed on MY tombstone that I was the FIRST man to quit the rotten old hulk." A very faint applause greeted this, but it died away before it hardly began. This was no time for jesting; it meant too much.

When at length the names were all affixed, cheer after cheer rent the air; it was deafening. Our world seemed to have gone wild.

General Call is an old man now; and he is a strong Union man. Chancing to look toward him I saw that the tears were streaming down his face. Everybody cannot be suited and we are fairly launched on these new waters; may the voyage be a prosperous one.

Nearly everybody seems to be happy and satisfied. The Supreme Court Judges, into whose hands the document just signed, has been placed, have carried it to Miss Elizabeth Eppes to engross or adorn it with blue ribbon; the judges selected Miss Bettie because she is a granddaughter of Thomas Jefferson. I hope President Jefferson likes our Ordinance—I believe those who are gone know all we are doing here below.

Father says the rest of the proceedings of this convention will be confined to business matters and though he is planning to attend, he will leave me at home and let me go on with my studies. I wonder if I can collect my wits enough to learn my lessons. I will have Saturday to rest up in and Lulu will make us some candy.

The Diary leaves off and the story takes up the course of events.

SECOND CONVENTION, APRIL, 1861

From this time on the South was an ever-increasing scene of activity. There was much to be done; the forming of a new government was a task in itself and before anything could be done in that direction for the different states, a Southern Confederacy was formed and again a convention assembled in Tallahassee to provide for the entrance of Florida into this compact. The wisest heads were needed to draw up a Constitution, which would provide for changed conditions while holding fast to the old.

Jefferson Davis was elected President of the Confederacy; a wiser choice could not have been made. A man of unblemished character, of high intellectual ability, accustomed to command (for he was a born leader of men) a statesman of the highest order. The South had none better, if as well, fitted for the position. An able cabinet was selected and President Davis was inaugurated at Montgomery, Alabama, the first capital of the Southern Confederacy.

The war clouds grew so black that there was no longer any excuse for trying to delude ourselves into the belief that the seceding states would be allowed to depart in peace. Abraham Lincoln having broken his solemn promise to the South, in April the *"Shot was fired which was heard around the world."* The war was on—God help us. Volunteers had been many and now there was

"A hasty marshalling of armed bands."

There were no hirelings in the Southern army, no substitutes, no German Mercenaries, but true-hearted sons of the South, ready to lay down their lives for the land they loved. The women of the South had never known what it was to work with their own hands but now nothing, which could contribute to the welfare of the soldiers, was too hard for them to do. Dainty fingers sewed on uniforms and flannel shirts and, later on, when no cloth could be had from which to make these needed garments, they learned to spin and weave and knit and sew, that their loved ones might be clothed.

The first troops to leave home for the war were the 1st Florida Regiment and they were ordered to Pensacola to secure the forts there. It was a fine body of men and we were proud of them, but it made our hearts ache, too.

Dr. Bradford volunteered as a surgeon in the Confederate service but the Secretary of War requested that he would remain at home and furnish supplies to the army, as this was as necessary as anything else, and

Dr. Bradford, with his large plantations, could do so much. But he did not like this, he had come from a long line of fighters and the impulse was strong within him; his father and grandfather had served in the War of the Revolution and his maternal ancestor, Oliver Cromwell, of England, had the courage of a lion, and he has left us that famous saying which will never die, "Rebellion to *tyrants* is obedience to *God.*"

The Doctor had plenty of what we slangy Americans term, "backbone," and he made another effort to get into the army, but there seemed to be no place for a lame man, so he stayed at home but he was always looking out for every way in which it was possible to serve his country.

The white men in his employ had all entered the service and negroes had taken their places. In the yard at Pine Hill stood an office consisting of one large room with several windows and a large fireplace, this the Doctor had used as his business office. Now it was fitted up as a bedroom, with every comfort that could be devised. In each corner of this twenty-four foot room was a bedstead, not a small hospital bed, but an old-fashioned double bed. The mansion was roomy and two of these rooms were also fitted in the same way and then the Doctor gave notice at the hospitals and camps that he was ready for sick and wounded soldiers. It is needless to say they were sent and, throughout the four years of warfare, these beds were seldom empty. The doctor was a skillful surgeon, besides being a physician. Mrs. Bradford had the kindest of hearts and was a true doctor's wife. She knew much of medicines and her skillful ministrations had brought solace to many a sufferer. They had abundant means and plenty of good servants, so they were well equipped for the work they had engaged in. Mrs. Bradford, like the wife who is so praised and lauded in Proverbs, "looked well to the ways of her household," and her many maids were taught to spin and weave and the quantity of cloth turned out from her looms was astonishing. This cloth went to the soldiers of the Confederacy. There was dire need of all that could be woven, for the blockade was enforced so rigidly that but few blockade-runners could evade it and we had to depend upon our own efforts to supply what was wanted.

Dr. Bradford was an analytical chemist and in the forests about us were many medicinal herbs; from these he manufactured drugs to take the place, in a measure, of those we could not possibly get.

That blockade was a cruel and an inhuman measure, even in war. To cut off from suffering women and babies the medicine they needed because some soldiers might be saved by their use; but then Sherman said, "War is Hell." Our enemies certainly did all they could to make it so.

We have told you of Mr. Hopkins, the New Yorker, who had come South and married into the Branch family. As a matter of course, when war was declared the South looked with more or less suspicion on these pseudo-Northern men, they would bear watching, they said. This seemed true in one sense but unjust in another. Soon after war had been declared, a small boat came into port at Saint Marks. There were three men aboard and theirs was a tale of shipwreck. The man-of-war on which they served had been wrecked off the Florida Keys, and in this small boat they had escaped. This sounded bad when our people were suspicious of all strangers and they were arrested and carried to Tallahassee, where, on exmination, they proved to be Lieutenant Seldon, of the United States Navy, and two of his crew. They had been on a three-years' cruise in foreign waters and had heard nothing of the political disturbances nor of the war, in which the United States was involved. Lieutenant Seldon was paroled and his men held as prisoners of war. We have told you that Mrs. Hopkins had spent much of her youth in Washington city. She had known Lieutenant Seldon there and Mr. Hopkins invited him to stay at Goodwood, while he remained in Florida. The offer of hospitality was gratefully accepted and this simple act was construed by some to indicate disloyalty on the part of the kind-hearted master of Goodwood. The fact that Mr. Hopkins had encouraged all his clerks to volunteer in the Confederate service; that he had given to each one his uniform and other necessary equipment at his own expense, should have made these doubters ashamed of themselves. But as the war dragged its slow length along and Mr. Hopkins never let an opportunity pass to aid the cause, suspicion was lulled to rest.

The Union men everywhere, whether of northern or southern birth, were looked at askance at first, but as these same Union men, one after another, volunteered their services and went to the front, all this was forgotten and we were one united people, having but one aim, the protection of our homes.

Believing that the clearest idea of the conditions which confronted us in these trying times can be gained by little daily happenings, we return to the pages of the diary and ask your attention to the events chronicled there:

March 3rd, 1861.—Father has volunteered. Mother was bitterly opposed but though Father yielded to her in many things he would not in this. I wish I was a boy; even if I am young, I could go with him if only I were not a girl. It will beak my heart if he goes.

March 17th, 1861.—Brother Amos has been a member of the Governor's Guards for a long time; that is, ever since the company was organized last October and he did not tell us until tonight that the Guards volunteered two weeks ago. Sister Mag was wild with grief at first but Mother tried to comfort her by insisting that there would be no fighting—just talk of war and reconciliation would follow. Brother Junius came in to supper and he told us he and Dr. Gardner and several others were raising a company in this county, to be called the Dixie Yoemen. Richmond Gardner, Captain; Joel Blake, 1st Lieutenant; Junius Taylor, 2nd Lieutenant; Jimmie Conner, 3rd Lieutenant. These men must think there will be war or they would not be preparing for it. This is extremely exciting.

April 17th, 1861.—Yesterday we had a picnic on Lake McBride, the occasion being the presentation of a flag to the Dixie Yeomen. The ladies of the Bradford neighborhood embroidered the banner and though cousins Martha and Rebecca Bradford designed and selected the silks, we, every one, did our part in the work. Even if the stitches were few, when the fingers were unskilled, those few stitches represented the deepest love for our country and her brave defenders.

The flag was presented by Miss Bradford and received by Captain Gardner. Both made fine speeches and, when that was over, we served an elegant dinner under the magnificent Live Oaks, which have stood guard over the lovely lake for many centuries. After dinner there was target practice and boat-riding; this does not seem like war.

The 1st Florida Regiment went to Pensacola today. Oh! this is like war. In the Leon Artillery, Captain Hilton commanding, Edward Bradford and Mr. Routh and many others of our Tallahassee friends. In the Leon Rifles were many more, but it was the Madison Company, Captain Richard H. Bradford commanding, which hurt me most. The entire Bradford family adore Cousin Rich, he is so young, so talented, so handsome and Sir Galahad himself was not more spotless than he. When the call for volunteers was made in the court house in Madison, Judge Vann made a stirring and patriotic speech. He pictured the grimness of war as well as its glory and when he had finished he stood beside the table, where a blank sheet awaited the signatures of those who should respond. For a moment the silence of death rested on the crowd assembled there, then Richard Bradford stepped forward and affixed his name to the paper which meant so much. Others came quickly and in a few minutes the hundred men needed for the company had signed and they elected Richard Bradford captain, and he the youngest man there.

I have often heard that "history repeats itself," and it is surely true sometimes. The book Miss Brewer sent me years ago about Mrs. Nancy Bradford, of New England, is very like Mrs. Nancy Bradford of Florida. In her diary the Mrs. Bradford of Revolutionary days was telling of the dangers which surrounded her husband and their five sons, all of whom were in the American army. She told of the heartaches, which she knew and the privations they suffered.

Our Mrs. Nancy Bradford has five sons also and four of them have volunteered in the Confederate army; the fifth would like to enlist also but he is just a little school boy and must wait awhile. I hope the war, which is just beginning, will not last that long. One of her sons is in West Virginia with General Lee, one has joined the Dixie Yeomen, one went to Pensacola in the Leon Artillery, and one, the Benjamin of the household, is captain of the Madison Volunteers. Aunt Nancy is something like our mother in appearance, she is just as tiny but she is even fairer and where our mother's eyes are blue and her hair a golden brown, her hair and eyes are of the lightest shade of brown you can imagine. I love her dearly and I tell her she dresses like Jenny Wren in Mother Goose, "For I will wear my brown dress and never look too fine." Our mother dresses in the fashion and she likes silks and laces but Aunt Nancy thinks it is wrong to attach any importance to dress, beyond being neat and immaculately clean. Both of them are members of the Methodist Church but their ideas differ on many points. When I asked Mother to explain this she said, "Our Lord looks at the heart and not the dress, read your Bible carefully and thoughtfully and you will find that our Heavenly Father requires nothing of His children but obedience and love." I shall try to remember this, to obey and to love.

May 9th, 1861.—We hear many rumors and the papers are filled with alarming paragraphs, just enough to keep us "on the anxious bench," yet not enough to give much real information. We have been hearing hints of a blockade but last night the news reached us that the United States Government established on the 6th of May, a blockade of all Southern ports, beginning at Pensacola. This is bad but the South has so many bays and inlets along her miles and miles of sea-coast that it seems almost impossible to prevent the entrance of vessels that wish to come in. The Southern Confederacy needs everything you can mention in the way of weapons and munitions of war; neither have we manufactories, where these can be made. Nearly every day some new company is organized and the need for arms grows greater all the time. Cousin Bettie Bradford has been at school in New York and now she is in a great hurry to get home before it is too late. Cousin Johnnie has gone on for her but nothing has been heard from them as yet and the family are feeling anxious.

May 11th, 1861.—The wanderers got home last night, the direct route was so closely guarded that they had to come across country to Vicksburg, on the Mississippi and, taking a flat-boat there, come south until they reached a landing at one of the large Louisiana plantations, where they got off. Cousin Johnnie explined the situation and tried to hire a conveyance of some kind to travel to the next town, but the planter was the soul of hospitality and entertained them until the next morning and then sent them on in his carriage to a place where a livery stable was kept. Here they purchased a horse and buggy and thus they reached home. Cousin Bettie has been at school in the North for four years, with just a short visit at Christmas.

June 11th, 1861.—Perhaps it would be as well, my dear Diary, to write here a short sketch of the Bradford neighborhood at this time. The war is an established fact and a shadow lies across the hearts of the Southern people. It may be that the North feels it equally with ourselves, but I cannot think so. This is the reason why. We did not want this war. It rested entirely with the North whether it should be WAR or PEACE. We wanted peace but war was forced upon us and now that it has begun we will do our best to win. May *The God of Battles help us.*

Coming southward from the Georgia line you reach the Bradford neighborhood at Pine Hill Plantation, the home of Dr. Edward Bradford. He has no sons, only daughters, but he has three sons-in-law in the army. The next place is Oaklawn, the home of Captain William H. Lester. The Captain's head is white, he gained his title in the Indian War but he has three sons and a son-in-law in the army. Then comes Greenwood, where Dr. Holland lives with a house full of daughters. His only son was among the first to volunteer and he also has a son-in-law in the service. Mr. Thomas A. Bradford comes next. Walnut Hill Plantation lost its mistress some years ago and the affairs of the household are administered by four beautiful and capable daughters. There are three sons also and these are in the Confederate army, as well as a son-in-law, who had won the fifth daughter from the old home. Water Oak Plantation is the home of the youngest of the Bradford brothers. He has four sons in the army.

This completes the entire number of men eligible for military duty and you see no one is shirking this duty. While the men have gone forth to meet the foe the women are not idle. The blockade established by President Lincoln has cut us off entirely from the rest of the world; we must depend upon our own resources and we are trying to utilize them all. Father says we never know what can be done until we are pushed to the wall and that is just where we are finding ourselves now. And this is only the beginning.

So far we have plenty of cloth for some purposes but uniforms are more necessary than anything else at present and no suitable material can be had. Of course the men of wealth can and do, buy up all in reach, but there are so many hundreds who must be clothed. The factories of North Georgia and Alabama are running day and night, turning out "Butter-nut Jeans" from which the women all over the South are fashioning uniforms. We are knitting socks, too, for they are needed; the dainty hosiery of pre-war days will not stand the necessarily hard usage of camp life. I learned to knit when I was quite small and now I am very glad of it; we try to see who can complete a pair of socks in the shortest space of time.

July 4th, 1861.—This day, which was once so filled with merriment and pleasure, is now a thing of the past, where we are concerned. Father and my uncles let the negroes go ahead with the usual Fourth of July barbecue. Father said it would not be right to curtail their pleasures because of our own troubles; so they are having a merry time today.

July 22nd, 1861.—Joy! Joy!! There has been a great victory for our side. Yesterday the Battle of Manassas was fought in Virginia and it was a complete victory for the Confederates. Our army chased the Yankees almost to Washington city. General Beauregard is the hero of the hour although there are so many who are heroic, it is hard to discriminate. Our loss has not yet been ascertained; nor do we know the enemy's loss. The telegraph office is crowded all the time and day and night the people are flocking thither for news of the great battle.

July 23rd, 1861.—Today we had a thanksgiving service at Mount Zion Church. Mr. Blake conducted the services and his text was "The race is not to the swift nor the battle to the strong but Thou, Oh Lord, giveth the victory." He made the most beautiful prayer I ever listened to and he prayed so earnestly and tenderly for those who had fallen in battle and for those who had lost their loved ones.

A telegram this afternoon tells of the deaths of Generals Bee and Bartow, both Georgians and both relatives of the Whitehead family.

July 27th, 1861.—Each day brings us fresh news from the battle of Manassas. One of our generals has gained a new name from his action while in battle; he is General Jackson, and he has been a professor in the Virginia Military Institute. He is a strict disciplinarian and his boys at the V. M. I. all knew better than to disobey and the soldiers in his command soon learned the same lesson. Then, too, all who come in contact with him in this new military life are impressed with the personal magnetism he exerts. Uncle Daniel, who was with him several days on business for General Lee, who is in command of the Division in which Uncle Daniel is a Brigadier General, says he is one of the most remarkable men he ever met. In the height of the Battle of Manassas General Jackson had his men drawn up in line facing the enemy; they stood firm, an unwavering line. The newspapers tell it this way. General Bee was trying to rally his Brigade of Georgians; men of undoubted courage, but under fire for the first time. As he waved his sword and urged them on his eyes fell upon General Jackson with his well-drilled Virginians, standing immovable. He cried out to his men, "See, there stands Jackson like a stone wall." Later in the day General Bee joined "The Immortals," but ere he went he gave to the quiet professor from the V. M. I. a name which will live forever.

July 28th, 1861.—Colonel Robert Howard Gamble is organizing "Gamble's Artillery," and Charley Hopkins has enlisted in that company and so have many others from Tallahassee. Aunt Sue brought a beautiful piece of French opera flannel and asked me to make Charley two shirts. I am a little doubtful as to my ability but if I find it too difficult I can get my Lulu to finish them for me; she sews so neatly and she makes all my clothes, under Mother's direction. These shirts are blue and they are to have real silver buttons, which Aunt Sue has had made at the jewelers. She says silver will not tarnish as common metal buttons might do. Mr. Pratorius is making Charley's uniform. I suppose I will learn all the different uniforms after awhile. The Infantry is gray, trimmed with blue, the buttons are of brass and the officers have gold lace on their sleeves, a chevron they call the design on the sleeves; a captain has three gold bars on his collar; the privates do not have any gold lace. Charley is in an artillery company and they wear a little red, but the uniform is gray, too. Cousin Willim Bradford is in a cavalry regiment and his gray uniform is trimmed with corn-color. They all look fine to me and I grow more patriotic all the time but Sister Mag says that is because I am not married. Ridiculous; I am just a child.

The Governor's Guards volunteered some time ago and now they are re-organizing and will serve as an infantry company, with Captain G. W. Parkhill as their captain. The name has been changed to "The Howell Guards," in honor of Mrs. Jefferson Davis, who was a Miss Howell. Soon they, too, will be going to Virginia; poor Sister Mag; she will be heartbroken I fear. The Captain is a fine looking man in his uniform but not so handsome as Brother Amos, who is 2nd Lieutenant in the Howell Guards. They are in camp now and are drilling every day.

August 1st, 1861.—The Howell Guards are going to Virginia on the 12th of this month. Poor sister Mag, she is not a bit patriotic and she is almost broken-hearted at this news. Her baby is more than a year old now, fifteen months old, and he is learning to talk and is so funny and sweet but even Eddie cannot bring a smile to his mother's face, she is the very picture of woe.

August 12th, 1861.—It is late at night but I cannot sleep so will write up the events of the day. The Howell Guards left on the mid-day train. A crowd had gathered around the depot to see them off. Mothers, wives, sisters, sweethearts and friends—all were there. Standing on the platform and looking around I marveled at what I saw. Women with bright, smiling faces, looking tenderly on the soldiers, who were ready to depart. Saying fond, loving words of advice and of hope; pressing the beloved gray-clad figure in a parting embrace; kissing the dear lips, maybe for the last time, and yet those brave women smiled. As soon as the train pulled out and the soldier boys could not see, the scene changed. Sobs and tears, wild outbursts of grief on every side, and yet, this had been suppressed lest it grieve those brave hearts, who were going forth to battle for home and country.

On the way home Eddie seemed to try to see how entertaining he could be, he took my handkerchief and wiped his mother's eyes, he kissed her over and over, then he put on somebody's big glove and gravely offered her his hand, saying, "Tell de popes howty." That brought a smile; Niobe herself could not have resisted the bright little baby face and the piping little voice.

Many a prayer goes up tonight from anxious hearts. May God bless our dear soldiers and may God bless the South.

September 15th, 1861.—All the troops are not sent

to Virginia, the Dixie Yeomen have been incorporated into the Fifth Florida Regiment and they have gone to Palatka to be drilled. So far the troops, which have been sent had been drilling for some time and were considered fit for service but these fresh companies have to learn.

Brother Junius went to Palatka, and we miss him very much but it is not like he was going away off. Palatka is so much nearer than Virginia, and then, too, they are fighting in Virginia. I must tell you my Diary what happened to Buddy. (I forgot, Mother says I must call him Cousin William.) But this is what happened. He has been practising medicine in this county for twelve years and everybody loves and trusts him. When the men composing the Dixie Yeomen came forward to be sworn into the Confederate service, first one man and then another, until nearly all had spoken, said he could not take the oath nor sign the Roster unless Doctor William Bradford would consent to resign and stay at home. Some of these men grew quite eloquent about it. They said they could not leave their wives and children unless the doctor would stay with them. "I should be obliged to desert," said one man, "if Doctor Bill was not in call, when my home folks got sick." So after much discussion he consented to resign. I know his mother rejoices in this for she has consumption and is never well. His young wife and baby need him, too, but then so many wives and babies have to suffer. This is a great compliment to our doctor and Father and Mother are delighted. He is their adopted son, you know. They love him as if he was their very own and no brother could be dearer to me.

October 10th, 1861.—War has come home to the Bradford neighborhood! . . . Last night, October 9th, Captain Richard H. Bradford was shot in the breast and instantly killed, while leading his men in an attack on Santa Rosa Island. He was everybody's darling. We were so proud of him, too. Father went to bear the sad news to Uncle Richard and Aunt Nancy. May God help them for this is hard to bear. Cousin Edward Bradford, his brother, is bringing his body home. The telegram said they would stop over a few hours in Madison and the casket would lie in state in the court house there, that Madison might do him honor. Then they will come on and he will be buried in God's Acre at Pine Hill.

Mr. William Routh was killed also, he was engaged to be married to Cousin Sallie and she fainted dead away when she heard the terrible news. Oh! War is worse even than I thought.

October 12th, 1861.—Cousin Rich was buried today. Crowds of people came and Governor Milton delivered an eulogy on his spotless record. His is the first blood shed on Florida soil in this cruel war. All his brothers were present except Cousin Johnnie, who is in Virginia. His two sisters are so distressed. When the services at the grave were over a military company came forward and fired three times across his grave, it was horrible.

Three weeks ago Cousin Rich came home on a short furlough. He came by Pine Hill to see us and after he had said "goodbye," he stood a moment with his cap in hand and looked about him.

"This is a lovely place," he said. "I hate to say goodbye," and in another moment he was gone.

We never know what the future holds for us. I will not write again soon for Aunt Nancy wants me to stay some with them. I am so fond of cousin Rob and little Susie and maybe I can help a little bit.

November 1st, 1861.—School had opened on the first of last month, but, after the trouble which came to us, mother let Miss Sadie go to visit her sister for a while. She came back on the 15th and the other girls have been going to school while I was away. This morning I began again, there are no others in my class so it did not really make much difference. Miss Sadie does not teach Trigonometry, so I have laid that aside until Father feels better and can help me with it. I feel so strange—and the war news hurts me as it never did before. I seem to be looking for bad news all the time. Father says I must try to overcome this feeling, he has given me a poem to learn and I think I shall copy it here:

"Let us try to be happy,
We may if we will,
Find some good in life
To o'er balance the ill.

"There are times when
The lightest of spirits must bow
And the sunniest face
Wear a cloud on its brow.

"But the deeper our own grief
The greater the need,
To try to be happy
Lest other hearts bleed.

"Let us each in all earnestness
Work for the best;
And leave to our God and
Our conscience the rest

"Still holding this truth
Both in word and in deed
That who tries to be happy
Is sure to succeed."

In the Bradford neighborhood death had been a frequent visitor; tragedy had not passed us by; every household had lost one or more,

"There is no flock however watched or tended,
But one dead lamb is there,
There is no fireside howsoe'er defended,
But has one vacant chair."

and now we saw, in the near future many vacant chairs, any day might bring us sad tidings and in this sorrowful foreboding all had a share. Winter was approaching in Virginia and warm clothing must be sent to our soldiers. Not only clothing, but blankets and shoes as well. So far we had not felt the blockade and, with extensive coast line, we had not thought it possible for an adequate blockade to be established. Now we were beginning to change our minds; the South had exhausted some of the necessaries of life, how would we supply the need? On almost all of the large plantations, spinning wheels and in some cases looms were kept. These had been handed down from a preceding generation and only the old negroes knew how to use them. In nearly every "quarter" some old woman could be found, whose day for hard work was past and who employed her time in spinning either wool or cotton into knitting yarn, from which stockings and socks were knit by other old people, for the benefit of their friends and families on the plantation. Here was a start in the right direction. Carpenters were called in and new looms patterned by these old ones. A man with a turning lathe, who lived in south Georgia, made fine spinning wheels and the old negro women taught the art of spinning to the younger ones. Soon the white women took up the work and the whir of the wheel and the noise of the baton could be heard in almost every home.

Shoes must be had. Dr. Bradford, for many years past, had carried on quite a number of industries; to these he now added a tan-yard, where hides of beeves, which had furnished meat for the plantations were placed in vats. Vast quantities of tan-bark was hauled to the tan-yard and soon the hides were converted into leather and speedily this leather was made into shoes. "Where there's a will there's a way," they say.

On Pine Hill Plantation lived Henry Fort, a most unusual type of his race. To his master and mistress, he was invaluable, inasmuch as he was perfectly honest; always truthful, and, though he was not an educated negro, he had a remarkable aptitude for figures and he who would cheat Henry in making change must rise early, indeed.

When it was not convenient for the owners of Pine Hill to go to town and supplies of any kind must be bought, Henry was often given considerable sums of money and sent to do the shopping. He had only one fault and he rarely let that fault get the better of him, but sometimes he found in Tallahassee something stronger than water and on such occasions he came home hilarious, in the extreme.

When the first call for troops for the Confederate Government was made Dr. Bradford not only volunteered himself but he dismissed all the white men in his employ, that they, too, might volunteer. He expected to close the sawmill, the shingle mill, the brickyard, everything, in fact except the grist mill, which was a plantation necessity and the wheelwright's shop and the smithy, which were also necessities; but this same Henry Fort and others of his comrades begged so hard to be allowed to run all these industries that permission was given and we really believe they astonished even themselves by their success.

This had been going on for more than two months when the Battle of Manassas was fought. About the first of August some repairs were needed on the engine which ran these mills and a machinist named John Cardy was summoned from Tallahassee to mend the engine. He was a Northern man, and in some way he made himself unpopular among the negroes who worked with him on the machinery. Henry Fort had been sent to town to purchase some groceries and it so happened that he was one of the first to hear the news of the great Southern victory; he immediately proceeded to tank up with some of "Damon's best," and, when he reached home, he was more than talkative. He had bought a new carving set and the box in which they had originally been placed was gone, Henry knew not where. He was brandishing this ferocious knife in his hand while he told the news from Manassas and he grew hotter with every word spoken and hurrahed loudly for the South. Suddenly he spied John Cardy coming around the corner. With a wild whoop Henry sprang from the admiring group by whom he was surrounded, and calling as he went, "I ben wantin' to kill some Yankees all day an' Ise gwine ter begin wid John Cardy." Away went John Cardy and closely after came Henry. The grove was enclosed by a thick hedge of Spanish bayonets; double gates opened on the public road; a thirty-foot walk was on either side of the residence; but it seemed as if poor John Cardy could see none of those. Back and forth he ran along the bayonet hedge, Henry pursuing. Finally he was cornered and with the sharp points of the Spanish daggers sticking in his back, he fell forward on his face yelling loudly for mercy. It had happened so quickly we did not realize the danger but now help was given, for Dr. Bradford had no mind to allow murder on his premises. Henry was coaxed into the kitchen, where Adeline assured him she had a cup of hot coffee for him, and while she was preparing it he fell asleep. John Cardy went back to town that night and though the job was a good one and his money always ready as soon as the work was done, never again could he be persuaded to come to Pine Hill. So it is on the stage of life, tragedy and comedy go hand in hand.

Letters came often from our soldiers in Virginia and in the West. They were unaccustomed to the hardships of camp life, and indeed, as yet, real hardships had not been encountered, though of course, they missed the comforts of home. In most instances even the privates had taken along some trusted servant, who looked after his master's needs. There was no lack of money and so far all the real necessaries could still be had. The Confederacy was engrossed, heart and soul, in striving to meet the problem of arms and accoutrements. Nitre beds were in evidence everywhere and hopes of sufficient powder seemed about to be realized. While all this was going on Mrs. Bradford was getting her youngest ready to be sent off to school in the Old North State. She, herself, had been educated in Raleigh and when, in the summer of 1861, Governor Branch wrote and urged that his "little Susan" be sent to him, that he might take her to Raleigh and see her safely placed at the same school her mother had attended, it sounded good to the home folks and, though she, herself, was opposed to this change, all arrangements had been made and, as an old friend of the family was going to Richmond and would take charge of her on the way, the day of departure had been fixed. We will let her tell why this plan did not materialize:

THE DIARY

December 1st, 1861.—Father was reading what I had written about the Battle of Manassas and he said, "My baby has forgotten to write of school plans. They should be recorded by all means. In years to come you will read of it with great interest and it should have come before the account of the battle." As he thinks it is not too late to tell of it I will write it here, though I do not like to think of it. I was so opposed to it at first and so disappointed when I had to give it up. In June, last, Grandpa wrote to Mother, urging her to send me to Raleigh to school. Mother was educated in that city and many of her old friends still live there. I would probably have their children as classmates. Grandpa, himself, would take me to Raleigh and see to all details necessary. His plan was for me to go on to Enfield with cousin Johnnie, who was then at home on a furlough and would see me safely in his hands. I could visit Grandma and himself until school opened. He said Raleigh was so far in the interior that there would be no danger of the enemy reaching it and he could think of no safer place in these days of war. He went on to say he thought the war would be over in sixty days; a great many people think so. Father was opposed to this but Mother thought well of it and though I hated the thought of leaving them, Mother told such entrancing tales of school life in Raleigh, that I soon became reconciled. Then, too, I dearly love to please Grandpa. Mother graduated with first honors and her father was so delighted that he gave her that lovely set of jet and gold, which I have always admired. I thought to myself, I, too, can study hard and perhaps I can get first honors and Father and Mother may be proud of their "ugly duckling" yet. Though the blockade is much more effective than we had any idea it would or could be, it was still an easy matter to fit out a school girl.

In the fall of 1860 uncle Arvah had bought an unusually large stock of goods and when, in the following January, Florida seceded, he wired his commission merchants in New York, to buy such goods as he was in the habit of supplying himself with, to the value of the cotton in his name, which they held in their possession. When these goods arrived, and they were shipped immediately, the bills of lading showed one hundred and forty-two thousand dollars worth of merchandise. So Mother had no difficulty in finding pretty materials; she and Lulu made my dresses and Mrs. Manning made my underwear. They were so beautifully made that I told sister Mag it was almost like her bridal trousseau. My traveling dress was brown, a soft, rough-surfaced material of wool, with small flecks of gold color woven in. There is a long cape, lined with satin of the same shade as the dress, quilted in small diamonds. My hat is of beaver felt, the color of the dress, three fluffy little ostrich tips are fastened in with a gold arrow. The cape, too, is fastened with three gold clasps. Such a pretty dress. But I will not wear it to North Carolina, for as soon as I had made up my mind to go things began to happen. The Battle of Manassas did not seem to alarm them but when the enemy attacked the coast of North Carolina, Father and Mother were quite positive that I must stay at home. So, war interferes with everything, even with education. It may be all for the best, I am sure it is, since Cousin Richard was killed. I believe what made Father and Mother change their minds is the discovery that the enemy are sending spies through the country to cut off telegraphic communication, when they get ready to attack. It would be dreadful to be cut off from your own home folks.

December 20th, 1861.—I spent today at Uncle Tom's. His daughters are just the smartest, busiest people I ever saw. Cousin Mary Bernard and her three children and cousin Frances with her five are there, while Captain Bernard and Cousin Tom are at the front and Christmas is at hand. There are but few toys to be had, so they are dressing a large Christmas tree with most of the decorations of home manufacture. It is a beautiful tree. They have taken the bright-hued autumn leaves, dipped them in wax and pressed them with a warm iron; these are arranged in clusters and they reflect the light from dozens of tiny twisted Confederate lanterns. Long ropes of "Sodom Apples" lend an added brightness and strings of pop-corn make you think of the snow, which comes at Christmas in colder lands. It is so good of these kind, loving aunts to do so much for the children for I know they work with heavy hearts.

Mr. Routh and Cousin Sallie were to have been married in November, he could only have a three days' leave of absence and the date was not quite certain, so she was almost ready with her preparations when the news of his death reached us. Her wedding dress was made and waiting and only a few last little things remained to be done. She fainted dead away at the terrible tidings and the next day she locked herself in her room and folded and put away, every article which had been made, in a big Saratoga trunk, locked it and hung the key around her neck. She is so pale and sad, it gives me the heart-ache to look at her. And yet, this is a part of *war*.

December 25th, 1861.—Christmas night! No festive gathering tonight. We did not have a Christmas tree. Mattie and Eddie hung up their stockings but they had so many things they might better have hung up a two bushel sack. I found a number of gifts on the lightstand beside my bed, when I awoke this morning. The grown folks had presents, too, but somehow the flavor of Christmas was not there. The servants and all the hands on the plantation came as usual and Father had fixed for them, just as is always done. He says they are just children and must have their pleasure the same as ever.

They shouted, "Crismus gif," they sang and danced, they had the "Sweetened Dram." Gifts were not lacking, good wishes were spoken just the same but, was it in my imagination, or was there really a difference?

Uncle William and Aunt Mary came and brought the children but Uncle Richard and Aunt Nancy did not come—their sorrow was too fresh and keen. Cousin Rob came and of course Cousin William and Cousin Sarah came but we missed the others. Aunt Sue is sick and that, too, cast a gloom over the day. Sister Mag had a letter this morning from Brother Amos. She had not heard for some time and this was written somewhat after the fashion of my diary. Of course he wrote a lot of her and Eddie, with messages for the rest of us.

He also told her why the letter was so long delayed. The snow is deep there now as the Howell Guards are stationed at Evansport, on the Potomac and they cannot mail a letter every day. He thinks it is funny that they enlisted first as a Cavalry company, then they were Infantry and now they are serving as Artillery, manning a battery of big guns.

He wrote of many of the Tallahassee boys; John Day Perkins, he says, is the very quietest man in camp; he rarely makes a remark of any kind. He says the battery has sunk several small craft and recently the battleship Pennsylvania went down. When they were first stationed there Captain Parkhill tested the boys to see which were the best marksmen. He found he had enough skilled men to fire the guns but the very best marksman in the company proved to be Nick Eppes, a stripling of seventeen, as pretty as a girl and looks like one, too. He was placed in command of the biggest gun in the battery and, when the Pennsylvania was sighted, few of the guns struck her except the shots from the big guns, which went to the mark every time. The Pennsylvania sank and still lies beneath the waters of the Potomac. Talking it over afterward, John Day surprised them all by remarking, "Nick didn't shoot all those turkeys for nothing." The company cheered and clapped so enthusiastically that he was encouraged to speak again, "I had rather be at home shooting turkeys than here at Evansport shooting Yankees." The applause was louder than ever and they all voiced John Day's sentiments. Brother Amos says Dick Parkhill is as gay and full of fun as ever; he makes love to every girl he meets, does it, "to keep his hand in."

Frank Papy is low-spirited and almost sick. Brother Amos is coming home in March to stay three weeks and Sister Mag can hardly wait. We will all be delighted to see him. He is the most hopeful person I ever met; "the war will be over in thirty days"—"sixty days"—

"ninety days"—I do not know what comes next but I do know he is a very pleasant person to talk to—you feel so cheered up. He wrote, too, that the War Department has ordered all independent companies to be merged into the different regiments. The Howell Guards will enter the 2nd Florida Regiment in General Perry's command.

*   *   *   *

Again we take the pen to supplement "The Diary." The army of Northern Virginia had gone into winter quarters. Until the Spring opened there would be little or no fighting, but the soldiers from the South felt the inclemency of the weather far more than the others. So far blankets could be had and there was no scarcity of provisions.

> "Hope springs eternal
> In the human breast"

and all, or nearly all, thought the war would soon be over. The winter days and nights were long in camp and the soldiers formed classes to study various subjects. Some studied Latin and Greek, some history, etc., etc. Many different biographies were brought forward, especially did they feel an interest in the famous warriors of both ancient and modern times. That created a taste for general literature which is a wide field.

Is it any wonder that the world never saw such an army before? Yet despite all this there were many who could not even write the few words home which would have given such comfort to the anxious heart of wife or mother or sister, waiting—always waiting. It is true some kind-hearted comrade would write that letter home for his less favored brother; but it requires an effort, just at first, to tell of one's ignorance.

For three years a young and extremely delicate woman came once a week to our house to ask for news of her husband, who was in Captain Taylor's company.

She could and did write to him, but he could not write himself and so he asked his captain to mention him in his own letters home and we would tell his wife the news. This went on for three years. Some days she would be so exhausted from the ride of four miles, that she would be obliged to stay all day and go back in the cool of the evening. Her maid, "Old Holland," who had nursed her as a baby and whom she called "Mammy," took excellent care of her and watched so tenderly beside her couch while she slept the hours away. In the summer of 1863 came the sad tidings of his death; he was killed in the Battle of Gettysburg and left on the field.

We feared she could not stand the shock, she was so weak and frail, but apparently she was stronger than she looked. Her mammy took entire charge of all her business affairs and they lived on together in the little home her dead soldier had provided. We went sometimes to see how they were faring and then, one winter morning Holland sent word that she was gone and help was needed to lay her to rest.

We have told you of the improvised hospital at Pine Hill. Some of the soldiers who came to be taken care of could not read or write. On one occasion an elderly man who had been wounded in the head, was desperately ill with high fever but it passed off and in a few days he could sit up and move about the room. Going to take him his breakfast, we found him sitting on the front steps, his head in his hands and groaning heavily. "Do you feel worse, Mr. Wells?" we questioned.

"No, mum, I don't, but I wants ter see my ole 'oman. She ain't writ ter me in a long time an' I can't nuver writ nothin' ter her, 'cause yer see I ain't eddicated." We offered our services, which were gratefully accepted and, in trying to get the correct address, we found she did not live so very far away after all. He could take the train in Thomasville and get to the town of Boston in a short time. He had thought it was hundreds of miles away. Jordan was summoned, a team was brought around, a lunch prepared and Mr. Wells was quickly transported to his "ole 'oman."

Ignorance is pitiful in a way, no matter where you find it. One handsome young mountaineer, who was sent to Pine Hill to be treated for a double break in his right thigh, was not so fortunate as Mr. Wells, inasmuch as his home was in the Cumberland Mountains and not so easily reached but he was more fortunate in being perfectly satisfied. Give him a knife and something to whittle and he was happy and while his hands were at work he whistled softly under his breath and his tune was always the same, "The Girl I Left Behind Me."

We thought of a lithe, slender figure of some mountain lassie; we pictured the young pair at the mountain spring, the moonlight casting shadows around them as they vowed eternal faith and love. We wove quite a romance, but we were destined to a ridiculous awakening.

On the morning of his departure, after a stay of three months, he gave to the servant who waited upon him a folded paper, directing him to give it to the young lady of the house when he had gone. Always when a soldier departed from this hospital his needs were carefully looked after, his clothes put in order, new ones supplied if needed; a lunch was put up for him and then the family gathered around to shake his hands and wish him well.

This morning all these preliminaries had been gone through with and goodbyes were being said. Taking the hand of the young lady aforesaid, he blurted out, "You is de gal I ben a whistlin' about; you is de gal I is aleavin' behind me, but I is acomin' back, ef Lincoln's boys don't find me."

The girl was abashed and indignant but it would

never do to hurt the feelings of a soldier boy just leaving for the war, so she had to restrain herself. The folded note proved to be a poem (?) of many verses, arranged to be sung to the tune of "The Girl I Left Behind Me," and written in the style of the author's conversation. It was evidently a work of time and patience and was certainly original.

One cold March day, when the spring winds were fairly sweeping the earth, an ambulance drove up to the door; Dr. Bradford went hurrying out, his assistants following closely in his wake. The ambulance contained four badly wounded men; one poor fellow looked as if he was already dead. Restoratives were applied and soon all four of them were comfortably in bed, their wounds dressed by Dr. Bradford's skillful hands.

We knew not who they were nor from whence they came; the wounds were not quite fresh nor had they been attended to and there seemed to be some mystery in this. Shortly before their coming a skirmish near St. Mary's had been noted in the papers, but no account of killed or wounded; it seemed to have been so slight as not to receive more than a passing notice.

We asked if they had been wounded in this skirmish but no satisfactory answer could be elicited. They had evidently been exposed to the weather, it had rained hard two days before and they had been wet and the clothes had dried on them. All hope of obtaining information vanished with the night, for they had high fever and three of them developed pneumonia and were very ill.

For days we thought they could not live. The fourth a grouchy, silent fellow, had no word to say and, when his comrades began to improve, he vanished as mysteriously as he came. Efforts to find out the command to which they belonged were fruitless. The hospital in Tallahassee had not sent them; in fact knew nothing concerning them. At last they were well enough to move on and they sought a private conversation with Dr. Bradford when the mystery was unravelled.

They belonged to Colonel Evans' Georgia Regiment and at St. Marys they were not far from their homes. They were wounded, but not too badly hurt to travel. They asked leave of absence to go home and it was refused. Then they took matters in their own hands. In Tallahassee, where they had been on one occasion, they presented a forged note to the negro driver of the hospital ambulance, the negro could not read so they asked him where he was going. He told them he was returning from Pine Hill to Tallahassee. They asked several questions as to where this place was? What was done there and, the negro being very communicative, they soon had their plans laid. Telling him that they knew all that and were quizzing him, they read him the bogus note, which was really just a scrawl, saying: "Transport these four soldiers to Pine Hill."

They got in, the driver put whip to his horses and as the distance was not great, and he soon announced, "Here's de Doctor's." Scowling terribly, they told the thoroughly frightened negro if he dared to tell he had seen them or that he had given them a ride, they would kill him.

"Doctor," the spokesman said, "we are not deserters in the true sense of the word; we meant to report for duty as soon as we were able and now we would like to go back and help to fight, but if we go back to camp we will be hung as deserters. Can you help us? You have saved our lives once already; can you save us again?"

It was a difficult problem, but the doctor would try. He wrote a letter, which was calculated to move even a heart of stone and sent a man on horseback to Lake City, where Colonel Evans with his boys was encamped. The messenger was gone a week, a long, anxious week to those poor soldiers, but when the answer to the doctor's letter came it was satisfactory. They were to report to Colonel Evans at once and he would arrange matters with the captain of the company to which they belonged. In conclusion he wrote: "You are doing a good work, may Heaven bless you."

There is much more to tell of this; of those who came to be treated at Pine Hill but we will let it wait, while we tell of conditions in the Confederacy and the action taken by other nations as to the war being waged.

We had expected to be recognized by the nations of the Old World. In this we were disappointed; Spain alone held out the hand of brotherhood. Some promised "neutrality," a few observed it. We believe there was in some countries, a sentiment favorable to the South but fear kept it under. All the world stood off and watched the unequal fight go on.

AGAIN THE DIARY

March 8th, 1862.—I do not like Dr. Cleveland. I wonder how much longer he is going to stay? This morning while we were sitting at the breakfast table he was contending with Mother about the "sweet-briar." It seems he has spent much time in England, perhaps he is an Englishman, but he insists that there has never been any "sweet briar," or as he says, any "true Eglantine" in America. I think it is rude of him to be so positive with Mother, but Father says, "all scientific men love to dispute with the laity." At last, when we were rising from the table Mother said, "Sue, show Dr. Cleveland the sweet briar by the school room."

We went down the walk to the frame where it grew and I pointed it out to him. Now this happened to be the very tangle of vines into which I threw my algebra, on that memorable day when Miss Damer made me pick it up. The vines are all thorns and they scratched me dreadfully. Dr. Cleveland inspected the vine, pinched a leaf, smelled it, sniffing loudly and then he said, "This is the true Eglantine."

"Mother told you it was," I replied.

He took from his pocket a small sketch-book and pencil and proceeded to make a picture of it, not a finished drawing but just a sketch. He replaced the book and pencil in his pocket and, trying to speak very pleasantly, he said: "When I get to my drawing materials I shall make and send you a pretty picture of this Eglantine, it is very rare."

"Do not trouble to do that, please, I have no pleasant associations with that thorny tangle," I answered, and we returned to the house.

The mail had arrived in our absence and the family were gathered around the library table; aunt Robinson handed me a letter from Brother Junius, saying as she did so, "Here is another birthday gift for you."

Dr. Cleveland, who was apologizing awkwardly to Mother for contradicting her so flatly as to the sweet briar, turned to Father and asked, "Her birthday, is it, how old?" "Sixteen," said Father. "Indeed—" went on the talkative man of science, "I should never have imagined it—there is none of the *'beaute du diable,'* which we naturally associate with that age." "No," said Father, "and I am glad of it, I do not want my baby to grow up too fast."

Then the whole crowd proceeded to discuss me as calmly as if I had been one of my own dolls. It was embarrassing but I found out what they thought of me. Among other things, I learned that I was bluntly truthful and would have to learn that Madam de Genlis' "Palace of Truth" was not practical and a white lie could sometimes be used to advantage. Mother's constant teaching of the Ten Commandments will, I think, make even white lies difficult for me, though I do try to be polite.

I had some pretty presents even if it is war times,

and I got a nice letter from Brother Junius, written two days ago so I would get it today. Brother Amos is here and Sister Mag is happy, we are too, for all love our jolly soldier boy, he has been at home for ten days and he has only two weeks furlough. It will be hard for Sister Mag to let him go.

There is something I have never told you, my Diary; ever since that day in August of last year, when we went to the depot to see the Howell Guards off to Virginia, Sister Mag has never failed to lock herself in her room for awhile every day to pray for her husband. I did not know just at first what she was doing, but I heard her tell him she never let a day pass without asking God to take care of him and he might know, wherever he might be, that her thoughts and her prayers were following him.

I felt real mean to have overheard this, for it was never intended for my ears, but I had sung Eddie to sleep and was holding him in my arms in the dark, waiting for Nellie to come for him, and they were talking on the porch just outside.

March 13th, 1862.—Brother Amos left this morning and our hearts ache for both of them. The women of the South have much to bear. Father takes me with him every other day to search for certain medicinal plants and roots, from which supplies for hospital use can be made. Medicines of all kinds are scarce in the Confederacy. Occasionally a vessel will run the blockade but not often; the Yankees have succeeded in making us very uncomfortable, to say the least of it.

Last week we sent to the hospital in Richmond a case of iron tonic for convalescents. We are now making a decoction of Boneset for chills and fever; this having been tried at home with good results was considered good enough for our dear soldiers. We make a salve too, from the leaves of what the negroes call "Jimson Weed." It is healing and soothing and the small quantity of spirits of turpentine, we add to it, makes it more effective. Another salve is made from the root of the elder, grated and stewed in lard. With this salve goes a decoction of elder flowers, these used in conjunction are a preventive of gangrene and will sometimes cure it. Oh, if our poor soldiers could only have half the medicines they need; it is so hard to see them suffer for simple things that all the world besides can have. I think this blockade is devilish.

March 15th, 1862.—Sister Mag has a daughter, born this morning. Poor little girl. She will, in all probability, never see her father's face. I do not believe the war is going to end in even ninety days. Sister Mag is very ill tonight and I have Eddie upstairs with me, that he may not disturb his mother. He is as sweet and good as can be. When I told him about his baby sister he said, "Don't bring her upstairs, let her be Aunt Pat's baby, I is yours." I certainly love him.

March 16th, 1862.—The entire family wrote to Brother Amos this morning, he will surely find out he has a young daughter. As scarce as paper is Eddie had to have a whole sheet to write his letter on. He looked so in earnest that I asked what he was writing? He said, "I is sayin', Father come home and wear de beautiful cloes." He admires the gray and gold as much as the rest of us do.

March 23rd, 1862.—This is Eddie's birthday, Adeline made him a cake, (no white sugar to ice it) and by great good luck I found in my doll things, which have been packed away, two toy candles which delighted his heart.

Though the weather is still cold in Virginia the army seems to be on the move and I am afraid we will hear of more battles soon. If I, who have only brothers and cousins in the army, dread this so, what must it be to the poor wives and mothers and fathers? Uncle Richard has never been the same since Cousin Rich was killed.

April 5th, 1862.—Sewing societies were organized long ago and every neighborhood has one. Ours meets first at one house and then at another, and all of us sew steadily all day long. Mother cuts many of the garments and Mrs. Manning helps her, that is, when they meet with us.

Peter and Mac make packing cases and it is astonishing how many garments go forward from the Bradford neighborhood.

I did not know much about sewing at first; at the beginning I made Charley Hopkins two flannel shirts but I am ashamed to say Lulu did most of the sewing. Now I can take any kind of a garment and make it entire, even the buttonholes, though Sister Mag says my button holes "gape." I mean to improve on them. I have to do my book-keeping early in the morning and sometimes I have to work at night to finish up the day's work. Since we have been sewing so steadily I have given up my horseback rides. Father does not approve of that. I take a good deal of exercise in other ways, however, and I feel well and strong.

May 1st, 1862.—Father has engaged a book-keeper to come next week. He says it keeps me too close. This man is an Englishman with a wife, a small son and a brother-in-law; a strong, healthy man, who looks as if he ought to be in the army but he says being an Englishman he is not subject to military duty. Uncle Henry got his arm cut off just above the elbow, in the shingle mill and this young man is to take his place. They live in the house formerly occupied by the sawyer, Mr. Wheeler.

Father is so terribly afraid we will develop consumption because our grandmother Bradford died of it. That is why he requires us to spend so much time in out-door exercise. I am a little sorry to give up the book-keeping for I felt that I was helping, but there is a plenty to do in other ways. Fighting is going on all along the line but the telegraph wires have been cut and no certain news comes to us.

May 5th, 1862.—We are continually hearing rumors of a fierce battle at Williamsburg but we do not know on what these rumors are based; we have no telegraphic communication and for weeks the mails have been so irregular as to amount to no news at all. No letters; no passing; just no news at all that can be relied on. We can only hope and pray.

May 10th, 1862.—There are rumors that McClellan has been removed from Richmond and McDowell appointed instead. With this new commander we may expect more fighting. "A new broom sweeps clean," they say. Sister Mag has made up her mind to go to the front where she can be at hand if Brother Amos should be wounded. This dreadful waiting, waiting, has almost broken her heart. In June she will take her children, Eddie and the baby girl, whom her father has never seen, and go to Richmond. Sister Mart will accompany her and, of course, there are nurses for both babies. The whole neighborhood is interested and is busy embroidering pretty things for the children. No other trimming to be had in this blockaded country. But that is the least of all the inconveniences.

The book-keeper is getting on quite well with the work and Mrs. Ansell is a really cultivated woman, she comes to every meeting of the Sewing Society and seems as patriotic as the rest. Her little son sticks to me like a burr.

May 16th, 1862.—There is light skirmishing around Richmond, so say last night's papers; somebody is killed in these skirmishes—God help the South. A letter from Grandpa insists that Sister Mag and Sister Mart stop with him at Enfield; trains to and from Richmond pass his home every day and night and daily news from the front comes from reliable people. If Brother Amos should be wounded she could get to him right away. Then, too, it is almost impossible to procure accommodations in Richmond, it is so crowded at present with the divisions of the army, changing from point to point. Sister Mag wrote at once accepting his invitation; it hurts me so to think I cannot see my darling Grandpa; he cannot come to Florida, while this war is going on.

May 27th, 1862.—They have gone. It is bad enough to give up the sisters but it is even worse to let the children go. Mother says I love them too well. But she loves them as well as I do if the truth was known. The girls have promised to write us every day, that is, if the writing paper holds out; nearly everything is scarce and hard to get. At last I am growing taller, and pretty soon my dresses will all be too short. Mother is having a piece of checked homespun woven and she is going to make me some dresses for next winter from that; the dresses she made me last fall for the trip to Raleigh are getting too small as well as too short. A growing girl in these days doesn't stand a ghost of a chance.

June 2nd, 1862.—The wires are in working order and they bring us news of two big battles near Richmond, Seven Pines on the 31st of May and Fair Oaks on June 1st. The list of "killed, wounded and missing" will come later. Mother is not well today, we are afraid she has some fever.

June 11th, 1862.—A letter from Sister Mag; the trip was a safe one and much pleasanter than she had anticipated; Grandpa and Grandma well and glad to see them; Eddie loved Grandpa right away and wants to follow him everywhere he goes. Now for the best part; Brother Amos is safe and sound. I had a letter from Cousin Joe in the same mail. He was almost broken-hearted when Cousin Sallie would not let him volunteer at the first when his schoolmates did, but

Cousin Sallie told him he was all she had in the world, his father was dead; he did not have to go until he was eighteen and she wanted him to go to Chapel Hill, study as hard as he cound until the week before his eighteenth birthday and then come home and join the army. He did not want to do this but he has always been a most devoted son and he yielded his wishes to hers. He is coming back now to join Colonel Scott's Battalion and he is happy.

June 12th, 1862.—We have good news from the army of Northern Virginia; General Robert Lee has been appointed Commander in Chief. President Davis says there is not a more able officer in the Confederacy.

I finished my hundredth pair of socks today, usually I knit at night. We do not need a light to knit, but I wanted to finish this pair to complete the hundredth. I am learning to spin. The next pair I knit will be yarn of my own manufacture. Aunt Robinson, who taught me to knit, has completed three hundred pairs of socks and some stockings for herself. I do not believe I would ever have the patience to knit such long legs.

I am going boating this evening with Cousin Florence and Jewel Holland and Hattie. McBride is a pretty lake.

June 20th, 1862.—The tannery, under Mr. James, is a complete success. Father sent to Gadsden County for a shoemaker, and three of the black boys are working under him, learning the trade; he has three sons and they are motherless. John, the eldest, is fourteen years old, but is very small for his age; David is twelve and Nathan is nine; they have never been to school in their lives and Father wants me to teach them two hours every morning. I have taught Frances right along, since Grandpa gave her to me but I do not know if I can "instill knowledge," as Dr. Cleveland says, into such unpromising specimens. However, I will try.

June 27th, 1862.—Brother Amos has been to Enfield

to see Sister Mag and the children, though he could only stay twenty-four hours. He thinks his daughter is the prettiest baby he ever saw and Eddie wants to go back to camp with him.

Sister Mag says the wounded men are passing through Enfield every day. As soon as they are well enough to leave the hospital they are sent home or to some nearby place to be nursed back to health and other wounded men take their places in the hospitals. This is necessary for the fighting is almost continuous.

July 1st, 1862.—Mother would like to omit the 4th of July festivities, but Father says the black folks must not be defrauded of their rights, so the preparations for the barbecue go on as usual. I cannot see that the war has made them a bit different unless it has made them more particular to do their work well. I believe we can trust our servants for if they had any unkind feelings they would certainly show it now. I am afraid my new pupils will not learn as rapidly as Frances. I am trying to teach them to read and write at the same time as she was taught. John tried a while on his slate and then he said, "I could do better if I had a pinter." I thought he meant if I pointed out the letters to him but when that was tried he explained what he wanted. "I ain't a wantin' nobody to pint places fur me, I wants a pin-pinter lak doctor is got." He had seen Father take his gold pen from his pocket to write with and it looked good to John's eyes. Nathan draws frogs over his slate and David will not look at either book or slate, but my copy-book says "Patience and perseverance accomplish all things."

Three days of each week are devoted to sewing for the soldiers. Often we sew steadily for days at a time, that is when we are getting up a special box to be sent by some soldier, who has been on a visit home and is returning to camp. Cousin Henry Bradford will take the box we are making ready now, he is a Major and certainly looks handsome in his beautiful uniform, just a single star on his collar and chevrons on his sleeves.

When we were at Old Point Comfort in 1857, I thought the blue uniforms with the gold epaulets were splendid; I wonder now how I ever liked them. Brother Junius is in camp near Tallahassee, at a place called Six-mile Pond. The 5th Regiment came up from Palatka last night. They have been drilling since last August and lately they have been guarding the St. Johns river; now they are to go to Virginia very soon. Captain Bernard has brought his family to the neighborhood to stay with Uncle Tom while he is away; Cousin Tom's family have been there for some time. Uncle Tom is the only man left on the place; his hair is as white as snow, his three sons and Captain Bernard are all in the army; that is the way all over the length and breadth of the land. We who live on plantations have the advantage of our city friends, for we have so many negroes around us to help in all ways and to raise provisions, both for the home and for the army. We are entirely cut off from the rest of the world and if these things could not be raised we would be obliged to starve. So much for the blockade.

July 3rd, 1862.—We went yesterday to see the soldiers in camp. Brother Junius is as brown as a berry. I did not know blondes ever burned brown. I thought they only turned red. His uniform is extremely becoming. He did not get it until after he reached Palatka, so we had not seen him in it before.

There are two regiments beside the 5th and their tents make quite a show. We saw them drill, they looked fine, but the hot July sun must make them very uncomfortable. Mother took a large hamper of good things to eat and I heard her tell Brother Junius to share with the men who were far from their own people, said she would bring or send a similar hamper every day.

Mattie was delighted to see her father and she cried when Mother said it was time to go home. She said, "Mother, can't we take papa, too?" The seven days battles around Richmond have filled the hospitals to overflowing; nearly every home is in mourning and the sound of "Rachel, for her children weeping," is heard on every hand. We have so many dear ones in the army of Northern Virginia, and so far, we have not lost a single one. Father in Heaven we thank Thee. Mr. Blake preaches such beautiful, comforting sermons. I mark his text each Sunday and try to remember all he says. I told Mother, one Sunday when she was sick and could not attend church, what he had said in his sermon and she suggested that I get a blank book and write all I could remember of all his sermons. Next time we go to town I will get a book from Mr. McDougal.

July 5th, 1862.—Brother Junius spent the day with us yesterday. He gave us such an entertaining account of the winter on the St. Johns. He likes army life better than he expected. He says he never was fond of hunting and when he has to really go "Man-hunting" he will not like it at all.

He thinks they will break camp about the middle of August.

* * * * *

The Diary leaves these new and untried Florida regiments in camp on Six-mile Pond and on the eve of departure for Virginia.

Around Richmond the fighting had been raging for more than a month and now, the Capital having been saved for the time being, our generals were giving the enemy a taste of invasion, or at least a threat of it. The 5th Florida reached Virginia just in time to participate in the second Battle of Manassas, which was fought on the 28th to 30th of August.

Fresh troops marched into the thickest of the fight —the dead and dying on every side—with orders to advance steadily in the face of the enemy's guns. They obeyed orders—they had come to fight and nobly they did their part. Many a good man bit the dust that day; many an orphan and many a widow were left behind.

The 5th Florida received its "baptism of blood" that day and we at home, were proud indeed. September, hot and murky came in. Both sides were burying their dead; that done they were on the march again. On the 17th of September the battle of Sharpsburg, as we Southerners call it, was fought. It was a bloody field and when the news of the day was wired to waiting men and women, it carried bad news to Mrs. Whitehead at Enfield. Among the wounded she found the names of her husband, four cousins and two brothers-in-law. Immediately she boarded the train for the front to find her husband. Her sister accompanied her and with the help of the nurses, managed to keep the babies alive, but Mrs. Whitehead, herself, had no thought for anything but her wounded soldier.

Going straight to headquarters, she obtained a pass which would take her into all the hospitals in the city. To one and then to another she went, until all had been visited but she could not find him; at last she met one of his comrades, whose bandaged head and arm showed what he had been through. He told her where to find Captain Whitehead and his brother. They had found a room in the rear of the Richmond Hotel in which mattresses were laid all over the floor; mattresses of the rudest construction, and the room was full of wounded men, some of whom had received attention from a surgeon, while others had not been attended to at all. She said it was like going into a butcher shop, or rather to the shambles.

John, Captain Whitehead's faithful servant, who had followed him day by day since the beginning of the war, was with him; it was John who had procured this room and offered it to his master's friends. She sent John to find a surgeon and he had the good luck to find one, who had just come in on the train, to offer his services.

Captain Whitehead was shot in the foot and the minie ball had torn the foot almost to pieces and then imbedded itself in the ankle; an exceedingly painful wound.

Two days later Mrs. Whitehead was on her way to Florida with five wounded soldiers to care for. Money can do something, even in war times and she had succeeded in making them as comfortable as their condition would allow. Her sister and the nurses were still caring for the babies; their mother had not given them a thought.

Throughout the ensuing eight weeks a scorching fever seemed about to lap up the life of Captain Whitehead, but the doctor finally located the ball and, when it was extracted, his recovery was rapid, though he was never able to walk on the foot without a crutch or a stout stick. We told Mrs. Whitehead she was a heroine, but she said no she was only a half-crazed wife. Not all were so fortunate as she, the demand for black dresses, for crape, for mourning veils, stripped the Confederacy of these emblems of mourning and, after that, you could not tell, when you saw a bright dress, how much of bitter sorrow was hidden beneath it.

At Enfield, Governor Branch was mourning the death of his nephew, almost his son he was, General Larry O'Bryan Branch, who was killed in this same Battle of Sharpsburg, at the head of his column of North Carolinians. A brave man, in the prime of life; he had given his life for his country. News of his death had not been received and Governor Branch was waiting at the station, hoping to hear from him, when he saw approaching a train heavily draped in black. "Who is dead?" he asked, and when he was told he bowed his head in grief; he was eighty years of age, his head was as white as snow, yet in other ways time had touched him lightly. Now his heart was broken; he was never the same and in less than four months he had left all wars and rumors of wars forevermore.

As the winter drew near it was thought the army would go into winter quarters but the season was mild and heavy fighting continued, winding up the campaign of 1862 at Fredericksburg, one of the fiercest and bloodiest battles of the war.

In Florida, the entire household at Pine Hill were engaged, heart and soul in trying to help Captain Whitehead to escape the death, which then seemed inevitable. By the 6th of December he was well enough to be propped up in a carriage and driven forty miles to a reunion of the Whitehead family, held at the house of the oldest of the brothers. This reunion took the form of a house party, given in gratitude and thanksgiving for the lives spared, even though the bullets had not missed their mark.

Again we yield the pen to the writer of the Diary:

* * * * *

December 1st, 1862.—It seems strange to think of fun and gaiety again, when we have been through so much of grief and horror. So much nursing, too, watching through sleepless nights, trying to soothe through the days of wild delirium, making one cooling poultice after another and wondering all the while if anything would ever help the poor sufferer.

December 4th, 1862.—Now, that the bullet has been extracted, Brother Amos is improving rapidly and he tells us many interesting things as he lies there so helpless. Last night his thoughts turned to the battle of Seven Pines; it seems that he, with a party of his company, was detailed to help to bury the dead. Some of those he found were acquaintances and two were kinsmen but the deepest interest with him centered in two young strangers, who were found clasped in each others arms. One wore the blue uniform and the other was a lieutenant in a Maryland regiment and wore the gray. They were of the same size and figure and when he looked into the poor dead faces they were exactly alike. He was so sure they must be brothers that he examined the papers in the pockets of each, and, sure enough, they must have been brothers—maybe twin brothers, as the last name was the same. In each boy's pocket were letters from the same place in Maryland and though these letters were simply signed "Mother," the writing was identical. They looked to be boys of twenty or perhaps less. He buried them still in that close embrace. The pine tree, beneath which they were found was carefully marked; some cannon balls were picked up and piled above them and when brother Amos returned to camp he wrote to that mother and told her all this.

I wonder why they were on opposite sides in this gigantic struggle. Will the poor, bereaved mother send and take them home or will they sleep on, under the Virginia pines? Brother Amos says he sent the contents of each boy's pockets to the mother in Maryland. How her poor heart must ache.

Now brother Amos is able to sit up and can even stand with his crutches and we are going to a house party, at the home of his oldest brother. Mr. John Whitehead is too old for army duty and he is also too fat for a soldier. Three of his four brothers have been wounded and are convalescent and he is having a family reunion. Sister Mart and I are going, too, for the Whitehead girls are dear friends of ours. Mother has made me some pretty clothes and it would make a funny picture if I could portray the great amount of turning and fixing she had to do to get me "something out of nothing," she says. We Southerners are copying Burns' heroine, who "Gars auld cloes look amaist as weel's the new." I really believe I forgot my Scotch just there and should have written "noo." I wish I could take my black mammy with me, it is bad getting on without her but she always has a baby.

December 6th, 1862.—We have been here three days; there are nine girls in the party and twelve gentlemen, young ones I mean; then there are two married couples with little children and our host and hostess, who are just lovely to us all. We have music and dancing at night, go riding whenever we feel like it and there is a nice boat on the Flint River which is very near the house. Albany is not far, if we want to shop—but there it is again—we have plenty of money but the stores are almost empty. When we went in yesterday, all we could find to buy was some delicious molasses candy. There is a cotton factory somewhere near here where they are making cloth for the army. I am going to see how they make it.

December 15th, 1862.—We have news of a great battle in Virginia, Fredericksburg, a terrible battle in which our side won the victory and the enemy suffered severe losses. How I wish the war would end; it throws a cloud over everything.

All the gentlemen visiting here have been wounded but all are getting well; they expect to report for duty very soon. Brother Amos is the only one who is permanently disabled. He says he is going to offer his services to the Commissary Department as soon as he is able. He says a cripple can do what is required there, just as well as anybody. Sister Mag says he shall never leave her again. Father and Mother are missing us but in another week we will be at home.

December 20th, 1862.—Last night we sat up all night, getting Harry ready to get off this morning, early, for Virginia. His sister and nieces were packing clothes, putting up provisions for him to take back to camp with him and I was finishing the last pair of socks I had on hand, that makes six pair I have knit for him. He wanted me to kiss him goodbye but Mother does not approve of caresses. All my playmates, with a few exceptions, have been boys and Mother's rule is "hands off." I am not allowed to waltz with any but cousins and she does not exactly like that.

Captain Mac Whitehead and Major Whitehead go tomorrow. Other people are coming but these soldiers who are going, are so near and dear and these new-comers are only just "company." It makes a great difference.

December 25th, 1862.—We reached home on the 24th but it is not like Christmas. No frolicking for anybody as Cousin Martha died yesterday morning and will be buried here tomorrow. Everybody loved her and grieves that she has gone.

Aunt Sue is in trouble, for little Mary Eliza is sick unto death and Father and Mother are with her today. She has typhoid pneumonia and she has always been delicate. Father has seven sick soldiers but none of them in danger at present, although he thought two of them would surely die the first part of the week. He has been fortunate so far, for he has not lost a single patient.

Brother Amos stood the trip very well and can handle his crutches better than at first. He can walk about in the house but has to have help to go down the steps. There are so many poor crippled soldiers. Oh, if this terrible war was over!

December 27th, 1862.—Mother has a letter in the mail, which has just come telling of dear Grandpa's illness. He went out on the ice to direct the man who was using the ice plow and took a violent cold. We feel very anxious. Mary Eliza is no better.

The papers say the armies have gone into winter quarters and we will have no more fighting until spring.

January 3rd, 1863.—My dear, dear Grandpa is dead. I loved him so well and now I will never see him again. Mother was all ready to start to North Carolina today but a telegram came telling the sad news.

Mary Eliza died in the night and she will be buried here tomorrow. There is trouble and sorrow on every side. It proved to be whooping cough poor little Mary Eliza had and Mattie and I have taken it. I thought it was a baby disease but it seems grown people can have it.

Our men in camp are suffering for blankets. Mother has sent all of hers and she has several of the women on the place at work washing and carding wool, to make comforts to take the place of the covering she has sent to the army. She has already sent all the linen sheets to the Reid Hospital in Richmond; not as sheets but rolled in bandages for dressing wounds. We have used most of the table cloths to scrape lint, for this blockade cuts us off from any supplies for the sick or the wounded.

Father has taught Nan to make salve and we ship it every week. She keeps the pot of salve going all the time for our poor soldiers. They need so much and we can do so little.

January 8th, 1863.—Cousin Sam Donelson came last night. I have not seen him since the summer of 1859 and I would never have known him. Instead of a slender, pale boy, he is a splendid looking man. He is on Uncle Daniel's staff, with the rank of Lieutenant.

Aunt Margaret left her home at the beginning of hostilities in the West. She had the farm wagons packed with belongings of the negroes and they walked behind and drove a herd of fine cattle uncle Daniel had raised. Old Aunt Purdy rode one saddle horse and Grace another and so on, until all the numerous riding nags were safely on the road and all the old and feeble negroes had a means of transportation. It is a wonder they got away but she managed to locate them in middle Georgia, where they are still waiting for the war to be over.

Cousin Sam is young and daring, he is having a good time in the main and he doesn't care how long it lasts. He says Uncle Daniel has grown thin; they are pleased, as, indeed, we all are, at his promotion to be a Major-General. I am sure he deserves it. I love him dearly. He was so good to me when Father was so ill at his home in Tennessee.

March 12th, 1863.—More bad news to write in my diary. Sweet little Susie died before day this morning. She was so pretty. Except cousin Rich, she was the best looking one of the family. She loved him devotedly and ever since he was killed she seemed to be thinking of him all the time. When she was dying she asked to be buried beside him. Our "God's Acre," is filling fast. Aunt Nancy is so frail we fear she cannot stand this fresh blow.

March 20th, 1863.—Mattie and I have the whooping cough very bad. She cannot retain her food, though I do not suffer in that way, it is extremely painful. When the spells of coughing take me the blood oozes from my eyes, nose and ears. Three doctors have been called in and they say they never saw such a case. It is well I am not going to school this winter for I do not believe I could study.

Sam Donelson went back to the army of the West today. Mother is with Aunt Nancy.

March 6th, 1863.—It is hard to even think, because I want to see Grandpa so bad. We were going to him in the summer and now I will never see him again. Father says I will see him in that beautiful Heaven, which he loved to talk of but it seems so far away. Grandma has sent me a lock of his lovely snow-white hair, but there is no comfort in that, for it only makes me long the more to put my arms about his neck and kiss the soft thick hair which glistened like silver.

His will has been read and he has left Uncle Kinchen and Aunt Amy in Mother's care for the remainder of their lives; all their children were given to Mother, so they will not be separated from their family. Father has sent money to pay their way down and Uncle Kinchen is such a good traveler, they will get on all right.

Grandpa was buried in the cemetery at Enfield. He had stated in his will that he must be brought to Florida and buried beside Grandmother in our "God's Acre," but when he was dying he told them not to try to take his body back to Florida, the whole country is in such an upset condition on account of the war and he did not know what complications might arise. I wish he could have been brought here so we could take him flowers every day. I know what I can do, I can bear in remembrance the many talks we have had and try to be just what he wanted me to be.

CHAPTER XV

REFUGEES FROM TENNESSEE

AT the beginning of the war in the West the most feasible route for the Union Army would be to follow the line of the Louisville and Nashville Railway. Marching along the Gallatin Pike to Nashville, the enemy would pass directly in front of the splendid residence which General Donelson, a short while before, had erected on his stock farm, which had long been the admiration of the surrounding country. At state and county fairs he carried off many a prize and many a blue ribbon. The undulating acres of this lovely farm rolled back from the pike; huge elms made inviting shade here and there, while the whole surface was covered with luscious grass. A bold stream flowed through the place, sometimes it flowed quietly through beds of fragrant mint then, curling and purling amdist huge boulders, gaining volume at every turn, it dashed over a steep declivity and here stood a mill, its high wheel turned by the force of the waters.

Back, out of sight from the pike, the wheat fields and corn fields told why the mill was there. This was altogether too tempting a piece of property to be passed over by the invaders; besides its value, it was the property of a "Rebel General, who was, even then at the front in West Virginia." Mrs. Donelson realized this and made hasty preparation for taking departure.

On a grain and hay farm many wagons are employed and to these wagons the strongest and best teams were hitched. The negroes were directed to pack their clothes and bedding, she and her children packed theirs and the smoke house was emptied of provisions. Sides of bacon, the far-famed Tennessee hams, long strings of sausage were tied about the wagons, while tubs of lard sat on the floor. Provender for the teams and the cows, which were being driven in front of the train of wagons, carriages and riders of the blooded horses of which the General was so proud.

The long cavalcade set forth on its uncertain journey just thirty-six hours before the advance guard of the Federal Army entered the city of Nashville, through which they had been obliged to pass on the southward way.

Pushing on as rapidly as circumstances would admit of, they succeeded in reaching Marietta, Georgia. Here Mrs. Donelson rented a farm, installed the travelers and, taking with her the two youngest children, hastened to join her husband at the front. Of course, she could not be with him; often she did not see him for days, even weeks but she was in touch with the army. If he should be sick or wounded she could reach him speedily and, while she waited her strong, capable hands found much to do for those who had not been so fortunate as to escape the enemy's bullets. Many a soldier blessed Mrs. Donelson's motherly heart and ready hands.

When in January, 1863, Governor Branch died at his home in the Old North State, it was found that he had willed to his daughter, Margaret, a fine plantation in Leon County, Florida. It proved to be a great gift, for the Yankees were steadily advancing into Georgia and again the Donelsons were in danger of capture. They had learned to pack by this time and once more they took the road.

Walnut Hill Plantation was about four miles from Tallahassee, a neat, six-room cottage, with orange trees and walnut trees shading the broad porches and a lake lying at the foot of the hill on which it stood. At the back, built on the slope of the hill, stood a large barn with sheds for cattle, a carriage house, a large garden enclosed by a "wattle fence" and just below, beside a stream, which flowed through the hammock of bay and magnolia was a dairy, ready for use. It looked like Heaven to these poor wanderers. The spring campaign had opened and the war was no nearer its end than it had been a year ago.

In March little Susie, youngest child of Mr. and Mrs. Richard Bradford "went home." She was a quiet, gentle child, never strong and, after the death of her beloved "Rich," she grew gentler and more silent until, when the March winds blew their fiercest, she slipped out of life. Her mother did not long survive her, when the air was filled with the scent of honeysuckle and jasmine, she too, entered "The Pearly Gates," to find her loved ones.

Captain Taylor had been brought home on a stretcher, hardly alive and almost a skeleton. He had not been wounded, but pneumonia had done the work. A few weeks of nursing and he was ready for duty again for the soldier of the South did not linger when his country called.

By this time supplies of all kinds were scarce and hard to get in the Confederate states. Everything which we thought could be sent to the soldiers was carefully put aside until such time as it could be forwarded. Mrs. Bernard was packing a box to send to her husband in General Lee's army. She had new clothes, a pair of shoes, a hat of her own manufacture, some handkerchiefs, also homemade, a large cake, some rusks and another very useful article, a crock of soft soap. This was an unusual box, it was rare, indeed, that so many of the necessaries of life could be gotten together. Of the soap, Mrs. Bernard was especially proud. She had made it herself and Captain Bernard had written her more than once of the scarcity of a detergent of any kind; it was this fact, that had inspired the soap-making.

The box reached camp in safety, the eatables were thoroughly enjoyed, the clothes were more than welcome. Everything arrived in good condition except the "butter," which was completely spoiled, had turned a dark yellow and they "took it out and buried it, reserving the crock for other uses." Imagine how that good housekeeper and loving wife felt.

There were no lights in the South except those of home manufacture. We had candles of wax and of tallow, candles of bayberry, tapers of twisted shucks, standing in saucers of melted lard, "Confederate lanterns," said lanterns being loosely twisted strands of spun cotton, dipped in crude turpentine and rolled around a green hickory stick of suitable size. These were placed in the open fireplaces in summer and gave a pleasant light for ordinary purposes, though you could not read or sew by them. In winter a blazing lightwood fire settled the question of lights.

We were now in the third year of the war and we had learned to supply, in a measure, our wants. We had learned to do without many luxuries, which had formerly been looked upon as necessities and we had accepted conditions and thanked God it was no worse.

While we were doing without nearly everything, nearer starvation than we had ever thought to be, suffering, when sick for want of proper medicines, wearing the rough homespun, which was all we could get, the North set up a hue and cry because the prisoners of war did not have the comforts of life. Southern captives in Northern prisons were not given the comforts of life and yet there was no blockade of Northern ports, no scarcity of the necessaries as was the case with us.

It was difficult to hold communication with friends from one side to the other. Before letters could be sent across the line they were subjected to a strict espionage, often they were not allowed to be delivered, and so sometimes the prisoners had been dead for months before we knew of it, some one would be exchanged and tell the news. The South had some friends in New York City and, through them, Southern prisoners were frequently supplied with clothing, but for these kind hearts the men in Northern prisons, exposed to the rigors of a climate to which they were unaccustomed, would have died.

Murphreesboro was the scene of a stiff fight, the army of the West, though it had met reverses, was still ready to do battle when called upon. Never on earth was there a braver body of men than these—the soldiers of the Southern Confederacy; the men who wore the gray.

In Virginia there was fighting all along the line; there was wanton destruction of property; there was terrible loss of life and Sherman, who, afterward, declared "war is hell," was right. Sheridan, after one of his raids across the valley of the Shenandoah, said, "A crow flying across the valley would have to carry his provisions with him." The non-combatants of Virginia were suffering horribly; there was certainly no Christian charity in the army of the Potomac.

General Donelson was dead. A severe stomach trouble attacked him and though he was faithfully and tenderly nursed by his devoted wife, and though Dr. Quintard was with him all the time, the medicines necessary to check the disease could not be had—the Confederacy was blockaded. Mrs. Donelson came to Florida. No need to follow the army now, her heart was broken—all was dark—for,

"The light of the whole world dies
When love is gone."

Since the beginning of the war we had suffered reverses; we had spent days of fasting, humiliation and prayer; we had won many a splendid victory and we bowed our heads in earnest thanksgiving for God's mercy. At Chancellorsville we had seen

"The noble oak which propped
Our cause go down"

And now we found ourselves facing the fiercest struggle of the war.

RESUMING THE DIARY

June 3rd, 1863.—I have been sick, dear Diary. I have not been able even to think at times and I am a *fright.* The fever made my hair drop out and I am wearing a black silk cap, which makes me look like the picture of the Jesuits.

So much has happened since I wrote here last. I miss Susie and Aunt Nancy and I am so sorry for Aunt Margaret. The whole country misses Uncle Daniel for he was such a fine officer, so splendidly equipped to command men.

My pupils have all gone away. I did not know when they went but the father died and the boys are scattered among their relatives. I hope they can go to school for they were actually learning a little.

Father says I can resume the book-keeping when I am well again. The call for troops made it necessary for Mr. Ansell and Mr. Edmondson, the brother-in-law, to enlist or leave the country. Rather than return to England they took the oath of allegiance to the Confederate Government and have joined the Gamble Artillery; that is, they expect to be in Colonel Gamble's command. Mrs. Ansell will stay on in the house provided for the mill manager.

Dr. English has written to Father in regard to a wounded soldier he is bringing with him from a hospital in Virginia. The doctor went on to see his nephew, who was wounded in a skirmish near Harper's Ferry, but when he reached the hospital his nephew had been dead two weeks. He found there a young Virginian, whose injuries were severe and painful; the surgeons in attendance said he was shot through both lungs, the bullet making what they term "a clean wound," entering on one side cutting its way through and leaving the body in a direct line. They think if he could get to some quiet place, where his wound could receive close medical treatment he might recover. Of course Father wants him to come here.

We always keep Charley when the doctor goes and he is with us now. He is like a little brother to me and Father and Mother are more like parents to him than his own father. The doctor is a scientific man, not an M. D., but a Ph.D., and a long list of other letters, which mean so much to him. He is so wrapped up in his researches that he does not find his own young son very interesting. Charley is happy here, however, and we love the poor motherless boy.

June 10th, 1863.—Dr. English came today and with him Captain John Yates Beall, the soldier he had written about. Captain Beall is young and very good-looking. He has the front room up stairs, where he can be cool and we have our orders to make no noise. He must not talk and he has to take nourishment every three hours. Father dressed his wound and left him to sleep a while. I hope I do not forget and make a noise.

Sister Mag, with her family, and Sister Mart have gone to Bath, where Brother Amos has a furnished house, left to him in his father's will. It is large and pleasantly located, built expressly for the summer-time and cool and airy. Brother Amos has never recovered from his wound and the doctors, who have examined him, say he will never be fit for service again, but he says he is going back, just as soon as he feels well again. That is the spirit which animates all our soldiers.

Mother keeps surprisingly well. We are so glad of it for it is impossible to leave home in search of health in these busy days.

June 12th, 1863.—Our patient, the newest one, likes his quarters very much. Father and Mother wait on him themselves, they are so afraid something may go wrong. The piano is kept closed and Mattie's poodle has been banished *pro tem.*

June 17th, 1863.—Vague and contradictory rumors fill the air; we seem to be upon the brink of a change some way. The army of Northern Virginia is on the move and we can only pray and work, for it grows more difficult with every passing day to provide the barest necessities for our brave boys at the front. Never did men fight under greater disadvantages. The armies must be supplied even if the home-folks starve. We do not let them know how we have to stint ourselves. They must not have our burdens to bear in addition to their own.

June 28th, 1863.—The army of Northern Virginia is pushing on to the invasion of the North. In this land of ours a curious species of fault-finders has developed. While the men, the true men, are at the front, struggling with might and main to save the South from destruction, there are others, poor weak-kneed cowards, who stand on street corners and criticise President Davis and the generals in command of our armies.

These cowardly back-biters have never smelled gun powder, they are Carpet Generals and yet, to listen to them talk, you would think that the only thing needed to insure victory would be to put them in command. I turn sick with scorn when I am obliged to be present while they are exploiting their wisdom.

July 2nd, 1863.—Yesterday fighting began on Pennsylvania soil. The army of Northern Virginia, the bravest army in the history of wars, may, even now be struggling with the foe. Oh, how horrible it is to know that those you love are in such danger! There must be aching hearts at the North as well as here. I feel for all who suffer and it seems to me the bond of brotherhood, which once united the two sections, ought to make us kinder in our judgments; more merciful in our actions. But war is a monster and destroys charity.

July 3rd, 1863.—Another telegram brings more news from Gettysburg—such awful news—death and destruction and perhaps defeat. God help our poor country. Holding my breath I listen and tears come, though I try to be calm. So many of our brave men, who went forward can never come back. Oh, this horrible, horrible WAR!

August 18th, 1863.—Tonight we had with us at supper two of the heroes of Gettysburg; John Nash and Nicholas Eppes. They were recommended for promotion by their colonel, for gallantry on the battle field of Gettysburg. On that field, where deeds of daring, which will live forever, were done, what did these boys do that could be singled out? They must have distinguished themselves for the War Department to notice and promote. I wanted to ask about the great battle but they were leaving home as they had, only a short hour or two ago, said goodbye to those they loved. They were on their way to the army of the West, even now fighting Rosecrans army. They were going to face death, just as they had faced it at Gettysburg, and so, I could not ask questions which would call up scenes of blood and agony.

When they had said goodbye and were out of sight Aunt Robinson said, "Mrs. Bradford, isn't it a pity for that pretty boy to be killed by the Yankees? He is enough like Sue to be her brother." Mother shuddered. "I am glad he isn't," she said, "I am afraid it is not patriotic but I am glad I have no sons."

It used to be a grievance to poor mother that, as Johnnie expressed it, "Aunt Patsey's boys were all girls," but she seems to be taking comfort in it now.

August 20th, 1863.—Captain Beall has improved

amazingly, he can now speak in a natural voice and is allowed to converse when he feels like it. At first his voice was so weak and it hurt him to speak, so he made signs for his wants. He is very pleasant, the doctors, who come now and again to see him, say his lungs are still in bad shape and he requires just the care and good nursing he is getting here. Father has inserted silver tubes in his right side to draw off the pus, which has collected there. The right lung is not healing as the left one has done and they forbid him to think of going back for months to come. A winter in Florida may make him as sound as ever.

Today Father took him for a short ride in the buggy. He drove Dabney, who is old and steady, so he would not be jolted or jarred. I wish Sister Mart was at home, she could play for him and entertain him. I have taken up the book-keeping again but it is not quite as heavy as it was because the saw-mill is not running. The hands who formerly did the work at the mill are needed in the crops that more provisions may be made.

The people who live in town and have no plantations to draw upon, have a bad time indeed. Father often sends articles of food to his friends in Tallahassee. Judge Baltzell said he had not tasted meat for weeks, so Father promptly sent him a ham, smoked after the most approved North Carolina fashion and it was touching to see how pleased the judge was. He often sends things to Major Beard, too, and none of us ever forget Bishop Rutledge, when something good is on hand. The Bishop eats like a bird, he has so little appetite, and has to be tempted to eat.

September 1st, 1863.—The children have not been well at Bath, so Brother Amos is bringing his family home next week. The War Department will not accept his services, so he is going direct to his plantation on Lake Jackson and try to make lots of syrup, sugar and meat for the armies in the field; such as this is certainly needed.

We are busy spinning, weaving, sewing and knitting, trying to get together clothing to keep our dear soldiers warm this winter. Brother Junius writes that he has worn all his under garments to shreds and wants to know if it would be possible to get some flannel, or some kind of wool goods to make him some new ones? We have tried but none can be had, so I am spinning some wool into knitting yarn and with some big wooden needles I have I am going to knit both drawers and shirts for him. I am so impatient to get to work on them and see if my plan is feasible, that I spend all the time I can at the spinning wheel. I know the shirts can be knit, for I made some for father last winter which he found quite comfortable but I am somewhat doubtful as to the drawers. After awhile we will learn how to supply most of our needs.

Cousin Rob did not have a hat when he was getting ready for school, which opens today, so I plaited palmetto and sewed it into shape and Aunt Robinson, who knows everything, pressed it on a block and then I sewed a ribbon around it and there it was, a sure enough hat and very becoming. He sat near and admired the braid all the time I was making it. I had no shoes except some terribly rough ones that old Mr. McDermid made and Cousin Rob tanned some squirrel skins and made me a pair of really beautiful shoes, nice enough to wear with my one and only silk dress. This dress, you must know, is "made of Mammy's old one" like Jim Crack Corn's coat—Little Diary, I am afraid you do not know very much of Mother Goose.

September 25th, 1863.—The telegraph wires are up and working again and the news we get is both encouraging and distressing. A great victory has been won at Chickamauga, but at such a fearful loss of life. It is said to be as bloody a battle as Gettysburg and it lasted three days, beginning on the nineteenth of this month.

We have such glorious news of the courage displayed by Gen. Finley's Florida Brigade. They are in Longstreet's Corps and they formed the entering wedge, which broke Thomas's line; they charged with the bayonet three times with dreadful loss, before Thomas gave way. It is grand, it is heroic, but oh, those poor boys and their wives and mothers! Sometimes I am glad I have no real, true brothers for wouldn't I love them just a little better than these I have?

September 29th, 1863.—This is Mother's birthday and the house is full of friends who have come to show their love for her. She is just the daintiest little lady in all the land and she is so gracious to everybody; it makes no difference who it is, and I believe that is one reason so many people love her. Father thinks she is perfect and he does not countenance the least disobedience to her wishes.

Some wounded men from the west came on the train to Tallahassee yesterday, only a few, however, and there is plenty of room in the hospital, so Dr. Geddings did not send any out to Father; if more come he will send them.

October 4th, 1863.—I saw something awful this morning; I wish I had not seen it. We were taking a box of hospital supplies to the depot, to ship to Richmond and, when we turned the corner by Fisher's Green, a group of soldiers were standing there. It was early, the sun had been up but just a few minutes and it shone bright on the group. I always look at soldiers, but I am sorry I looked at these for they had two poor fellows, who had deserted and been caught and, while we were looking, the squad fired and the deserters fell dead. Isn't it perfectly awful? I didn't think it ought to be done. So many are killed in battle and lives are worth more than that. To kill them when maybe they meant to come back. I am afraid I shall not sleep a wink tonight.

October 27th, 1863.—We went to the salt works today and, though I am tired and dirty and have no good place to write, I am going to try to tell you about it.

A year ago salt began to get scarce but the people only had to economize in its use, but soon there was no salt and then Father got Cousin Joe Bradford to come down from Georgia and take charge of some salt works he was having installed on the coast. He had plenty of hands from the plantation but they had to have an intelligent head and then, too, it is a rather dangerous place to work, for the Yankee gunboats can get very near the coast and they may try shelling the works.

Though they have been in operation quite awhile this is my first visit. Father brought us with him and we will stay three days, so he can see just how they are getting on. We are to sleep in a tent, on a ticking filled with pine straw. It will be a novel experience.

I am so interested in seeing the salt made from the water. The great big sugar kettles are filled full of water and fires made beneath the kettles. They are a long time heating up and then they boil merrily. Ben and Tup and Sam keep the fires going, for they must not cool down the least little bit. A white foam comes at first and then the dirtiest scum you ever saw bubbles and dances over the surface, as the water boils away it seems to get thicker and thicker, at last only a wet mass of what looks like sand remains. This they spread on smooth oaken planks to dry. In bright weather the sun does the rest of the work of evaporation, but if the weather is bad fires are made just outside of a long, low shelter, where the planks are placed on blocks of wood. The shelter keeps off the rain and the fires give out heat enough to carry on the evaporation. The salt finished in fair weather is much whiter and nicer in every way than that dried in bad weather, but this dark salt is used to salt meat or to pickle pork. I think it is fine of Father to do all this. It is very troublesome and it takes nine men to do the work, besides Cousin Joe's time; and Father does not get any pay whatever for the salt he makes.

We expected to have a grand time swimming and fishing. We are both good swimmers, but Father and Cousin Joe will not allow us to go outside of this little cove. Yankee gun-boats have been sighted once lately and there is no knowing when the salt works may be attacked.

October 6th, 1863.—Yesterday morning we got up with the sun and had a bath and some clean clothes, then came breakfast of corn hoe-cake and fried fish. Mother wanted to pack a basket of eatables for us but Father said we must eat camp fare, so the only thing we brought along in that line was a jar of preserves, for Cousin Joe, and some coffee. Breakfast was fine and when it was over we went fishing, still inside the cove. After dinner we went to Newport and had a bath in the sulphur spring. There we had some delicious October peaches, and we also saw many of our soldier friends in Colonel Scott's battalion. I admire Colonel Scott most sincerely, he is a Pennsylvanian by birth but he came in early life to make his home in Tallahassee. His home was a little way out of town and his wife and babies were his world. When the war began he volunteered his services to the Confederacy; it had not been expected of him because of his Northern birth, but there is no better friend to the South. He says it is his country. He was in the mercantile business but he has developed unusual military ability and he seems never to tire. Last winter he took cold, being so constantly in the marshy coast region, and rheumatism followed the cold. He still suffers and at times he has to have assistance in mounting his horse, but he drills his men regularly and last night one of the boys told me of the burning of the bridge across the St. Mary's river.

The enemy were advancing. The only hope of stopping them was to burn that bridge and Colonel Scott and his cavalry were miles away. Night was fast coming on, when the Colonel walked into camp and said, "Boys, I want volunteers to go with me to burn St. Mary's bridge; we may get back or we may not, I am going." Very nearly all wanted to go but Colonel Scott picked eight young men, almost boys, the most of them. He was so stiff from rheumatism that they had to put him on his horse, but "there is a *spirit* in man," and he led them off in the darkness.

Rapidly they rode; through brake and briar their way lay, but they reached the river not one moment too soon. Each soldier carried, tied to his saddle, a supply of fat pitch pine. The tramp of the enemy's cavalry could be heard approaching. Lighting their torches, they had the bridge blazing merrily in the twinkling of an eye.

By this time the Yankees were in sight and a howl of rage went up, as they discovered the blaze. Swiftly the gray figures disappeared into the night and, though volley after volley followed them, not one was wounded. Five of the eight I know and am proud to claim as friends.

Tomorrow we go home. Cousin Julia has enjoyed it hugely—apart from the pleasure of seeing her father, it is her first visit to the coast and everything was new to her. I think our Florida coast is more attractive than the Virginia seashore, though it is rank heresy to say so.

THE STORY CONTINUES

Perhaps it would be as well to explain to our readers what was served at the good suppers mentioned in the diary. Nothing which could be sent to the army was eaten at home, but there was much in country homes, which would not bear transportation, in the primitive modes of the times. So we ask that you imagine a table, either with or without a tablecloth, usually without; on the polished surface were dishes of broiled or baked chickens or a roast of mutton, for that was a meat which we could not send, except to nearby camps; delicious batter bread, hot, with fresh butter; vegetables, daintily prepared, maybe a sweet potato pone, dear to the Southern palate.

On rare occasions a cake made of brown sugar, or syrup, as the case might be; and cut glass bowls filled with custard, also made with brown sugar and flavored, usually, with leaves from the nearest peach-tree. Sometimes the cake was lacking and then pans of syrup bread took its place. Baked eggs were always liked and salad could easily be had, for we made our own vinegar in great abundance from fruit juices. So you see when these suppers are written of you may rest assured that none of these eatables could have been sent to the army, which had first place in every Southern heart.

THE DIARY RESUMED

November 2nd, 1863.—Now, while Cousin Julia is with us, I am trying to make things as pleasant as possible for her. All the boys are away in the army, so we have what Aunt Dinah calls "hen parties." We have been the rounds of the family to dinings; we have had picnics, to which we have taken the children from the various families in the neighborhood, rides on horseback, walks to look for chinquepins and hickory nuts and now we want some evening parties. As Cousin Julia is a minister's daughter and does not dance or play cards, the question of amusement is a little difficult, but we will play games and next week we will set the ball rolling with a musicale. We have several fine musicians in the neighborhood and mother never fails to have plenty of good things to eat.

Brother Amos and sister Mag are with us and they are splendid help in entertaining. He is still on crutches but is as jolly as a cricket and she is so sweet everybody loves her.

December 4th, 1863.—We had that musicale last night and it was fine. We had an unexpected guest; in the afternoon cousin Mary wrote a note asking if she might bring Miss Maria Eppes. She had come to visit at Greenwood. Of course we were glad to have her and when she came we were delighted; she is beautiful, and has such charming ways. I have a picture of Lieutenant Mecklenburg Polk, which he sent me by Cousin Sam. He must be remarkably handsome if he looks like his picture and I have framed it in pine cones, the kind that grow on the short leaf pines. It makes a very pretty frame and it occupies a prominent place on the mantel. I do not know this fine young soldier boy, but whenever I look at the picture it seems to recall some one whom I have known; just a fleeting impression, which I cannot quite grasp.

Last night Maria Eppes saw it and she called out in a rather excited tone: "Where did my brother's picture come from?"

I told her who it was but she could hardly believe me, and said, "It is exactly like Nick."

I knew then why the face looked familiar and I told Maria of the night her brother took supper with us. Then she told me of the part he took in the great battle of Chickamauga; of Finley's Brigade, of which his regiment is a part, how they charged the enemy with the bayonet three times before they succeeded in breaking General Thomas' line; how they yelled as they drove the enemy down Snodgrass Hill; how terrible the fighting was; how the ground was covered with dead and dying men and of the awful groans of the wounded horses.

They had a truce for a short time to bury their dead, not really a decent burial, but just a trench, in which they were laid. The battle lasted three days and covered many acres of ground, miles, it seemed to those engaged.

Just think, exactly one month before, Lieut. Eppes was sitting so quietly at our table, he and cousin John, and so soon after this bloody battle came to them.

Maria said her mother had a letter that morning, telling of the battle of Missionary Ridge and the crossing to Lookout Mountain, where another battle was fought. Maria says her brother escaped almost by a miracle at Missionary Ridge, as most of his comrades were either killed or taken prisoners. We have heard that cousin John and cousin Henry, who were in that battle were taken prisoner and thus far we have not heard where they were carried.

Maria is very glad her brother is safe so far, but then you never know what you will hear next. Maria says if I will send Lieutenant Polk's picture back, she will give me one of her brother and I can have the original as well as the photograph, too, funny, isn't she? I do not expect ever to see either one of them.

Cousin Julia had a nice time last night; she likes Hattie better than any of the girls. I do not wonder at that for she is delightful company, so witty and so original. When I have girls staying with me Hattie always entertains for them and then when she has company I reciprocate. It makes it pleasanter all around. Captain Lester and my father "spoil their daughters" the neighbors say, but it is a fine thing to do, according to our way of thinking. It gives us a good time even if we are spoiled. I don't think we are bad girls either, and how we do love our indulgent fathers.

CHAPTER XVI

CAPTAIN JOHN YATES BEALL

WE leave the girl of the diary to her spinning and knitting, while we tell of some happenings, which she does not record.

The Battle of Gettysburg, which should have been a complete victory for the Confederates, was lost by *a mistake.* We do not criticise, we have no unkind words to say; nevertheless, from that day the Confederacy, slowly but surely, lost ground. Such a magnificent display of courage and of endurance was never before witnessed—such slaughter was sinful.

Captain Junius Taylor went into the battle with nearly the full complement of men in his company and he brought off from that hard fought field *seven men fit for duty.* He, himself, saved the colors of his regiment (the 5th Florida Infantry) by springing forward as the color-bearer fell dead to the ground and, catching the flag from his dead hand, he tore it from its staff and thrust it into his bosom.

Even our enemies admired the coolness and matchless courage with which those gray columns marched to their death.

> "Tell it as you will, it never can be told,
> Sing it as you may, it never can be sung,
> The story of the *glory* of the *men who wore the gray.*"

Captain Beall, who had found such kind friends in the quiet of this lovely home, had so far recovered as to go to Tallahassee on a visit to Dr. English. His place at Pine Hill was almost immediately filled by an elderly man from South Carolina; a gentleman and a scholar, whose health had completely given way under the stress of military life. Colonel Colcock was very different from Captain Beall, needing less care, in a way and requiring all the time of a listener, for he was very talkative.

In the little city of Tallahassee, noted for being the *habitat* of the bluest of blue blood and also the centre of hospitality, there congregated a society of intelligence and brilliancy. The society of that day and time resembled descriptions we have seen of the Salons of the French. Courteous, knightly gentlemen, graceful ladies whose "savoir vivre" proclaimed them "to the manner born," exchanged gay badinage, sparkling wit, or discoursed more seriously, but not less charmingly, of more weighty matters.

In one of these handsome homes lived one of the ladies of whom we have spoken. The wife of a wealthy planter, who did not, however, live on his plantation. Her house was visited by the *elite* of her own and other cities. In these days of war and distress two cousins of Mrs. Williams had taken refuge under her hospitable roof. The elder of the sisters, Miss Fannie O'-Bryan, was still in the prime of life, cultivated and attractive, she made many friends, but it is of the younger sister we will write. Several years Miss Fannie's junior, she was also blessed with a larger share of beauty; modest, unassuming, gentle and with a tender light in her eyes that suggested all lovable traits, it was surely no wonder that Captain Beall fell, a willing victim, to the manifold attractions of Miss Martha O'Bryan.

Dr. English and Colonel Williams were the best of friends and the day was not what a day should be, without at least three games of chess between them before the bed-time hour. So when the evening drew near Captain Beall was duly presented to the Williams family. The two old gentlemen were soon so engrossed in the intricate game they were playing as to be lost to all that went on around them. Mrs. Williams and Miss Fannie were equally absorbed in the mysteries of "heel and toe" as they knitted away on socks for the soldiers.

Outside the house lay a lovely flower garden and live oaks, which probably had witnessed the meetings of Seminole youths and maids. All this was bathed in the whitest, brightest moonlight on this warm September night, and the garden seemed to hold out beckoning hands to these young people. So they descended the steps and, walking hither and thither, through the mazy paths, breathing the fragrant air and feeling the magic influence of that patron saint of lovers, the moon, they quickly came to understand that to them had come that most wonderful of miracles, "love at first sight."

The winter in Florida, which the physicians had ordered for Captain Beall, met with no farther objection from him. Dr. English and Colonel Williams lived on the same street, only two blocks between and these young lovers spent much time together and when at last he was allowed to return to his command he pleaded that they might be married before he left. But she must have time to get ready; girls of that period were not so hasty as now. When he reached Richmond he was examined by a noted physician and pronounced unfit for duty and the War Department offered him the place of Secret Agent to England for the Confederacy. His parents were English and he had many relatives in that country, it was a most suitable appointment. He wrote to his "lady faire," begging her to accompany him on his mission. He used every argument to persuade but she had brothers in the Confederate army and she could not bear to leave them, when any day she might hear they were killed or wounded. It was a bitter disappointment to him but he declined the offer made him and entered the secret service of General Lee's army. Perhaps we may as well tell all of this sad story, here and now.

The winter of 1863-'4 wore slowly away and Miss O'Bryan heard infrequently from her lover, as his position made any correspondence hazardous. As the spring came on, the terrible news reached her that he was in a northern prison, sentenced to be executed as a spy. Letters came from him, heartbroken and filled with love and despair.

John Wilkes Booth was a friend and class-mate of John Yates Beall and he thought he could exert some influence with President Lincoln. He went to him at the White House and recited the facts of the case. He pleaded for mercy. President Lincoln listened attentively, he was evidently moved. When Booth concluded, Mr. Lincoln gave his solemn promise, pledged his sacred word that Beall should not be hung. Booth was satisfied for he believed he had the promise of an honest man.

When Booth heard his beloved friend had been hung he fainted away and this fainting fit was followed by brain fever. When that had run its course and poor Booth could move around again, he bought him a pistol and all the world knows what happened to Abraham Lincoln.

On the morning of the 15th of April, 1865, the New York papers came out in deep mourning and in flaring headlines, telling the people the South had murdered Lincoln. To this day he is looked upon as a martyr and yet the truth remains that he died because *he did not keep his sacred word.*

For days Martha O'Bryan prayed to die but death does not come when it is wanted and she lived to be eighty years old and all through those long, long years she never ceased to mourn that she did not go to England with John Yates Beall.

We have digressed to give these facts; no history records them. President Lincoln was a kindly man but a weak one; no doubt he intended to keep the promise he had given but Seward was stronger than he and on Seward's shoulders rests the blame for the assassination of Lincoln.

We go back now to the fall of 1863, fighting had been universal in both armies. The skirmishing around Chattanooga had culminated in the great battles of Chickamauga and Missionary Ridge. The year closed with high hopes for the Confederacy; there were rumors of recognition on the part of England; there were whispers of help from our friends at the North; report said they were tired of war and that influence would be used to bring about an early peace. Just how Heavenly that sounded in our ears none may know.

Severe cold at the beginning of the year 1864, forced both armies to remain inactive but soon came milder weather and there were signs of renewed activity. Disease, caused by lack of proper food, decimated the Confederate ranks.

Virginia and Tennessee, in the days before the war, had been among the finest agricultural communities in the world. Blessed as to soil and climate, with slave-labor in abundance, there was, practically no limit to the foodstuffs which these great states could produce. The "cattle on a thousand hills," the vast number of blooded horses, the heavy fleeced Southdowns, the fat hogs, the well-stocked poultry yards, all these contributed to the prosperity and plenty of the land, while the well-filled granaries gave assurance of food for man and beast.

Now all this is different; the contending armies had here swept back and forth for nearly four years and these once prosperous states are almost a desolate waste. Georgia, too, had been invaded and here, also, the hand of the destroyer could be plainly seen.

So it came about that little Florida, with a sparse population and poor railroad facilities began to be looked to as the source of supply for the army of Northern Virginia and the army of the West. Every effort had been made by the Florida planters, from the very beginning of the war to increase food production, and now they redoubled their activities along these lines. We did not realize just what we could do until this necessity came upon us.

In middle Florida were large plantations, formerly devoted principally to the growing of the fleecy staple; some cotton must be had for it was needed, but only what was really needed was planted. Vast areas of cotton lands were planted in corn, sugar cane, rice, wheat, sweet potatoes, etc. The range cattle proved to be greater in number than had been anticipated and every train out from Tallahassee carried both meat and bread to our hungry armies. Sugar and syrup went, too, for, deprived of sweets, scrofula might develop. So we toiled and saved at every turn lest our soldiers should suffer.

Do not imagine, however, that all was gloom and desolation in these years of war. We have omitted the pages of the Diary devoted to social pleasures. So far the sad side has been presented to your view.

At the beginning of the war we felt that frolicking of any nature would be like insults to the heroic men, who had gone forth to fight our battles; but later on we discovered that it was unwise to banish gaiety from our lives. She is a wise little maiden, this Gaiety; she knows that the bow that is bent too long loses its spring. She knows that "a merry heart doeth good like a medicine" and we were convinced of her wisdom and so, we welcomed this wise and frivolous damsel again to our arms and tried from that time on to make the visits of the soldiers to their homes a round of gaiety and pleasure. They appreciated it and it did not seem to them, as we had feared it would, that we were heartless. No, we welcomed them with joy; we fed them with all obtainable dainties; we sang, we danced, we made merry in all ways, and then when the parting came—we wept bitter tears but we dried them as quickly as possible and went to work to make some needed article to send to them. God bless our soldiers.

When we reopen the diary and turn its pages, the curtain rises on scenes which change with kaleidoscopic rapidity. The Battle of Olustee; death and sorrow; wounded men and tireless nurses; and then we seem to see the girlish diary writer bending delightedly over party finery, and joining in the "war gaieties" of the hour, with all the zest and enthusiasm of her years. But so it has been since the world began; sunshine and cloud, joy and sorrow and thus it will be till the end of time.

AGAIN THE DIARY TAKES UP THE CHRONICLE

February 9th, 1864.—For more than a year we have not attended large parties nor have we given entertainments. Of course we have had our friends with us in social intercourse and enjoyed it, too, but we were wearing black and, while we do this, it is not suitable that we should be seen in gay places.

We are taking off black now and there is some talk of a great big affair at Goodwood. This has put us to thinking of something to wear; a far more difficult problem than that which confronted "Miss Flora McFlimsey of Madison Square."

Sister Mag is living in Georgia now, but we get letters from her nearly every day. Last night, when mother opened and read a letter from her, she gave me a key and told me I could search through the big black trunk in the attic and see if I could find anything worth having. I had never been allowed to do this before and it sounded so interesting I could hardly wait until morning. As soon as breakfast was over I rushed up stairs and what do you suppose I found? That trunk was full of party finery sister Mag had worn when she was a young lady. It has not been so very long either, for she was married in 1859.

CHAPTER XVII

THE DEPARTMENT OF SOUTH CAROLINA, GEORGIA AND FLORIDA

WHEN, in 1861, the Southern Confederacy came into being, one of the first things done by the Secretary of War was to divide this Southern Confederacy into departments, suited to the exigencies of the situation. Naturally the deepest interest, for us, was held by the Department of South Carolina, Georgia and Florida, that being our own immediate section.

The first commander assigned to this department was General Trapier, of South Carolina. He made Tallahassee his headquarters and, it is needless to say, added greatly to the social life of that city. General Trapier evidently had an eye for beauty and apparently had selected his staff officers in accordance with his love of the beautiful. One couple in particular, Major and Mrs. Edward Anderson, were the admired of all beholders; they were the cynosure of all eyes, whenever they walked abroad. Long years after this Major Anderson became Governor of South Carolina and, if his picture in Munsey's Magazine, could be believed, he was just as handsome in middle life as he had been in youth. Everybody, who was *anybody,* entertained the General and his staff. The war was new and so were their uniforms. Direct from Paris these uniforms were, and beautiful beyond description. We did not think there would ever be any real fighting and "all went merry as a marriage bell."

For some unexplainable reason no general remained long at the head of this department. To the eyes of the uninitiated it seemed like a game of that most intricate of games, chess, where kings, queens, castles, knights and pawns moved from place to place as the master mind directed, while the bishop dispensed his blessings, "on the fly."

We did not bother our heads very much about all this, however, and it was *"Le Roi est mort! Vive le Roi!"* Several different generals had succeeded one another in the Department of South Carolina, Georgia and Florida, when, in 1864, General T. R. R. Cobb was sent to us and, contrary to custom, selected our sister town of Quincy as his headquarters. This did not trouble us, for by this time Tallahassee had known so many military changes; so many bodies of troops from all points in the South had been encamped here, that we began to feel as if we knew everybody.

Florida, by this time, had attained a position of considerable importance in the eyes of the War Department at Richmond. As the Confederate lines became more and more contracted; as large areas of country, which had formerly helped to feed the Confederate army, were devastated by the occupancy of first one army and then the other, it became somewhat of a problem whence the necessary supplies would come.

All eyes turned to little Florida. The Yankees sought ways to occupy the state and the Confederates bent every effort to keep them out. Only a few troops had been kept in Florida but now it was evident that our government saw a need for more. Regiments from Georgia were sent to Lake City. Troops from Alabama waited near the Florida line. General Dickenson and his men showed great activity and there was in the air a sense of "something doing."

The enemy had possession of Jacksonville, St. Augustine and some other places. All our ports were blockaded and it was not the fault of the watchful Yank that a few venturesome old blockade-runners continued to find their way up the Suwanee, or in and out among the keys, along the Florida coast.

An enemy we had with whom we were unable to cope,

the diabolical deserter. From some of the counties, lying adjacent to the waters of the Gulf of Mexico, soldiers had been *conscripted* and the Confederate Government did not realize that "a man who is forced is a man to be feared." The price they paid for this knowledge was a terrible one. The women of this land of deserters would go on visits to their kinsfolk and friends in the interior. They would "spy out the land," prolonging their visits until some news of military movements could be gained, then back home they went to tell what they had found out to these deserters, who lost no time in rowing a small boat out to the blockader and proudly telling the news they had gleaned. In this way the Yankees were kept informed as to what Colonel Scott was planning; how many troops had been sent in from other states; if the arsenal at Tallahassee was full or empty. This system of spying was very effective but later on a way was found to put a stop to it.

These men, who were so treacherous and disloyal, belonged to a peculiar class; they were, for the most part the descendents of criminals, who had taken refuge in the bays and swamps of the Florida coast. Their hand against everybody and everybody's hand against them.

All laws, statutory and Divine, were defied by them; they held human life so lightly that they did not hesitate to take the lives of others nor to risk their own. Hidden away in the coastal forests, secure from the hand of the law, they led lives which, in many instances, would have shamed the very beasts, who shared with them this wide wilderness. Born criminals, they had no sense of honor.

"Desperate cases require desperate remedies," and when, in the fall of 1864, they would creep up in the dead of night and apply the torch to all houses in reach, it was plain that drastic measures must be taken to stop them. The Confederate Government was more than loth to make war on women and children but men, women and children were engaged in this cowardly warfare, where the torch was the weapon. We did not know, when we saw double-pen log houses going up just outside of Tallahassee, for what manner of encampment these houses were intended. We counted nine as we rode by, each of the nine had two large rooms with chimneys of "stick and dirt" and a passage way between the rooms. There were doors and windows, no glass but comfortable shutters.

The planters had been called upon to erect these houses but no questions were asked; nor could we guess the use to which they would be put. To add to the mystery several wagon loads of firewood were hauled in and deposited in easy reach of these houses. It was a nine-days wonder and then came the solution.

Wagons were sent down to the god-for-saken country, of which we have told you, each house was visited. The women were told to get their belongings together and pack them on the wagons. If they had chickens, pigs or cows, the men in attendance would drive them after the wagons. Some of the women sullenly obeyed, some raved and cursed and refused to obey and when this happened the drivers did the packing and they moved on.

A body of troops accompanied the wagons, and when each house had been emptied of contents and occupants, the torch was applied and the troops remained until each filthy cabin was in ashes. Four counties were traversed by "The Wagon Brigade" as it was termed. The work was well planned and, in spite of distance and danger, they did so well that ere midnight of that day the nine double houses were filled and an additional tent was pitched to accommodate the overflow.

The weather was warm and pleasant; these families had brought with them everything they owned; the houses were far more comfortable than those they left behind. It was "potato digging time" and the people of the surrounding country saw to it that there was no lack of "yams and cubas" and, besides this, meal, vegetables, milk and sometimes meat, found their way to "The Deserters' Camp." They could not have been more kindly treated but a guard was stationed around the camp. This was necessary for the protection of our own people.

Many of the women were sulky, a few were smiling and pleasant. Some were violent, using the worst language possible to imagine and making dire threats of what their men would do; but these threats did not trouble us much, for while the "Wagon Brigade" was at work these same men were not far distant, just out of sight, and yet they made no attempt whatever to come to the rescue. Cowardly and treacherous, as might be expected of the betrayers of their country.

But we are going far afield, our story deals with the early spring of 1864. About ten o'clock, on one of the loveliest days of spring, Dr. and Mrs. Edward Bradford walked in their flower garden, admiring the fresh unfolding of leaf and bud. Just beyond was the front entrance to Pine Hill and they saw, entering the gate, five or six Confederate soldiers. Now this couple loved nothing so well as to entertain our soldiers and, advancing to meet them, they found these men were the advance guard of Colonel Henry D. Capers' Battalion of Artillery. Upon farther questioning they found the battalion was near at hand.

They had camped the night before on the Thomasville and Tallahassee road and had broken camp very early and were beginning to think of dinner. Dr. Bradford invited the battalion to dine with him and Mrs. Bradford, like the good housekeeper she was, hurried to make the necessary preparations. The smokehouse doors were opened and hams, sausage, pickled pigs feet and corned beef were soon on the fire. A dozen or more cooks went to work, it was a frolic for all, both white and black.

At the foot of the hill was the saw mill, a number of darkies brought wide planks and others hurriedly knocked up supports for these to rest on and in an incredibly short space of time two long tables stood in the grove.

In the mansion, Mrs. Bradford had prepared a table, which had a seating capacity of thirty, but this was only a beginning. It was almost impossible to get flour in Dixie, but "egg bread" made a good substitute. Such piling dishes and plates of fried sweet potatoes, eggs *ad libitum,* fried with ham, scrambled with butter, boiled hard and served with crisp lettuce, green and fresh; milk in abundance, even for that crowd and the dinner ended with fritters and pancakes, with plenty of delicious Florida syrup.

Plenty and to spare for all and yet Mrs. Bradford never ceased to regret that there was no time to get chickens ready for her guests. While they waited for dinner some of these young soldiers furnished delightful music for her entertainment. Hearing the piano, she turned in at the parlor door and saw one young soldier laddie at the piano, another was tuning the guitar and still another had taken the violin from its case and was drawing the bow across the strings, in a manner which proclaimed his knowledge of the instrument. Several fine voices joined in and to say that their hostess was pleased is to put it mildly indeed. Afterward she was heard to say that Capers' Battalion was the first body of troops she had ever seen where "every man was a gentlemen." Could she have paid them a higher compliment?

Colonel Capers said they were not due in Tallahassee until the following morning, so he would camp at some convenient location. Two hours after their departure,

Dr. Bradford had Randal bring a wagon to the yard and in it he had him put a barrel of hams, a barrel of meal, a barrel of Florida syrup and the spaces he had filled with sweet potatoes. Randal was to drive along the road to Tallahassee and, when he found Colonel Capers' Command, he was to stop and deliver the eatables, which, he was to tell him, were for supper. You never read a nicer note than the Colonel sent in reply; this note is still treasured by the family.

The next morning the Battalion moved on. Very near Tallahassee, on one of the loveliest hills in Old Leon, shaded and sheltered by majestic magnolias, a clear, cool spring bubbling up from the hillside, the encampment was made. No spot could have been better suited to the purpose. To the east of the camp stretched an open field, just the ground for the drill and the parade.

Again we make our exit and leave the girl of the Diary to tell what she found out concerning this fine body of artillery-men:

February *, 1864.—I did not write yesterday, nor for three days before that and now I cannot quite remember the date. We have had a delightful visit, or rather two delightful visits, first at Goodwood and then at Woodstock; just the two pleasantest places that you could imagine. I am sure no girl ever had two sweeter aunts than Aunt Sue and Aunt Nannie; both are charming, each in a different way.

Eliza Lane was at Goodwood with us and, when we went home with her, I was so glad to see dear little Sallie, who is so anxious to be "a grown-up young lady" too.

Aunt Nannie has a beautiful bride staying with her, Mrs. Dr. Goldthwaite, from Mobile, as well as I can

* This diary was written in pencil and in many instances the dates are almost, or quite, illegible. The month and year are plain but the figures are not so plain; particularly is this the case during the years of warfare, possibly the pencils were poor, or the paper might have been. At any rate we ask our readers to be lenient if some little mistakes occur.

remember. She told us of her wedding, which took place some ten days ago. Dr. Goldthwaite had thirty-six hours leave of absence, so there was need for haste. There is a dearth of young men, when you get away from a military post and she had twenty young ladies for attendants. The groom, the minister and the bride's father were the only men present. They left immediately after the ceremony for Tallahassee, where Dr. Goldthwaite thought he was stationed but, much to his disappointment, his regiment had moved on, so he left his wife with Aunt Nannie. Everybody is just as kind as possible and tries to make things cheerful for her and she is as pretty and sweet as can be.

But I am not telling you of the exciting day we missed. On our way home, opposite the Berryhill Place, to be exact, we saw a number of soldiers, preparing to camp. We could see that it was a battery of artillery but that was all, we could not even go slowly by the camp, for Father and Mother are very strict in their ideas and, while some girls do not mind stopping to talk with any stranger who wears the gray, we have been told not to do it. So we went on, wondering as we went, who they could be?

As we drove in at home, we met uncle Randal with one wagon and little Randal with another, we thought nothing of this, but no sooner had we entered the house than Mother and Mattie began to tell us all we had missed. This same battery of artillery had dined at Pine Hill that day.

Mother was enthusiastic in her praises of Colonel Capers and his command and Father was so taken with them that he had sent the wagons we met to take them some supper. Well, we can't have everything. When uncle Randal came home he brought just the nicest note of thanks you ever read to Father, for his kindness to him and his men.

February --, 1864.—We did not hear anything more

of the Colonel and his boys yesterday but this morning we have a note from Aunt Sue with a postscript from uncle Arvah, telling us of the arrival at Tallahassee of a battalion of artillery, which had encamped on the Magnolia Hill to the east of town. Aunt Sue says we must pack our prettiest clothes and come prepared to stay with her, while they are encamped so near Goodwood. She wants us to help her entertain them. Uncle Arvah's P. S. reads like this, "In these days of hard fighting it is your *duty* to do everything you can to add to the pleasure of these soldiers, who are here today and gone tomorrow. Tell Mrs. Bradford and the doctor this, with my love."

Sister Mart and I are hoping Father and Mother will realize that the path of duty lies that way. Aunt Sue says they have a fine brass band and she is going to have some of them over as often as they can come; won't that be fine?—That is if, we can go.

February --, 1864.—We have been at Goodwood three days now and there is so much to write about. The first night Aunt Sue invited all the social world of Tallahassee to meet Colonel Capers. He came, attended by fifty or more of his men, the artillery uniform is beautiful and it is particularly becoming to Colonel Capers. I am sure he knows it for I notice he keeps one end of his cape thrown back over his shoulder, bringing the red lining next his face. He wore a vest of fine red broadcloth, buttoned up with round balls of silver for buttons and that added much to the beauty of his uniform.

When I was introduced to him, he said, "I am pleased to make your acquaintance, Miss Bradford. I have already had the pleasure of an acquaintance with your father and mother," and then he stood there and gave a glowing account of that most unique dinner at Pine Hill, and he added, "I wrote a full description to my wife before I slept that night."

Lizzie Wirt pinched my arm and whispered, "Horrid creature—I hate married men."

The music was good and we were soon dancing the Lancers. My partner was Sergeant Clayton, young and handsome and a graceful dancer. The couple opposite were evidently talking about us and presently the gentleman, who was one of the sergeant's comrades, said, "Clayton, you and Miss Bradford are enough alike to be brother and sister."

"Yes," answered my partner, with an apologetic look at me, "As soon as I entered the room I noticed the strong likeness to my sister and when I was introduced was sure we must be related, for my name is Edward Bradford Clayton."

Of course we claimed kin on that; Uncle Arvah says all Southern people are kin anyway. It is just a part of being born South of Mason and Dixon's Line. I like the new cousin very much and he told me a great deal of army life and of his commander, whom he loves dearly.

February --, 1864.—I have found out a good deal about Colonel Capers and all I hear makes me admire him the more. I will try to write this like history, my little Diary, and you must take care of it for future generations.

When Georgia seceded, Henry D. Capers was in command of the Marietta Military Institute. This was one of the best schools in the South. Many fine men had graduated there and some of the very best civil engineers in the Southern army had studied the profession at Marietta.

When the wise men of our country met at Montgomery, to organize a government, Henry D. Capers promptly offered his services, in any capacity where he could be useful. He was accepted and was made Chief Clerk and Disbursing Officer of the Confederate Treasury. Here he served until the spring of 1862, when he resigned, to enter active service in the field. The Treasury Department was loth to give him up and resolutions were drawn up expressing their regret at parting with one, who had proved himself so capable and trustworthy. A fine sword was presented to him by Secretary Memminger, bearing a suitable inscription (the Colonel is wearing this sword now). I intend to read that inscription some day if the fates are propitious.

The War Department made Henry D. Capers a captain in the regular army of the Confederacy and he joined General Magruder but for only a little while. Captain Capers was longing for "his boys," who were so near his heart. When he left them they all volunteered for twelve months in the Confederate Army and became a part of the 1st Georgia Regiment. This Regiment was about to be disbanded at Augusta, Georgia, and, with a permit from the government, Captain Capers was on the spot, to organize the 12th Georgia Battalion. Can we not imagine his feelings, as one by one "his boys" were sworn in "For the war," and he realized that they were once more in his keeping? These boys tell many interesting things about their Colonel and they all adore him.

This may not be exactly like history should be written but I will learn to write better as time goes on.

February --, 1864.—Last night we had an impromptu musicale and Aunt Sue provided a delicious supper at the close of the evening. The Colonel's boys have something more to tell of him, whenever we meet. Last night Edward Clayton told me of the lectures which were given almost daily by the officers. Of course they have no books in camp but these lectures are an education in themselves. The boys are encouraged to ask questions and to debate on different points. Mr. Kellar, who is a mountain boy, says the Colonel taught him to read and write and now he is determined to get an education, when the war is over. He has a splendid baritone voice and we keep him singing most of the time. Mr. Seavy told me that sometimes when the boys tried to "run wild" the officers, especially Col. Capers, gave them talks, which were better than any sermon he ever listened to. Mrs. Capers must be very proud of this grand soldier of hers.

Good-bye little Diary, I have an engagement to go to ride this afternoon and must get ready.

February --, 1864.—By special invitation, we rode over the hills to the Camp today, to see the battalion drill. It was a dress parade and every man looked his best. I made a new (old) acquaintance after the drill was over. Frank Baker, the only son of Judge Bolling Baker, of Virginia. He is just as handsome as a picture and very pleasant. I could scarcely recall the little boy of years ago, who thought I was too small to notice. I think I must have grown just a wee bit.

The camp is beautiful; it is only a short distance from Goodwood and Aunt Sue told the boys to come over whenever they felt like it. She also offered them books to read, which offer was eagerly accepted. Tonight Mrs. Howard Gamble is giving a large party and I must stop writing and see about my dress. We cannot vary our toilettes to any extent in these days of the blockade.

February --, 1864.—Mrs. Gamble's party was delightful, the band gave us fine music, the camp provided plenty of partners and there are young ladies galore in Tallahassee. Last night one of General Cobb's staff officers told me the Capers Battalion had been sent to guard Tallahassee, in case of invasion. He said General Dickenson and General Miller and General Finnegan were all ordered to Lake City and several Georgia Regiments had gone on, too. Colonel Scott, he said, was guarding the Gulf Coast. I wonder if this can be true? If it is he ought not to be telling it around but

I shall not repeat it. I have not given his name to you my little Diary, but I cannot help thinking it is a pity for those who give parties to have punch. It certainly loosens the tongue and I do not believe this information would have come to me but for the big bowl of regent's punch.

I was dancing last night with a young soldier, from the mountains around Rome, Georgia, he was loud in his praises of Colonel Capers. "Do you know, Miss Bradford, I did not know how to read and write when I was sworn in? I felt terribly ashamed when I found how ignorant I was and the Colonel found it out and he taught me sometimes and, when he was too busy, some of the boys helped me and now I can read 'most anything I come across and I can write whatever I want to say. Besides that I have learned so much just listening to him talking with the other boys. I am not the only one who has been helped; there are twenty of us, all about the same age and all from the Rome country, none of us had any book-learning and he has taught us all." Isn't that a fine thing for a man to do?

February --, 1864.—Three days since Mrs. Gamble's party and I have been to ride with my new cousin every day. He has written to his mother in Athens, and she is so glad he has found some kinsfolk in Florida. It seems she knew they had relatives in this state but they were strangers to her and she had never mentioned them to him.

I told him what Mr. Kellar said about Colonel Capers and he said, "it was all true and then some more"—he seems to think Colonel Capers is the grandest man on earth. I told him I believed the Colonel had taught dancing and deportment along with other things, they are so well versed in the usages of polite society.

February 20th, 1864.—Two more Georgia regiments passed through today en route for Lake City. I am afraid that means a fight. God help us.

February --, 1864.—We have had a grand time but now it is over. We have had rides and walks and drives; we have had parties, picnics and serenades; we have had a merry two weeks and now our play-mates are gone. They looked so handsome and they held their heads so proudly and marched away with such steady steps. As they went they sang, "The Girl I Left Behind Me." Poor boys—I hope and pray they may some day come home again.

February --, 1864.—Blind Tom is to play at the Capitol tonight. We are going to hear him for he is too wonderful to miss. I am staying at Aunt Margaret's. Cousin Jim will take Mart and Sue and me to town. It is not very far and I had an invitation to go from a captain in a gorgeous uniform. I would have liked to go with him but Mother does not like us to go around without a chaperon. If I was at Goodwood, Aunt Sue would go; she is the very best aunt a girl ever had.

February --, 1864.—Blind Tom is wonderful! He plays the Battle of Manassas and, before he begins to play, his master tells you how Tom came to compose this piece. His master, Colonel Bethune, is so proud of him and Tom loves him and is so affectionate; just like some sweet-tempered animal that you have petted.

This Battle of Manassas begins with the booming of cannon; the rattle of musketry and above all the clear notes of the bugle. Faintly in the distance the strains of Dixie float upon the air, these strains grow louder and louder and mingle with the clashing of guns, the tramping of horses and the sharp commands of officers. He intersperses the music with the names of the different Generals, who took the most prominent parts in the day's work. How an imbecile (for Tom is plainly that) could ever be taught a connected description of Manassas, is certainly a miracle.

February 21st, 1864.—Yesterday a terrible battle

was fought at Ocean Pond, or Olustee, both names are used in the news sent to us of the fierce struggle between the Yankees and our troops. Many are dead on both sides and our loss would have been heavier if the Yankees had been better shots. Our soldiers are, the most of them, wounded in the head and the ground was fairly covered with small branches cut from the pines above. Those same pine trees were a great item for our men, they fought behind the trees like the Indians and like General Washington did, in his fights with the French long ago. The dispatch said "Lieut. Holland killed," so Mr. Robinson went down today with a casket to bring his body home. His wife wants him buried in Tallahassee, where she expects to make her home with her sister. The Holland family are grieving deeply, for he was the only son and brother,

February 22nd, 1864.—A message from the Tallahassee hospital to father tells him to prepare to receive nine wounded men from Olustee, they will be in tonight.

February 23rd, 1864.—There were ten men instead of nine, but we were ready for them. Eight of them are wounded in the head, the face, or in the shoulder. One was shot in the palm of the hand, while the tenth was shot in the foot. One of his comrades, who is not hurt much, laughs at him and says he knows that fellow was standing on his head.

The one, whose hand was hurt, is just a child. He says he cannot remember his mother. His father was killed at Gettysburg and, when he heard of it and saw his father's body brought back to Macon and buried, he could stay there no longer but ran away and came to Florida, where his uncle, whom he loved next to his father, was keeping the Yankees away from Tallahassee. He will not be twelve years old until August and he is small for his age, we call him High Private Watson. We do this because he expresses a great desire to be an officer, and he will not tell his Christian name.

Only two of our patients are dangerously hurt; one, a tall man about thirty, who has a very bad wound in his head and the other is the man whose foot is shot to pieces. Both of these have fever. The others say their chief ailment was hunger and now that they have had a good breakfast they will soon be all right and ready to take a pop at the Yankees again.

We will go in tomorrow to Lieut. Holland's funeral; we have beautiful flowers to carry.

March 15th, 1864.—This is the first entry for more than two weeks but we have been so busy and now I am going to write something that sounds heartless. Goodwood is to open its doors to society. The first time Aunt Sue and Uncle Arvah have entertained since dear little Mary Eliza's death.

This party is given in honor of General T. R. R. Cobb and his staff. He is now in command of The Division of South Carolina, Georgia and Florida and he is an old friend of the family as well. I felt at first as if I could not possibly enjoy a frolic of any kind but Aunt Sue is so dear and if she wants us we must go. Again the question of dress comes up. To realize just how much of vanity and love of dress one possesses it is needful to be obliged to plan and contrive as we war girls have to do. The big trunk yielded up its treasure and a dress of *crepe lisse,* very much tumbled came to light. It has a lining of satin and a sash of the same. Lulu is a wonder at pressing and making over and my part is suggesting and trying on. Let me tell you a secret, little Diary; "I have my second grown-up beau." I think I like the boys best, in fact, I *know* I like the boys best. That is because all my life I have had boy play-mates and now, that these boys look like men and are in the army, they still seem like comrades to me. They like me too; whenever one gets foolish and says silly things to me I laugh at him, and so, I do not lose my friends as I should if they were allowed to deteriorate into lovers.

March 21st, 1864.—The party at Goodwood was a grand success. The general and his staff were magnificently attired in new uniforms, just from Paris, via. Zeigler's Blockade Runner. As many of Colonel Scott's Battalion as could be spared at one time came in from Camp Randolph. There are quite a number of strangers in town and Captain Oliver, a wounded officer from a Maryland Regiment who is staying at Goodwood, was the lion of the evening. He has a lovely baritone voice and accompanies himself on the guitar. He sang "Maryland, my Maryland," so feelingly that it brought tears to many eyes.

General Cobb's band played for us to dance and we had a delightful time—as every one does when at Goodwood. I wore the *crepe lisse* dress and aunt Sue pinned white hyacinths in my hair. That grown-up person said they were perfectly lovely. The boys may not be able to make such pretty speeches but I still like them best.

March 26th, 1864.—I am so ashamed of myself. In all the excitement we have experienced and, yes, all this ill-timed gaiety, I forgot I had not finished the allotment of socks, which was to have been ready for the box, which is to be forwarded to the Army of the West. I have only three pairs ready and cousin Henry may come for them any day. Never mind, if I can stay awake to dance and play I can surely keep my eyes open to knit socks for our dear soldiers. Aunt Robinson, who is always forehanded and never "puts off for tomorrow what should be done today" has given me some disapproving looks but I have designs on her, though I have not told her yet. I must stop and—knit—knit—knit.

March 31st, 1864.—The box has gone and my socks were ready; that is, the requisite number went but I had to borrow one sock from Aunt Robinson, with the promise that I would knit another right away. I am going to Aunt Margaret's to stay a few days. Her girls are going to school at Live Oak and I do not see them as often as when they attended school here at Pine Hill.

April 2nd, 1864.—We did a mean thing yesterday. It being "all fools day", we issued invitations to a favored few to supper. Then we went to work to play a joke on them. We induced Betsey, who keeps house for the Donelsons, to help us. We made pies, beautiful looking pies, but they were filled with cotton instead of fruit. Green corn had just filled out enough to eat, so we had corn fritters, but cotton was shredded through and through the tempting looking brown cakes. We had hot biscuits, but they, too, were tough and unfit to eat because of the cotton kneaded in the dough. A beautiful bowl of salad graced the centre of the table, but instead of lettuce, hoarhound had been used. Now Mother would never have let us do this but Aunt Margaret is very indulgent and allows her daughters to do pretty much as they please. The company arrived, three young ladies and three soldiers from Camp Randolph. We took our seats at the table and Aunt Margaret made the coffee and the dishes were handed to the guests. It was only when we saw the blank expression on their faces that we understood what an unkind prank we had played.

Aunt Margaret arose to the occasion—Betsey must have whispered in her mistress' ear, for she touched the bell, which sat beside her plate and Rose and Charity came in and removed the dishes, which we had come to hate by this time, and Betsey followed, with old Aunt Prudy in the rear, with a truly good supper, a more bountiful one than we had provided and far better. Oh, how we thanked Aunt Margaret and she did not scold us one bit.

April 6th, 1864.—There was a concert last night at the Capitol for the benefit of the Martha Reid Hospital, in Richmond. Local talent, assisted by Quincy and

Monticello, furnished the music. Sister Mart was one of the star performers and there were a score of others. Pretty music they made and a pretty picture, too, as they all came forward to the footlights and bowed, when the curtain first rose. As one of the audience I had a good opportunity to judge.

Several gentlemen with fine voices offered their services and we had very fine music, both vocal and instrumental. They sang operatic selections; they sang soft, plaintive Confederate songs; they sang the world-old ballads that everybody loves and they sang patriotic songs and wound up with Dixie, sung by the entire assembly and followed by cheers so heartfelt as almost to shake the foundations of Florida's Capitol.

Quite a large sum was realized and many of the gentlemen present added hundreds of dollars to the original amount. The hospitals will need all we can send them, for every day brings us fresh news of skirmishing and often of battles. We are so far off from the seat of war here that it is hard to remember all the time how perfectly terrible it is.

April 7th, 1864.—Today I have no shoes to put on. All my life I have never wanted to go bare-footed, as most Southern children do. The very touch of my naked foot to the bare ground made be shiver. Lulu my Mammy, scolds me about this—even yet she claims the privilege of taking me to task when she thinks I need it.

"Look here, chile," she says, "don't you know you is made outen the dus' er de earth? Don't you understand dat when you is dead you is gwine back ter dat dus'?"

"Yes, Lulu," I answer meekly.

"Well, den, what is you so foolish fur? Better folks dan you is gone bare-footed."

I listen to all she has to say but a thought has come to me and I have no time to argue the point. Until the shoes for the army are finished, Mr. McDearnmid will not have time to make any shoes for any one else, this is right, for our dear soldiers must come first in everything, but I will stop writing now and get to work.

April 9th, 1864.—Today I have on railroad stockings and slippers. Guess what these slippers are made of? Whenever I go to uncle Richard's I see an old black uncle, hard at work plaiting shucks and weaving the plaits together into door mats. It seemed to me a lighter braid might be sewed into something resembling shoes, so I picked out the softest shucks and soon had enough to make one slipper. So pleased was I that I soon had a pair of shoes ready to wear. They are a little rough so I have pasted inside a lining of velvet. Everybody laughed, but I feel quite proud.

April 8th, 1864.—I am at home again and father and mother say they have missed me. The hospital patients are better and High Private Watson is begging to go back to his uncle. Father has written to him and described the child's condition, asking if he might send him to his relatives in Macon? No answer has come and the little fellow is too feeble to be allowed to go to camp, so Father is going to send him to Macon with Mr. Higgins, (who was wounded in the shoulder and is about well now). He has a short furlough to visit his home in Griffin and will take charge of him.

There are a number of soldiers sick with some kind of fever, which will fill the places these two leave vacant.

Brother Junius writes that he liked his knit undershirts and drawers so well that he wants me to knit him some of cotton. I will get to work on them right away. He writes that the army is almost constantly on the move and the soldiers have hopes of defeating Grant, in this Spring campaign and ending the war. I have taken care of all the letters he has written me; he writes alternately to Mattie and to me. Father says his letters would make a good history of the army of Northern Virginia. Last winter he wrote such entertaining accounts of the "night school" the soldiers had, not the primary grades either, but a classical school with oratorical efforts interspersed.

I have little time now for study, I still keep on with some studies and recite to Father, when he has time to hear me, or we talk it over when we are out in the woods collecting medicinal herbs. What I am most interested in at present is Upham's Mental Philosophy. I do not teach Frances now, she was so bad that Mother sent her to stay at the Horse-shoe with Aunt Pendar. She does not work in the field but takes lessons in sewing from Mrs. Manning.

June 2nd, 1864.—There are many aching hearts in our land these bright, beautiful summer days. If it was not for the little children, who do not realize the danger we are facing, I do not believe we could stand it. Bless their dear young hearts, which are so light that they overflow with merriment no matter how black everything looks to us.

Fighting is almost continuous now and there is not standing room around the bulletin board, to do more than get a hurried glance at the list of "Killed, Wounded and Missing." Oh, those horrible words, I seem to see them in letters of fire when I wake in the night.

Father has a very sick patient and Mother is helping to nurse him. Mrs. Manning, Aunt Robinson and I have been busy packing a large box of clothing to be sent tomorrow to the army of Northern Virginia.

A late supper of rice-cakes, Irish potatoes and squabs, cooked in Adeline's best style, finished the day. It is now 10 o'clock and everybody ought to be abed and asleep. We will not hear from the front tonight. May the news, when we hear it, be good.

June 4th, 1864.—Uncle Richard has just returned from Tallahassee. This morning the telegraph wires were working for the first time in four days. It brings us dreadful news, on the 2nd inst. a battle was fought at Cold Harbor, some of our Florida boys were wounded and two were killed. Colonel Henry D. Capers was desperately wounded and is now in the hospital. Seven of his battalion were killed; the names were not given.

August 8th, 1864.—This is a day of fasting, humiliation and prayer. Our armies in Virginia and in the West have suffered reverses of late and we have many such days. All who can, go to church; all the churches hold services. We take our knitting with us. Some stay all day, for they are fasting, but Father will not let us fast absolutely. He says "To keep your strength some food must be taken. Eat sparingly, but do not refrain entirely, for if you do you will not be capable of the best work and that is what our country calls for now."

The telegraph wires are down and we have heard nothing for days. What there may be for us to hear we do not know. Father in Heaven, take care of our poor boys!

August 11th, 1864.—Communication is established once more and Oh, the horrible, horrible news that has come to us! Capers' Battalion reached Petersburg just in time for that terrible explosion and a part of his command were blown to atoms. Frank Baker is killed and so is my little new cousin. Mr. Kellar will never sing for us again. When he said goodbye and we told him we hoped to have him back before long and hear his sweet songs again, he said, "If I don't come back I'll join the Choir as soon as I get to Heaven and I'll sing for you there."

It is heart-rending to think of death and destruction, bodily destruction, for those young boys, who were so thoroughly alive, who were looking forward to a speedy return home and the home folks who were waiting for them. Oh, it is dreadful!

CHAPTER XVIII

"MARTHY"

IN April, eighteen-sixty-four, faint gleams of hope for the Southern Confederacy appeared upon the horizon. The North was sick of war and when we say this we mean the representative people of the North. Speculators and profiteers did not want to see the war end; they were making fortunes; the like of which had never been known before. What cared they that so many perish, what to them were the breaking hearts of the wives and mothers and sisters? The fatherless orphans on every side did not touch their hearts; all they cared for, all they worshiped was the "almighty dollar", and because of these greedy vultures, the war went on.

In the air rumors were afloat of recognition for the Confederacy by European nations; this gave us a hope and we hugged it to our breasts with passionate fervor. In the meantime Grant had been placed at the head of all the armies the United States had in the field. He was a man of undoubted courage and grim determination; his famous saying, "I'll fight it out on this line if it takes me all summer," showed the true character of this man, who has been called "Grant, the Butcher." No sacrifice of human life appalled him, he had a task before him and what did it matter who suffered, while he accomplished his task? Lee, the splendid soldier, Lee, the Christian gentleman, was at a grave disadvantage, when they opposed each other; these two characters were so diametrically opposite.

It did seem as if the Lord, looking down from His throne on high, would have favored the man who, from his youth up, had kept His Commandments, but, long ago we were forced to believe that there is no "god of battles." And why should there be? God is Love, He cannot take delight in strife and bloodshed. Our prayers are of no avail, when we go contrary to His teaching and it is only in this way that we can reconcile to our own mind the earnest prayers and supplications which ascended daily, hourly, from the hearts of the Southern people. They were a god-fearing nation, sincere in all the professions they made; they had faith in God and yet, when the end came it was past belief.

In this Spring of eighteen and sixty-four, however, we had not ceased to hope, nor had we ceased to make every effort to succeed. General Lee moved on and in "The Wilderness" a battle took place, which almost equalled Gettysburg in slaughter. Spotsylvania was furiously fought and so it went on, sometimes one army was victorious and then the other. We of the South had services of thanksgiving and days when we sent up our supplications to the Throne of Grace and bowed our heads in humiliation because of defeat. Our hearts were still strong within us, for we knew we were *right* and we believed the Lord was on our side.

In the wildwood of Southern Georgia, a country sparsely settled, lived a widow and her large family of sons. She and her husband had come in the first years of their marriage, to this region of promise. Eight sons they had when the husband was killed by a falling tree. Kind neighbors came for the last sad offices; a rude pine coffin was made and a grave dug, beneath the largest pine tree in the enclosure. The poor, bruised and mangled body was placed tenderly in the coffin and six feet of Georgia earth covered it from sight.

Through the long winter the widow and her sons, lonely and desolate, did what they could to keep the wolf from the door. It is the fashion, in this land of which we write, to help one another and they did not fail in this instance. The winter was past and gone. About the little cabin door the wire-grass, diamond-studded with dew, sparkled in the April sunshine, lofty pines, straight and beautiful, showed a wealth of green above, and in the wire-grass, flowers of many hues lifted their sweet faces to the light. Within the cabin the world-old struggle was going on. An hour later a ninth son, a little boy who would never see his father's face, drew in the breath of life.

In South Georgia at that time, there were but few homes and what they termed "a settlement" often covered miles of territory. The vast pine forests, in their beauty and loneliness, had, as yet, attracted but a small number and they were of the courageous, high-hearted pioneer stock. This settlement was composed principally of North Carolinians. In the pine country of the Old North State, they had been reared and, when they sought out a new home, what was more natural than to seek a similar environment? These settlers were all "Methodist" and when, in May, the Circuit-Rider came on his yearly round, the father's funeral sermon was preached and the baby baptized and given the name of Sylvester.

When the Circuit-Rider could beg, or borrow (he was never able to buy) a buggy or a gig he brought his wife along and this time she was in evidence. An elderly woman whose hair was thickly sprinkled with gray; her face a living exposition of the Christian virtues. She was, indeed, a comfort to this sorrowing mother of many sons; so strongly did her heart go out to this bereaved sister that, on the following morning, when her husband was ready to move on, she announced her intention to stay and help the needy household. In vain the preacher urged her to accompany him; to her mind this was a call direct from God. It might be, probably would be, another year before the Circuit-Rider came this way again, but she was immovable. "Whatsoever thy hand findeth to do, do with all thy might," was evidently her motto and she turned a deaf ear to his objections and calmly proceeded to put the little cabin to rights and then to bathe and dress the tiny babe. She was indeed a gift of God to that stricken household. Into the mother's heart she infused fresh hope and courage. In kindly words she pointed out the great work the Lord had cut out for her; to train these fine boys to work in His vineyard; to raise them up to be a credit to the father, who had gone from them; to teach them, above all things, to be honest and true and to give to her, their mother, the love and obedience, which the sacred scripture enjoins. As they sat in the twilight, after the evening meal was over and the little ones were asleep, and the older boys played around or sat on the step and listened, all these things were talked over in a way so loving and so convincing that the words sank deep into the hearts of her hearers.

"Here a little, there a little
As a bird buildeth her nest,"

And who but God, Himself, could know the good she accomplished? The summer passed away; Autumn had come and the children were piling up pine cones for the winter's kindling, when the circuit-rider appeared at the cabin door. He had come for his wife and the feeling of blank desolation she left behind beggars description; but the mother had given her promise that her teachings should not be forgotten. So, day by day, she and the boys tried hard to live up to the light, which the preacher's wife had assured them, God let shine upon their path. All this time the little Sylvester was thriving and growing and every day he looked more and more like the father he had never seen. His mother loved all her boys but she felt for Sylvester an added tenderness, an even deeper love.

As yet there were no schools in this lovely country of pines or if, at long distances, a school house appeared in the wire-grass, it was sure to be a school to which a favored few had contributed and only their children could attend; so these boys grew up with no "book learning" but wise in many other ways. A considerable clearing had been made by this time and happy in her splendid boys the mother once more enjoyed life. 'Tis true the boys did not all stay at home, for "My son's my son, till he gets him a wife," is an old saying and, one after another, these handsome fellows found true mates and sometimes moved some distance from mother and home, but, to her, this was as it should be and so long as she could keep Sylvester she was satisfied.

Then came the War Between the States and, even in the solitude of these pines, the war cry was heard. Their ancestors, back in "North Ca'lina," had followed Green to Yorktown in Revolutionary days and in pioneer blood lurks no *cowardice,* so, one by one, these boys enlisted in the Confederate army. The pure flame of patriotism burned high in those brave hearts and they went forth to fight for home and country. The mother, too, was patriotic and she would have been satisfied if she could only have kept Sylvester, so strong and handsome he was, so young to go away, so like his father, so marvellously like him, that father he had never seen. They were gone, all gone and, alone for the first time in her cabin home, she knelt and prayed. The circuit-rider's wife had done a good work and, though God had taken her to Himself some years before, her spirit still lived in this desolate home. Nay, more, her spirit had gone forth with the soldier boys, and would be with them in camp and on the battlefield. "A word spoken in due season, how good it is."

At first the house had consisted of one room only, but as the boys grew up, room after room, was added and it was now a large house for that day and time. Built of logs, just as the first cabin had been, with puncheon floors and chimneys of "stick and dirt," reaching half way across the room and furnishing both light and heat to the inmates. Now the house seemed too big for her, so she closed a part and went to work to spin and weave, to knit and sew, until all Sylvester's wants were supplied and then the others came in for a share. Her needs were few; she had cows and hogs, poultry and a garden, these supplied her every want. No need to ride six miles to mill to get bread for just one, so she cleaned "big hominy" in the mortar, which, with its heavy pestle, sat always at the kitchen door. Lonely she was and sad, but it is a blessing to have some work which we feel obliged to do; work which will benefit those we love. And to her this employment brought contentment.

The oldest son was killed at Sharpsburg but she did not hear of it until near Christmas. A comrade, on furlough, brought the news, for neither mother nor sons could write nor could they read when others wrote. The boys could always get some more fortunate man to read a letter but those at home, far away from any such, letters were a poor comfort, indeed. Two of these brave boys were left on the field of Gettysburg and now they were fronting a greater loss. In the spring of 1864, Sylvester had a furlough of three weeks; his mother was wild with delight; her days were a paean of thanksgiving to God, that He had brought her dearly beloved safe again to her arms. A week passed and then "Marthy" and Sylvester stood before her and asked her blessing. They wanted to be married and the preacher was to be in the settlement next week. It was as if the Lord, Himself, smiled on their marriage for this was not the regular time for the preacher to come. With a little jealous pang at her heart, the mother gave the coveted blessing. Marthy was a good girl, she was raised almost under her own eye and Sylvester could find no better wife and then, too, as he said, "You won't be so lonesome when I'm gone with Marthy to keep you company." The days of the furlough sped swiftly by and the hour of parting came all too soon. As her boy had said, it was not near so lonesome with Marthy in the house.

Late one afternoon about the end of May, a stranger, who had lost his way going to Albany, stopped to get directions to go on. Of course they asked for news from the war? He had in his pocket a Macon paper, fully two weeks old it was, and it contained a list of the killed, wounded and missing from the Battle of the Wilderness. Reading it over to them, very slowly, for reading did not come easy to him, he read out "Sylvester Carter, missing." At first, in utter abandonment of grief, both women wept bitterly, then the mother, remembering her trust in God, spoke words of hope to the poor young wife. The paper did not say he was dead, it did not even say he was wounded or sick; it might be he was a prisoner and would be exchanged or it might be he had just got separated from the rest. So many things might have been and he would yet come home again. Marthy's sobs ceased, and both women busied themselves in getting supper for the stranger, for hospitality was one of the cardinal virtues in this settlement.

Always watching, always hoping, always praying, the summer wore away. Marthy's secret was a secret no more and the mother wept herself to sleep at night, because it had been borne upon her that this child that was coming, like Sylvester, himself, would never see its father's face. To Marthy she showed a cheerful countenance and there was need that she should. As the days went by, Marthy grew more and more restless, until one night when the moon was full and all the earth was flooded with its white light, poor Marthy broke down.

"I jus' got to hear from Syl, I'll die if I can't hear from Syl," she cried.

The old woman was easy to move now, for she, too, felt that she would die if she did not hear. They knew where the family of Sylvester's captain lived and, though it was sixty miles away, they prepared to make the journey. Before light next morning they started in a small cart, drawn by a large yellow mule, with ears that flopped ludicrously. A rocking chair was in the back and in it sat Marthy with pillows at back and feet. On the driver's seat sat our old friend of pioneer days; the same old spirit shone in her blue eyes and her grasp upon the reins showed determination.

It was a long ride and a hot one. Once having started, they could brook no delay and, except to let the mule eat and drink, no stop was made. They reached Pine Hill Plantation about eleven o'clock at night but the family were still up. Captain Taylor had come home for a week's stay and friends had collected to spend an evening with him. All had departed and we were just about to say goodnight, when this queer equipage drove up to the front door. Dr. Bradford and Captain Taylor went out to meet it and in a few minutes they came in, supporting Marthy in their arms. The ride had been too much for her and she could not even straighten herself, the ride had been so long and her position so cramped. Mrs. Carter stood it well and when Marthy had been comfortably placed upon the library couch and she was also seated, she told her story. "And now," she said in conclusion, "kin you tell me where I kin find Captain Taylor?"

Captain Taylor rose from his seat, such a splendid looking man he was in his gray uniform, he stood before her, he took the work-hardened hand in both of his.

"Mrs. Carter," he said, "I am your son's captain and I am happy to tell you I left him, not a week ago, safe and sound. He was reported missing but he turned up next day, shot in the foot but so slight a wound he did not lose a single day from it."

Joy never kills, they say, but Mrs. Carter, who had

stood so much, fainted dead away and Marthy lay still and cried. Dr. Bradford forbade any farther conversation until some supper had been eaten but Marthy had something to say. Scarcely able to walk she made her way to Captain Taylor's chair and dropping on her knees she seized his hands, covered them with kisses and tears, while she called down God's blessings on his head. It was like a very sensational novel and we were glad to get the wanderers both to bed.

Dr. and Mrs. Bradford were positive that Marthy should not be awakened in the morning and when she woke of herself, she must have breakfast in bed and rest, for as many hours as she could be persuaded to lie still. They stayed for two weeks and you never saw such grateful people, though we assured them it was a pleasure and a privilege to help them.

Captain Taylor promised to mention Sylvester in every letter he wrote home and we promised to let her hear right away if anything should happen to him. Mrs. Carter was a very interesting woman, and, in the two weeks of her stay with us, she told us much of her life story; of the nine sons she had given to her country; of the fatherless grandchildren the three dead sons had left and of her hopes and fears for the others but always the thought that hurt her most was: "The little child what's a-comin' won't never see its father's face." It was an obsession and we grew superstitious, too, and expected to hear of Sylvester Carter's death.

In April, 1865, the war ended and nothing had been heard of the Carters. Three years later a member of our family, riding through south Georgia, in search of a favorable site for a saw-mill, found himself only a mile or two from the Carter cabin. He went to see them and was received with delight. He had only a short time to stop but he had to go over the house and see that it was all just as Mrs. Carter had told it. The rooms added here and there as they were needed, the neatly hewed logs, the puncheon floors, white enough to eat off of, the home-made furniture and the last piece to be finished was a new cradle, which Sylvester had made for his little daughter, two months old. The grandmother explained that "the three children was all babies an' the old cradle couldn't be spared, when the little gal come along."

October 27, 1864.—I certainly do love to go to Uncle Tom's; I have always loved him and his daughters but the principal attraction just now is the crowd of children who are living with him "until this cruel war is over." Captain Bernard and Cousin Tom, both brought their families to Uncle Tom, when they enlisted in the army. Cousin Mary Bernard is a beautiful woman and she has four uncommonly good-looking little folks; Bettie, ten years old, is a demure, wee maiden, much smaller than Overton, who is only eight.

Ruby is just the prettiest brunette youngster you ever saw and Jessie, who is only two years old, is perfectly lovely and I love to get her in my arms. But we have a sweet little girl at *our* house and cousin William and cousin Sarah have two, who are hard to beat, but all of these, like Cousin Mary's, are quiet children. Cousin Tom and Cousin Frances have six and they interest me greatly. They are not quiet, not they. Such rollicking, frolicking, jolly boys you never saw.

Uncle Tom really adores them but he complains heavily of the liberties they take. No sooner does he settle himself comfortably on the front porch to read the newspaper than they absolutely swarm all over him. If he has a letter to write he runs them off but usually it ends in his rising from that aforesaid comfortable position and going with them to the pasture to catch a horse; to the lot to yoke up some calves to be broken for oxen; to the lake to paddle the canoe or perhaps to catch some fish, anything to get "grandpa," who is their idol, out in the open with them.

It is in vain that Cousin Frances says "Father, do not let these boys disturb you in this manner, Daniel has nothing to do but look after them." But she knows all the time that it is his pleasure to humor them.

I love this "rough and tumble" young army; they are like steps when they stand in a row and the eldest one is just a very small boy. I love to take them out of doors and listen to them talk. Yesterday we met at Walnut Hill, to sew and then, of course, we could not play, but the children came around and there was a steady stream of talk. The boys and girls seemed equally proud of the "Soldier Papa" as they called their absent fathers but today they had Christmas on the brain.

"What will Santa Claus bring us, Aunt Lizzie?" asked Sam.

Aunt Lizzie explained that the blockade would keep Old Santa out of the country.

"Don't you remember, Sam, when Captain Wheeler's boat was trying to enter the Suwanee and the Yankees captured him and all the nice clothes Grandpa had ordered and paid for, for you, were captured?"

"Yes," Sam remembered, and a silence fell upon the group, sitting around on the floor and, when conversation was resumed, it was rather a sad outlook for Christmas.

Sam was certainly needy; the clothes he wore were neatly patched in almost every conceivable place and like Joseph's coat, showed many colors. Sadly the boys talked of Christmas trees they had either seen or heard of; almost with tears they deplored the blockade and finally little Henry sobbed out loud, "Oh, God, please 'stroy de' 'Ankees." Some way must be found to help Santa Claus run the blockade.

November 3rd, 1864.—We have grown so expert in sewing and knitting and materials are getting so scarce that we have gone into a new business. The

Bradford neighborhood has inaugurated a Toy Shop. At Uncle Tom's there are ten children, four of Cousin Mary's and six of Cousin Tom's; at Cousin William's there are two; at Dr. Holland's, little George is to be looked after and Sister Mag has two, so we are making toys and it taxes the inventive powers to the utmost.

We have made rag dolls of all sizes. Some are dressed as babies, some are nurses, some are dressed in Confederate uniforms and some are fine ladies in hoop-skirts. We have made many kinds of animals of scraps of dark goods and a mock snow man of ginned cotton but Cousin Sallie has surpassed all the workers in the neighborhood by making a rooster a foot high, of watermelon seed. The natural color of the seed lent themselves beautifully to the breast and sides and she stained some of the seed to give the needed touch of red and to furnish the black tail which all common fowls seem to possess. It is such a success we are all envious.

We have a maker of books also and our Christmas tree will surprise the children who have been told that Santa Claus cannot run the blockade. We, ourselves, have gotten a lot of pleasure out of these preparations and I am sure the soldiers in camp will read with interest of these efforts to make their little ones happy. Of course we only work at this when other duties have been disposed of but we have several weeks still ahead of us and much more can be accomplished; we keep thinking of other children who must not be forgotten.

November 24th, 1864.—Three times a week Mother fixes up a basket to send in to the Tallahassee hospital, fresh butter and butter milk; fresh vegetables from the garden; any kind of fruit we happen to have and always two large loaves of delicious home-made bread. This last is a luxury as flour is hard to get. Father raises wheat and he has put in bolting cloths in his grist mill, so the wheat can be prepared for use. This morning Sister Mart and I carried the basket and I was so sorry for a patient, whom I had not heard of until today. It seems he was shot through the lungs, at the battle of Olustee, and has been here in the hospital ever since. Some of the people here, becoming interested in him, have tried to get him exchanged but have met with no success. He is slowly dying of consumption and he wants to go home. His family live up North, somewhere and Mr. Craig, who goes often to see him, says they are frantic to get him exchanged but they can do no more than the few who are trying in Tallahassee can do. Mr. Craig writes his letters home for him since he has grown so weak; he still cherishes the hope of going home but they say he would not be able to go now, even if the exchange could be made. It is pitiful! Sick in a strange land and for so long.

December 9th, 1864.—The poor, sick prisoner is sick and in prison no longer. He died this morning, died happy, too, for Mr. Craig, who sat up with him last night, says he could not see any harm in telling him the papers had come and now he was going home. He was so happy and he held Mr. Craig's hand and made his plans to start next day; asked if he would not go with him to Port Royal, where Southern authorities took their prisoners for exchange. He talked of his mother, of his sisters and told Mr. Craig they would write and tell him how grateful they were. Poor fellow. He was buried at sundown today, in the spot reserved for those who die in the hospital. His grave is marked and if his family should wish it, he can be moved when the war is over.

December 16th, 1864.—We have had company today, ladies from town to spend the day. I have listened to many a bit of gossip and heard some laughable incidents related. Life is a complex problem; it is like a kaleidoscope in its changing scenes. On one side all is gay and bright and on the other, sorrow and dark misery.

One of Father's favorite texts is this: "Trust in the Lord and do good," and it seems that is the only thing left for us to do. Father says I must remember that the Bible says there is a time for all things, a time to laugh and a time to weep and it is as much our duty to "rejoice with them that do rejoice" as it is "to weep with them that weep." So I have tried to forget the poor sick Yankee and his sad death and take part in the fun these ladies are having.

There are to be two or three weddings; at least two engagements are in sight, if not yet *une fait accompli.* One couple were married last week and parted at the church door; he to go to Virginia and she to go home to wait for him.

Lieutenant So-and-So was suspected of casting soft glances at a certain charming young widow, who still wears her weeds, and eyebrows went up and voices were lowered to a whisper, as the tale was recited of a certain aged Romeo and Juliet who are, at present, amusing Tallahassee society. Well, the day is over and I will not deny that I have laughed as heartily as if there was no war, but it is only to lose sight of it for a little while.

December 26th, 1864.—Christmas was truly delightful. The joy of the children, at sight of the beautiful tree and toys fully compensated us for the time spent in their manufacture. Such exclamations of delight; such squeals of joy; as they received the gifts and realized that the blockade had not kept old Santa out. I never saw a happier set of youngsters in my life. We, who are grown old in service, do not expect gifts any more but this morning I have two letters, one from the Army of Northern Virginia and one from General Forrest's Command in the West. Do diaries ever feel curious? I shall not tell you who these letters are from.

February 17th, 1865.—There is little but bad news

now. Sherman is a very Devil. If this goes on much longer Georgia will be desolate indeed, for his favorite weapon is the *torch*. Every State Capitol in the South, except Tallahassee, has been captured and we cannot expect to escape much longer. The Yankees come nearer every day and we lie in Sherman's path to the sea. As they advance they pilfer and burn; all valuables are stolen; all provisions are taken, of course, and the rest goes up in smoke. Mother asked Adeline if she could trust her to help her to hide her valuables from McCook's men. Adeline thought she could be trusted, so, with Jordan's help, they dug pits in unlikely places; secreted some small articles in hollow trees; hid the oil paintings under the floor of Adeline's own house; carefully wrapped the family portraits and put them in the loft above her head. Mother had implicit confidence in Jordan and Adeline had given her word to be true and the mistress felt that she need have no fear for her treasures. The walls look bare with only the big mirrors to break the broad expanse. We will eat off of vari-colored plates and dishes. The set of French china and all the cut glass are boxed and buried. "Fingers were made before knives and forks," mournfully announced Father, as he saw the silverware being packed, but something must be done to save them from McCook's men. Captain Lester will not believe they will ever get here. I hope they will not, but I am afraid.

All the girls in the neighborhood know how to shoot and we have agreed, if we cannot escape we will shoot ourselves rather than fall into the hands of the enemy as they are treating the women and old men dreadfully in Georgia. Another thing they are doing; in those old Colonial homes in Georgia are many handsome portraits, painted by famous artists; and of course family portraits are always highly prized. When the Yankees enter a house, where any of these are hanging their first thought is to destroy them. Sometimes they slit them to pieces, sometimes they shoot them up, sometimes they are piled and burned—and it is such vandals as this we have to deal with.

February 22nd, 1865.—Washington's birthday! I used to read of the War of the Revolution and wondered if it could be true; it seemed so unbelievable. I admire General Washington very much but I never once imagined war could ever be so real to me. I wonder when it will end? Some wars last so long and perhaps this one may last for thirty years. If it does I hope I will not live through all those years.

March 1st, 1865.—We have a new lot of sick and wounded soldiers in this morning; two of them, wounded and sent here because they will probably never be fit for duty again, were completely worn out when they came. Father gave them a hot toddy and mother sent them some soup and such things as they could take and, after a while they slept and woke about bed-time and felt like talking.

Mr. Blount, the elder of the two, is from the Army of Northern Virginia and, singularly enough, Mr. Glendenning is from the army of the West. They had never met until they were helped into the ambulance to come here. Both of them give depressing accounts of the different commands they are from. "Pessimists" we would have called them once, but now we hesitate. I believe, I must believe that our cause will succeed, we pray to our God for help and surely He will hear our cry.

It is late and Mother and I are waiting for Father. He never rests while there is anything to do, which will make his patients more comfortable. Father is so hopeful, too, he never gets despondent, he never lets an opportunity pass to help our beloved South.

March 2nd, 1865.—This is a sad day for all of us, dear Mother feels it most of all. When she was a child she had her little pony, "Winnie Wiggin", to ride to school, and after that she always had a horse which was all her own. Grandpa loved fine horses and mother did, too. When mother married, she knew she was marrying a young doctor, who had his way to make in the world but he found he could provide her with all she needed. For five years now, she has been driving, to her especial carriage, a fine pair of glossy bays, "Tom" and "Charley." These horses are the joy of Jordan's life and he spends much time in brushing and currying his beautiful pets. At the beginning of the war there were horses a plenty for the army, but, as time wore on more and more were needed and all we had were given up to the Confederacy; that is, all but Mother's carriage horses. We were spending the day at Live Oak and Jordan had brought the carriage to the door to carry us home, when Mr. Elkins came riding up and ordered the horses taken from the carriage. Jordan asked if he could not be allowed to take his mistress home? To this Mr. Elkins agreed but told him to have the horses ready for him at nine o'clock next morning.

They are gone now and of course it is right for our country to have them, but Mother will miss them very much. Since the other horses were impressed we have had Jordan to carry us to town twice a week for our music and French lessons, tomorrow is the day, I wonder if we can go? Father says we can have a pair of mules, that is if a gentle pair can be found.

March 4th, 1865.—We went yesterday and it was just too funny. Jordan came to the door at eight o'clock and sent Robert in, to tell us he was ready to take us to town. We were sitting at breakfast table but made haste to go and when we reached the carriage, Sister Mart declared she would not ride behind such a team. She was willing to ride behind mules, but not such mules as those which had been selected. Father said these were the only perfectly safe ones and we must use them. It was fun enough to watch those mules.

One is a large yellow mule, quite the largest I have ever seen, the other is a very small one, rejoicing in the name of "Kits." She is of a shiny black contrasting well with Robert's dirt-colored sides. "Kits" and "Robert," in place of the sleek, satiny steeds of two days ago. Kits has a striking peculiarity, she has unusually long ears and they always point in opposite directions. Jordan had attempted to make the harness fit but it did not speak well for his skill. At last Sister Mart was induced to get in the carriage and off we went. Our team traveled well and we were becoming somewhat reconciled, when we reached town and were opposite the postoffice. Here our new horses (?) met a wagon from Horse-shoe Plantation, drawn by some of their acquaintances. Such a greeting as they gave them, such braying, such rapid movements of Kit's long ears and the answer from the plantation team, woke the echoes. By this time a crowd had collected and Sister Mart burst into tears. I was sorry for her but my sympathies are mostly for Mother. She, for the first time in her life has no horses. I understand that Mother's pets are to serve in Houstoun's Battery.

Every day brings us news of fresh atrocities in Georgia. We come next, what our fate will be none may know. Last week, near La Grange, an old gentleman, over eighty, was taken from his home and carried miles away to a swamp. Here he was found two days later, bound hand and foot to a sapling, which had been bent and allowed to spring back. The poor old man was almost dead when he was cut down and died before they reached a place where a doctor could be had. This gentleman's only offense was, that he would not tell where his daughter's jewels were hidden, she was not at home and when she returned she found her house in ashes and her father dead. Why cannot the Yankees act in an honorable manner as General Lee's men do?

March 5th, 1865.—It seems we are not to be captured by McCook after all. Over the signal stations between the Light House and Tallahassee a message came this morning. Gunboats are around the light house and *colored troops* are landing and are now on the way to Tallahassee via Newport. Such excitement I never saw; Captain Brokaw called in the Home Guards and they came, from the farm, the stores, from all places, where old men were employed, they came hurrying in. Soldiers at home on furlough, (there are very few of these) came forward to take their places in the ranks of Tallahassee's defenders. The cadets from the seminary, west of the Suwanee, offered their services and there was even some talk of a company of women, to organize and help to hold the enemy at bay. It is four o'clock now and these hastily marshalled troops are gone. Tallahassee waits, waits for news of the morrow.

March 6th, 1865.—The battle is on and since daylight we have been listening to the booming of cannon. Natural Bridge, where the two armies met, is only eighteen miles (as the crow flies) from Tallahassee and these big guns can be heard plainly. This is our first experience in warfare at first hand and I do not feel quite as bad as I expected. I am so hot with anger, I would like to take part in the fighting myself. Now, while I am scribbling this, we are waiting at the depot, for there are no telegraph lines, no way to hear from the battle except by courier or by train.

Mother has been sending the nicest lunches to us to be sent down to Natural Bridge, for distribution among the soldiers; others are doing this same thing and I hope none will go hungry. Dick Long rode in a few minutes ago with a dispatch for the Governor. Of course we do not know what it is but we will waylay the messenger on the return and, if possible, stop him long enough to hear the news. There he comes now. It was impossible to get anything out of Dick. He positively would not tell us one thing, except how well "Yannie" behaved in the fight. Then he and Yannie were off like a flash. Well, I suppose that is the way for a courier to do his part.

It is night, the battle is over and we have some news at last. God has been good to us and the enemy was completely routed, though we were outnumbered four to one. All the troops were negroes but the officers were white, if we had not been reinforced at the critical moment, things might have been different but a Regiment of Georgians rushed in and the enemy fled, not knowing how many more might be coming. We lost two men, Captain Simmons and a private whose name I have not yet ascertained. Poor Mrs. Simmons, she has a little two weeks' old baby and has been very ill. After the terrible excitement of the last forty-eight hours Tallahassee should sleep well tonight.

We have a ten-mile ride before us but it would not be right to stay in town when Father and Mother will be anxious to hear the full account of the battle, before they sleep.

March 7th, 1865.—Today Captain Simmons was buried in the Tallahassee Cemetery. His poor wife came from her home and fainted at the grave. How horrible war is!

I had an invitation to go on a picnic to Natural Bridge today. How awful! I do not understand such curiosity. General Miller says dead negroes were actually piled upon one another in places and the river was covered with their floating bodies. General Newton commanded the Federals, one of his orders, picked up on the battle field this morning is horrible beyond belief. Let us thank God they were not allowed the opportunity to carry it out.

March 10th, 1865.—Not one of the cadets was hurt. Not many went, because none were permitted to go without a written permit from their parents and those who went are so proud and those who did not go are so chagrined. It is funny to hear them talk it over.

Charley says, "we stayed right behind General Miller and his staff all the time."

"Why was that, Charley?" I asked.

"So we could protect him," was the proud answer.

I did not dare to tell the dear little fellow that the commanding officer was supposed to occupy the safest position.

March 15th, 1865.—I am afraid we have the swell-head because we repulsed the enemy and made him take to his gun-boats. It seems to have put new life and hope in us all. The news from the armies is a mixture of good and bad; more funds are needed for the hospitals and Leon County is preparing for a concert, in which the entire musical talent will be called out and great things are expected. It will take some time to get this elaborate entertainment ready for the public, so the 9th of April has been appointed as the most suitable time.

Cousin Bettie will play *"Une Pluie du Perle"* and cousin Fannie Nash will play "Sleeping I Dreamed Love." Sister Mart and Cousin Jennie are practising a beautiful German duet. If I knew German I would tell the name but I cannot even be sure I would spell it right and I know I could never pronounce it. Everybody who is at all musical is in this concert but I am only a listener.

These arrangements were made yesterday. Cousin Jewel is going to play a lovely Nocturne. She is a genius in music and she thinks they are taking too much time in preparing for the concert. Isn't it funny how people differ even in little matters like this?

Father's fever patients are well again and returned today to camp but Mr. Blount and Mr. Clendenning will never be well again. The enemy have possession of the home, in the Valley of the Shenandoah, where

Mr. Blount used to live and Mr. Clendenning's mother lived in Atlanta, until the Yankees burned her out. Father will keep them until they want to make a change.

March 18th, 1865.—Do not think we have been neglecting either the knitting, the spinning and weaving or the sewing, while this excitement is going on. Lulu takes my work for me when I go away and she is more capable than I, where the sewing is concerned, though she is not so good at the spinning wheel. My knitting I always take with me, no matter where I may go. I have learned to knit in the dark and that is a very necessary accomplishment these candleless nights. My first diary was a small red morocco book, the pages were not ruled and I had great trouble writing straight. When I needed another I bought a book twice as large, from Mr. McDougal's bookstore. That one lasted until the war and the blockade had made paper of all kinds very scarce. In 1863 I needed another diary and this, in which I now write, is of the coarse, thick, rough paper, almost like wall-paper. I have to use a pencil because in the first place we have no ink, and in the next place the paper would blot if I tried to use it. We have learned to do without so many things we used to consider necessities. We make a substitute for ink but it fades in a short time and we have not been able, as yet, to make a fast color. So, as I am writing this, for my great-grandchildren, I am using a "No. 1" drawing pencil. Brother Amos got me a dozen in Augusta and advised me to hide them away where nobody could find them. I have taken his advice for I have become so attached to you, my Diary, I would really be distressed to give you up.

April 1st, 1865.—More distressing news of our dear boys at the front. In Virginia and in the army now slowly falling back before Sherman, starvation is staring them in the face. Johnston's men are fighting almost inch by inch; every foot of the way is contested.

In Virginia, "Lee's Invincibles," are falling from the ranks, fainting from lack of food. This is heart-breaking, and yet our people are hopeful of final success. I know I am as true to "The Cause" as any but it seems to me there is but little hope. "Whom the Lord loveth He chasteneth and scourgeth every son whom He would receive."

CHAPTER XIX

WHEN WE WALKED IN GETHSEMANE

THESE last days of the Confederacy were trying ones. Our spirits rose and fell, as the news at the telegraph office was good or bad. Day and night found a crowd around the office waiting anxiously, not always the same crowd but just as eager to hear. "Carpet Generals" were never wanting to place the blame for misfortune on this or that commander, but no one listened to them. There was an almost universal contempt for such as these. We were not willing to admit the possibility of defeat and yet we feared it.

With feverish energy we worked, hoping against hope. The negroes could not have behaved better than they did. Of course, after the landing of black troops at the Light House, they knew the enemy were very near and they very well knew what the defeat of the South would mean to them, but no word was spoken. There was not a shade's difference in demeanor, just the same respectful, good-natured servitor he had always been; just as willing to take any part they could in helping their "white folks." Many a thought was left unspoken in those days.

The 9th of April came and that night all Tallahassee, as well as many from the country round about, were assembled in the Hall of Representatives in Florida's Capitol. The scene was not one to be easily forgotten; the animated faces; the evident enjoyment and the smart sprinkling of gray coats and gold lace, from a nearby camp. But all this was eclipsed when the curtain rose. It was beautiful. At the back was a life-size portrait of General Washington; above this picture was draped the flag of secession, given to Florida, a little more than four years ago, when she had severed the ties which bound her to the Union and stood alone, a sovereign power.

Our town was justly celebrated for its lovely roses in those days and these were used in the greatest profusion, filling the air with their fragrance. In the centre of the stage stood a grand piano and a handsome Confederate flag waved over it. A score or more of Florida's fairest daughters completed a picture of rare beauty. When the cheers with which they were greeted had sufficiently subsided, the leader came to the front and announced that the opening selection was "Dixie," and the audience was invited to join in the chorus. Then came more cheers and one after another the performers carried out the part assigned to them. Sweet old-time airs were sung; operatic music enchanted educated ears; touching Confederate songs brought tears to the eyes of many.

A magnificent quartette was singing "The Southern Marseillaise," when a gentleman entered the door and advanced rapidly up the aisle, bearing aloft in his hand *a telegram.* All hearts stood still, and waiting was agony, for none knew where the blow would fall. Ascending the steps he stood at last upon the platform. Twice he tried to speak and twice his voice failed him. Then he made a mighty effort and in a loud and unnatural voice, he read:

"General Lee surrendered the army of Northern Virginia today, at Appomattox."

That was all but it was the death knell of all our hopes and for a moment a silence as of the grave filled the hall; then followed such a scene as we pray we may never see repeated. Tears and cries and lamentation, the bitterness of heart-broken woe. Men, women, and children, wept aloud as they realized the calamity which had befallen us. Few slept that night and the sun arose upon a miserable, broken-hearted people—far too miserable even to talk it over with each other. It was as though our nearest and dearest lay dead within the house.

The hours passed slowly in this Garden of Gethsemane and in those hours the Southern woman, throughout the poor conquered South, realized her *duty;* sacrificing *self* upon the altar of *love* and, putting her shoulder to the wheel, she made ready to help her men. They were crushed and conquered, these noble heroes, who, for four years had fought as never men had fought before. They were coming home to poverty and want, all was lost save *honor.*

First of all their comfort must be looked after; that was the duty which lay nearest to her hand. So, in every home, however lowly, a welcome was prepared, but how about those who were coming back to a chimney standing where once a home had been? If there was no roof-tree, there was a woman's warm heart, a woman's willing hand and nature was kind in these April days. They should feel and know we held them blameless for what had happened, our dear, dear boys.

These heroes of ours had gone forth so full of hope and courage, so handsome and trim in their "suits of gray" and now, they come in twos and threes, not in regiments and battalions; heart-broken, footsore and weary. Some were bare-footed, and on some, the gray uniform hung in tatters and many a manly head sank low on a woman's breast, while he wept the bitter tears of humiliation and defeat. God help us! We cannot believe we deserved to drink of this bitter cup.

If we could have had the kind of *peace* that General Grant had in mind at Appomattox; if we could have been entirely under the control of the United States Regulars, all might yet have been well, but we were turned over to the negro troops and, a little later, to the Freedman's Bureau. Then a horde of Carpetbaggers overran the country, inciting the hitherto harmless negroes to evil deeds of every kind, arresting white men on trivial pretexts, carrying them before a Military Court and after a trial, which was only a travesty of justice, pronouncing any sentence which seemed good to them. Several citizens were banished to the Dry Tortugas; some were incarcerated in local jails and those who were shrewd enough to see through the motives of these "masters of the situation" paid some money and went scot free. But before these Carpet-bag days, came the wild search for President Davis and his cabinet. When Petersburg fell it was a foregone conclusion that Richmond, too, would be taken by the enemy, so President Davis packed all valuable papers and such money as was in the treasury and, accompanied by the members of his cabinet, set out for a place of safety.

Near Athens, Georgia, lived Mr. William Carr, a gentleman of seventy or thereabouts. He had friends in Charleston, South Carolina, the family consisting of Mr. Holmes, eighty years of age and extremely feeble; his wife and daughter. Their home in Charleston had been completely demolished by the shells, which were continually thrown into the city and Mr. Carr invited them to stay with him until such time as the war should be over and they could rebuild. This they did, and when Yankee soldiers were scouring the state of Georgia for President Davis, they found themselves at the locked door of Mr. Carr's residence. They battered away at the big front door for some time, but the house was strong and well built and at last one of the posse found an axe, with which he smashed the door and they entered. Only three frightened women were in the house and the only man was poor old Mr. Holmes, who was at death's door with consumption. For several hours they had expected him to pass away but life still lingered. Entering his room they declared they had found "Jeff Davis," dragging him by his heels down the stairs, his head bumping on every step; utterly unconscious, he made no moan and though his wife and daughter begged piteously for mercy, none was shown. Getting him in the light they soon discovered their mistake. They left him lying on the ground while they explored the pantry and cellar, taking what they wanted then piled up the rest and put fire to it. In the yard a flock of ducks were feeding, these they shot to pieces, laughing loudly when they hit the mark. After shooting the dog and the cat, they lighted a torch which they placed under the steps. The ladies were busy with restoratives, hoping to help Mr. Holmes, so they did not see this but a faithful servant did and extinguished the flames, before much damage was done. Mr. Holmes was dead before his tormentors were out of sight of the house. When President Davis was finally captured he was imprisoned in Fortress Monroe, to answer the charge of "Inciting the Assassination of Lincoln." Of this crime he was as innocent as a babe unborn.

Again we give place to the writer of the Diary that she may tell her story in her own way.

CHAPTER XX

LEAVES FROM THE DIARY

APRIL 10th, 1865.—General Lee has surrendered the Army of Northern Virginia. Oh, I wish we were all dead! It is as if the very earth had crumbled beneath our feet. In our minds all is chaos and confusion and yet, outwardly there is no difference. The skies are just as blue, the flowers just as bright, the mocking-birds are flitting in and out teaching their young ones how to fly and tonight they will be singing just as gayly as if this crushing sorrow had not come to us.

Father walked the floor all night long, I do not know if Mother slept but I know that not one of us went to bed, though I fell asleep for a little while but Father's ceaseless tramp followed me even when I slept and he is still walking to and fro, from the front door to the back. He does not say a word and I can see Mother feels very uneasy. She is coming now with a cup of coffee and I am wondering if she can get him to take it. Father was so sure we would succeed.

April 11th, 1865.—McCook's men got us after all. About twelve o'clock today they came in sight, a long line of blue. I don't see how I could ever have thought the blue uniform was pretty, and yet, when we were at Fortress Monroe, and I was a small girl, I admired the officers so much, when they came to the Hygeia Hotel to dance. They look ugly enough today. Mother has never taken her treasures out of hiding and now she is feeling so safe about them, but I do not feel safe about myself or anything else.

April 11th, 1865.—At bed-time. Terrible as this is, I just had to laugh today, when Adeline walked up to six or seven Yankee officers, who were asking for the owner of the premises and said, "I'll show you where de silver an' de pictures an' de likenesses uv ole

Mistess an' ole Marster is hid; me an' Colonel Ashe is got 'em in uses house."

A stern-faced officer answered her, "You surely do not know the war is over and we have our orders to protect personal rights wherever we go. I want to see the owner of this place now to buy feed for our horses."

Adeline went away abashed and we have not seen her since though she is in the habit of coming to help Emeline with the dishes at night, while Aunt Morea is sick.

April 16th, 1865.—We have seen no more of McCook's men. It took a long, long time for the dusty column in blue to pass our place. The officers were very strict with the men and did not allow them to straggle nor did they let the men come inside the enclosure for any purpose; we were so afraid of them at first. Aunt Sue wants me to go to spend the night with her but I am not willing to leave the home folks just now.

This morning Father sent for all the men on the plantation to come up in the yard. They came and they seemed ill at ease and I wondered what Father sent for them to do. Well, my curiosity has been gratified. When they had filed into the back yard and stood silently around, Father said: "My people, I have sent for you to tell you that you are *my* people no longer; the fortunes of war have taken you out of my hands—you are free men now.

"It is no longer your duty to work for me and it is no longer my duty to feed and clothe you but I shall continue to do this until suitable arrangements can be made. I hope each of you will stay on at his accustomed work and I can assure you that my feelings toward you have known no change and will not unless you give me cause. We are no longer master and slave but we can still be friends."

Father's face was pale and his voice almost gave out

once but he got through it splendidly and the negroes seemed much impressed. Some of the men cried, some spoke regretfully, Uncle Ben came and stood near by, then others crowded around and found their tongues. Only two looked surly and had nothing to say, Luke and Tup. They went off muttering to themselves, a habit so many have. Mother says she is not going to say anything to them, she will let events shape themselves.

Tonight Lulu came as usual to see me safe in bed and when she had said "goodnight," she came back and, leaning over me, she said, "I'm always goin' to love my child," then she was gone. It makes me feel queer; life has changed.

April 17, 1865.—We have been very miserable the past few days. General McCook with his command were near Thomasville when General Lee surrendered and they pushed on to Tallahassee. Everybody knew they were coming and some things in the Capitol were hidden away but, just as it is in case of a fire, the most valuable possesions were left behind and the first Yankees who reached Tallahassee helped themselves. Well, it is what we expected.

For days the Union forces have been passing along the Thomasville and Tallahassee road; sometimes like well-drilled soldiers, sometimes straggling over the enclosures and entering the houses without the preliminary knock. It is very disagreeable.

Eddie is five years old now and he is a bright little fellow with the greatest admiration for "Toldiers," as he calls our men. This morning he was on the porch when a Union officer walked in and took, unasked, a seat. He had quite a pleasant face and I suppose Eddie did not know what the blue uniform betokened. The officer held out his hand to him and said: "Come and talk to me awhile, I have a little son at home just your size." Eddie went across and in next to no time he was sitting in his lap, and eagerly telling him of the events of the past few days.

"Toldier," he said, "Don't you hate the Yankees?"

"No," said the officer, "I am a Yankee, myself."

Eddie looked incredulous, he slided down to the floor, his lip quivered, his eyes filled with tears, as he stood before his new acquaintance.

"I am sorry I sat in your lap," he said. "I didn't know you was a Yankee. I thought you was a Toldier."

The officer flushed angrily; "Look good, my little man," he said, "See if you can find my horns and the cloven feet you expected?"

But Eddie would take no notice of him. He took refuge in his grandfather's arms and sobbed out, "I sat in his lap and just a month ago they killed my uncle Mac, my dear uncle Mack. Do you think, grandpa, that this Yankee killed him?"

The officer left the house without another word. I tried to comfort Eddie but found myself crying as hard as he did. Will our losses ever be forgotten or forgiven? Can our people, North and South ever be a united country with this *bloody gulf* yawning between us? The South did not want this war. We fought for our rights, we resisted oppression and now we are crushed and conquered. God help us!

There are wild tales told of the doings at Washington. I will not try to record them for, like as not, nothing we hear is true. Whether we believe or not, these wild rumors fill us with dismay. Our own especial soldiers have not yet returned and we have not heard one word from them since the surrender. Perhaps they will never come. Father is heartbroken and miserable; he cannot sleep and nobody in the house cares for food; the meals are removed from the table almost untasted.

April 18th, 1865.—There are several companies of negro troops commanded by white officers, stationed at Centreville only two miles away. We fear the effect this will have on the neighboring plantations. We hear that these troops are a part of those who came with

General Newton to attack Tallahassee. Generl Newton, himself, is in command at Tallahassee.

Miss Hennie, who is anxious to get back to her home in Memphis, went to see if she could get from him a passport to take her across the lines. Uncle Arvah accompanied her and they were both of them astonished and indignant at his reply:

"You are a very pretty girl Miss Winchester, give me a kiss and I will give you the pass."

She was angry beyond the telling, and this was her answer, "I'll die in my tracks before I would kiss you."

General Newton laughed heartily, as if it was a joke and not an insult. "Heigh-ho little Rebel, you'll get some of that knocked out of you before you get to Memphis."

Between anger and disappointment, she cried all night. I am not going to have a word to say to any of them. I might say too much.

April 19th, 1865.—This morning at breakfast Father said, "Ten days since Lee's surrender and none of our boys home yet."

We look for them continually but they do not come. A miserable uncertainty hangs over us and we do not know what to expect. Ever since I can remember Father has been trying to teach me "self-control," as he expresses it. He is teaching me to "fight my nerves." Mother has no nerves—so everybody says, and in these trying days she is the mainstay of the household; we all look to her for help and Father says I must be just like Mother. I wish I was, she is such a comfort to us all and I will yet conquer nervousness, which Aunt Robinson says I inherit from the Bradford side of the house.

April 19th, 1865.—It is bedtime and I am writing in my own room; usually I write in the library, where Father sits, but tonight I want to be alone. Oft I have repeated, perhaps repeated boastfully, those brave lines:

> "I am the master of my fate;
> The captain of my soul."

And now, I find I am but a broken reed, shaken by the wind. Let me write the day's happenings while I can.

This morning we sat on the front porch watching the road. Father sat in his big rocker and Mother sat close beside him; Brother Amos and Sister Mag were sitting back in the vines, playing with little Rebecca, who was in her mother's lap. Mattie was stretched out, full length on one of the porch seats, her beautiful golden curls falling to the floor. I sat on the steps and Eddie was spinning acorns beside me. Sister Mart is at Goodwood. For several days now the front porch has been the favorite place for the family to sit.

Mattie is wild to see her father and she rehearses their meeting, making it different every day.

I was watching Eddie and did not know there was anything to see, when Father said, "There they come." Entering the front gate, too far for my near-sighted eyes to distinguish one from another, were three Confederate soldiers. Poor fellows; they were pitiful. Thin and so browned by exposure, until they were hardly recognizable. Footsore and weary, on they came, Captain Bernard, stepping quicker than his companions.

We rushed to greet them but Brother Junius, who was next called out, "Do not come near me—send Bill to my room" and then he went rapidly away in the direction of the room which was always known as his.

Mattie burst into tears—"Papa, you are crazy," she wailed. Cousin Johnnie came last; his face the saddest you ever saw. Falling on the steps, he put his face in his hands and cried like a child. Cousin Johnnie, who of all men we knew was the most reticent and reserved.

Dear Mother always knows just what is best to do

and say and with her sweet words of welcome, her inquiries after the health of each one, the hot coffee and cakes which she has had ready day after day; all this helped to restore the composure of all.

Jordan took Captain Bernard home and Father had his buggy brought to the door and carried cousin Johnnie home himself. Father loves uncle Richard so dearly and I believe his sons are almost as dear to Father as if they were his own.

In the meantime none of us had seen Brother Junius. Bill had made sundry trips back and forth from the room in the yard and the kitchen; several kettles of hot water had been transported and then Bill got a pitch-fork and came out, bearing the clothes Brother Junius had worn, and proceeded to burn them.

An inkling of the truth must have come to Mother for she said, "Come in the house children, Mr. Taylor will be in after awhile."

Then Bill sent Aunt Morea to borrow the sharpest scissors. We did not see him until long after Father had returned and when he did get in the house he looked very different from the weary man whom we had caught a fleeting glimpse of. With his golden hair cut as short as Bill could do the work, his face clean shaven, dressed in a suit of civilian clothes, with immaculate linen and a white silk necktie, he was ready to be hugged and kissed and made much of by everyone, from Mother down to little Rebecca; though Mattie of course, came first. She was simply wild with joy.

Mother said he should not tell one word of happenings in Virginia until he had eaten a good, hot supper. She was right, as she always is. After supper we gathered 'round him in the library and he began by telling us of the trying times the army had been exposed to for weeks before the surrender; but not a soldier made complaint and not one listened with any show of patience, to the thought of laying down their arms.

On through the days, his story went until that fateful 9th saw the ragged remnant of the Army of Northern Virginia drawn up in line on either side of the road, to see their beloved Commander pass. He was mounted on "Traveler" and a splendid new uniform added to his fine appearance. His men cheered him all along the line and he acknowledged their greetings. Never had soldiers so loved a chieftain as these men in gray loved Lee.

The army waited; sometime passed and then they saw through unbelieving eyes, their general, riding slowly toward them. His head, usually held so proudly, was low on his breast and not once did he raise his eyes. He made no pause; no need for words to tell them what had happened. When the realization came to them those war-worn veterans wept like David, when the news of Absalom's death was brought to him.

Gladly would they have followed him into the "jaws of death" but this—it was more than they could bear. After an hour or so officers from General Grant came, with an order to stack arms and prepare to deliver to the United States authorities all army equipment. The entire Army of Northern Virginia were prisoners of war.

Again officers came from General Grant; these men must make oath that they would not bear arms against the government of the United States until such time as they should be exchanged. Still they were not disbanded. Another officer issued paroles and told them that a government transport would sail on the 11th from Norfolk to Savannah. They could go to Norfolk the next day and sail, that is as many as the transport would accommodate. A detachment of Grant's men went with them. The transport was old and did not look sea-worthy but they were hustled on board, until there was hardly standing room. They had no provisions, no money. To add to the misery of the situation the transport was fairly alive with I. F. W.'s and they, too, were hungry.

"This," he said, "will explain why I needed Bill and so much soap and water. Bill burned everything I wore, even my shoes and hat. Fortunately my trunk was well filled with clothing. Never in all my life have I felt so desperate, and, when those disgusting creatures took possession of me, I completely lost my self respect."

With this he laid his head on the library table and *sobbed.* Such sobs as I had never heard—dry, harsh, choking. The room shook with their violence. Oh! it was awful to see that great, strong, splendid man, so completely unstrung. Before his story was ended Mattie had left the room and when we found her she was doubled up on Mother's bed, and she had cried herself to sleep.

I sit here and wonder, wonder if all the dear "men in gray" feel as crushed and disconsolate as these? Is the home-coming painful to them all? Will they ever be able to forget? Will the time ever come when they can remember the glory, the honor, the magnificent courage they have shown, and take comfort in that? God help them and help us all.

Tomorrow we will take up our every-day life again, and in the little ordinary things of daily life the tension may be loosed. I will do as Father says and try to be like Mother.

April 22nd, 1865.—Aunt Margaret is going back to her home in Tennessee. She had letters today telling her General Fish had possession of her house as his headquarters. As soon as she can get the place she is going back. I will miss my jolly cousins dreadfully and Aunt Margaret too, but I know they will feel better to be at home once more. They have been refugees for four years and they must be tired of wandering.

Brother Junius looks more like himself. He has been

to Neck-or-nothing Hall and found the plantation in good order and his servants were so glad to see him. His cook was loud in her denunciations of John, his man, who deserted to the enemy a year ago.

"Dat sure is a sorry nigger," said she "ter up an' leffen Marse Junius doubten nobody ter wait on him nur blacken his boots."

His visit to his plantation did him good, we think. Father has conquered himself and you would never know how terribly he felt and must still feel, though, he is so cheerful and so helpful to others.

April 23rd, 1865.—I ought to be ashamed of myself and yet I am afraid I am not. For the first time in all my life I have laid hands in violence upon a *negro.*

It happened in this way. We were sitting last night in the back parlor, the two tallow candles did little more than to make the darkness visible, but it was moonlight outside. Since we have been in the enemy's lines, we feel suspicious of all unusual sounds at night and often we have discovered listeners, under the windows or the servants, employed about the house, have "toted news" to the camp at Centreville. So when footsteps were heard approaching, I looked out and saw some twenty or more half-grown negro boys and girls. When they reached the house they began to sing, to the tune of "John Brown's Body," these words:

"We'll hang Jeff Davis on a sour apple tree,
We'll hang Jeff Davis on a sour apple tree,
We'll hang Jeff Davis on a sour apple tree,
As we go marching on."

In the corner of the dining-room stood a new carriage whip, purchased that day by Jordan, who considered himself a judge of carriage whips. His mistress had given him money that morning to buy it and this is what he said when he brought it in, "Miss Patsy, here's de whup, its a rale sure nuf whale-bone whup and de lash is twisted silk."

I seized it as I passed through the dining room to get out in the yard. The negroes were evidently expecting to make us angry but they had not counted on the reception they received. I rushed in their midst and, laying the whip about me with all the strength I could muster, I soon had the whole crowd flying toward the Quarter, screaming as they went. One of them screeching loudly, "She dun outen my eye," another, "Oh, Lordy—Mammy ain't nuver laid it on me lak dat."

I would have followed up the victory but behind the magnolia tree a dark figure was visible and I did not know how many more there might be. It was over so quickly that no one realized what was taking place until the screams broke on the air. It amused the family to think for nineteen years I had lived on the plantation and never before had I struck a negro.

April 30th, 1865.—General Johnston, too, has surrendered and the last slender hope to which some of our people were clinging, has vanished. We have lost all save honor.

May 7th, 1865.—Aunt Margaret has been busily making her preparations for going home and yesterday she received notice that General Fish would evacuate her premises on the 20th of May. So she is leaving us tomorrow. Most of the servants she brought with her are going back in the same wagons they came in but some are not willing to leave Florida.

Cousin Jim and Mr. Horton will take charge of the train and Uncle Arvah is going as far as Tennessee, in company with them, as he may be able to help her with the military authorities at Nashville. This is the last night they will be in Florida. We spent last night with them at Goodwood and they sleep here tonight for this is ten miles on their journey. Captain Oliver is going along, too. John Branch is going. He will make his home in Nashville. As yet he has no plans for work of any kind. We Southern people will have to take the matter of employment into serious consideration, for the war has left us stripped of everything but land.

May 10th, 1865.—I felt bad over giving up the girls but they were so happy in going. I hope we will hear from them often. There is to be a picnic on Lake McBride tomorrow. At first I thought I could not go but Brother Amos says it is my duty to make things pleasant for the dear boys, who, now that they are at home, must be entertained, for they are, perforce, idle for a time. Some are fortunate enough to find employment but most of them will have to wait for an opening. So, I am going to that picnic and do my best to be amusing and entertaining; if I fail, the blame will rest on Brother Amos.

May 11th, 1865.—I went to the picnic and if I was not entertaining nobody was so ill-mannered as to tell me so and I can assure you I was entertained. So many gray-coated soldiers; so much to listen to; so many questions to be asked and answered. A delicious dinner, boat rides in the cool of the evening and then the pleasant ride home "in the gloaming." Cousin Henry was there and he told us of life in the prison on Johnson's Island. He was captured in the battle of Missionary Ridge and was exchanged just in time to meet the returning soldiers from Virginia. He had a terrible stay in prison. In the midst of plenty, they were given only barely enough to sustain life; this in retaliation for Andersonville. But they ought to remember we would gladly have given those poor prisoners all they could want if we could have gotten it. Little food; no medicines, almost no clothing, we could not help ourselves and we should not be arraigned for that.

Cousin Henry said sometimes they got so hungry they caught the prison rats and ate them. The prisoners vied with each other in catching the rats, just as they had in shooting deer or quail in the days of yore. There was a dead line, just an imaginary line, but it must not be crossed under penalty of death. One morning a large rat ran out into the open space and several Confederates gave chase. In the excitement one of the men accidentally went over the "dead line." Quick the guard raised his gun, flash, there was one prisoner the less on Johnson's Island that night. War is cruel; men grow callous. Is the spirit of Christ dying out of the world?

May 20th, 1865.—It is late at night and this has been a perfectly horrible day. For three days Sister Mag has been very ill; last night death seemed very near and this morning her dead baby was laid in a little white casket and buried in God's Acre. She does not know. She has known nothing for hours and the doctors give us little hope. Nellie and Fannie are nursing her. She may never be conscious again. Mother and Father do not leave her and poor Brother Amos is wretched.

Jane left this morning without bathing and dressing Rebecca, so that job fell to my share. I usually dress Eddie myself anyway but Rebecca is badly spoiled and it is difficult. I coaxed them out in the flower garden and then Mother sent me with some directions to the cook. Now, this cook is my own Emeline, who has always professed to love me dearly. I went to the kitchen, but she was not there. I looked around but could not see a single one of the servants who were generally, at that hour, busily employed, each one, in his or her portion of the day's work. I went on to Emeline's house and she was standing in the middle of the floor, tying on a sash of blue ribbon, which would complete quite a stunning toilet. "Emeline," I said, "Sister Mag is so sick and Mother sends the key-basket to you and she says have a good dinner, for Dr. Betton and Dr. Gamble will be here and she is leaving everything to you." Imagine how I felt when she answered thus:

"Take dat basket back ter your mother an' tell her if she want any dinner she kin cook it herself."

I was hurt and dazed. I had not slept all night and I pleaded weakly, "Don't say that Emeline, Sister Mag is so sick, the doctors think she will die."

"Dey do? Well, what is dat ter me? I ain't make her sick, is I?"

Silently I left her house. They are free, I thought; free to do as they please. Never before had I had a word of impudence from any of our black folks but they are not ours any longer.

Retracing my steps I stopped at the laundry door; Melissa stood beside the table ironing a snowy cloth.

"Melissa," I asked, "what has become of the other servants?"

Slowly she raised her big brown eyes to my face, "I thought you knowed dey wus all gone ter de meetin' out ter Centreville, dem black soldiers, an' de white man wid 'em is sont messages ter all de folks cum ter-day an denounce our freedom. He kin save heself de trubble; I ain't no bond an' 'pressed slave. I ain't nuvver knowed no mother but Miss Patsy, an' she ben mighty good ter me."

Mother did not have to cook the dinner, Adeline saved the day and though dinner was late, it was excellent and, by the time it was served, Sister Mag was conscious and the doctors say the danger is over. We are so thankful.

I have learned a lesson today: we must not expect too much of "free negroes." Nellie and Fannie could not have acted better than they did but of all the others on the plantation, only Melissa remained at her post and Adeline showed so much good feeling, such true sympathy, that I love her more than ever.

May 21st, 1865.—We have found out about the gathering of negroes at Centreville yesterday. More than a week ago a notice was sent to all the negroes in this and adjoining counties to come and bring well-filled picnic baskets. Lieutenant Zachendorf and the soldiers under his command had a message to them from the President of the United States.

When a large crowd had assembled Lieutenant Zachendorf proceeded to announce, in the name of President Johnson, the freedom of the entire negro race. They were told that they must show their appreciation of the great boon bestowed upon them by refusing to work any longer for those who had formerly held them in slavery. He proclaimed to these poor ignorant creatures the perfect *equality* of the races. He told them they were at liberty to help themselves to any property belonging to their former owners.

"You made it," he said. "It is all yours." This is outrageous. What the outcome may be none can know. Already we see a change in the demeanor of those around the house; a sullen air they have not had before. If this goes on, and we have no way to stop it, what will the end be? The terrors of San Domingo rise before our eyes.

May --, 1865.—Mother has been sick with fever for three days past and I have paid no attention to my diary. Last night such a mysterious stranger came to us. I, who have the reputation of having no curiosity, am fairly eaten up with it. Father knows but does not tell. He says I must not write down what happened as it might endanger our visitor. He says I must not even put a date.

Mother's illness was severe, she does not often have fever and we felt alarmed but she is much better this morning, even to the extent of eating a nice little squab, Adeline had broiled for her breakfast.

Something dreadful has happened dear Diary, I hardly know how to tell it, my dear black mammy has left us. I did not expect her to be the first to leave but it was not exactly her fault. Mother did not want

Hannah to go out to Centreville where all those soldiers are encamped and when she found Lulu was dressing her in her prettiest clothes to take her there to spend the day, Mother told her Hannah must not go.

Lulu reminded her that they were now free and if she saw fit to take her daughter into that crowd it was nobody's business.

Of course that angered Mother so she said, "If you disobey me in this matter you and your family must leave the place."

Lulu did not believe she was in earnest and came in as usual to attend to her duties but Mother was firm and Lulu had to go and I am inconsolable, though I would not have Mother to know it for the world.

I feel lost, I feel as if someone is dead in the house. Whatever will I do without my Mammy? When she was going she stopped on the doorstep and, shaking her fist at Mother, she said:

"I'll miss you—the Lord knows I'll miss you—but you'll miss me, too—you see if you don't."

Well, she is gone—I will try to wait on Mother so she will not miss her too much. I do not think Mother realizes they are free.

June 9th, 1865.—Nellie went away today and the parting between her and Sister Mag was pitiful. She has nursed Eddie all his life and for three weeks now, the three weeks Sister Mag has been so ill, she has been almost constantly at her side, while I took care of Eddie. He is sorely distressed but it is as nothing compared to his mother's grief at giving her up.

Nellie knelt on the floor and put her arms about sister, both were sobbing and both faces were wet with tears.

"I wouldn't leave you Miss Mag," she gasped out, "but my husband says I got ter go. He says if I don't go with him now I shant never come and he says I b'longs ter him now an' so I'll have ter go."

"Can't you persuade him to stay here with you, Nellie?" pleaded the almost heart-broken mistress, but no, he did not like country life, he had work in the iron foundry and would not give it up.

From the porch, just outside, Emperor Dulan's loud voice was heard, "Come on, Nellie—I shore is tired waiting."

He was evidently impatient and she could stay no longer.

"God bless you, Miss Mag, God bless Marse Amos an' de sweet chillun an', over everything else, may the Lord bless Marse Ned an' Mis' Patsey."

Another link broken and it is only the beginning of the end. I hope Emperor will be kinder than he sounds. I love Nellie, myself. She has been Sister Mag's maid for years, they grew up together, she has nursed the children and has been friend as well as servant.

I wonder what Aunt Harriet Beecher Stowe would think of the farewell of this morning? We were afraid the excitement would be too much for our dear invalid, but she is sleeping quietly; has been ever since she ate her very light luncheon at twelve o'clock. Adeline does not give us dinner until three o'clock, sometimes later, but she is such a good cook that nobody feels like finding fault with the hour.

June 15th, 1865.—Once more the family are every one well and this is a truly delightful state of affairs. Ever "sence freedom drapped," as the negroes say, we have not been permitted to ride horseback without a gentleman with us. Sometimes it was not convenient to find one and often we could not go but we young folks have determined to turn over a new leaf. We have made up our minds to drown our troubles in a sea of gaiety and with that end in view, we have organized a Riding Company, a Shakespeare Club, a Bezique Club and once a month a regular Dancing Party. This party to be held at whichever home in the neighborhood wanted us most.

The Riding Company will be commanded by Major Henry Bradford, late of the Confederate States Army. Being a cavalryman, he will be able to give us lessons in the cavalry drill.

The Bezique Club is a very informal affair. We have a handsome imported set of Bezique and any number can play it, but we also play any other game, which my be desired. Sad to relate, cards are looked upon with great disfavor in the neighborhood. Only at Pine Hill can the Bezique Club meet. It meets just any time the members please, the only proviso being that the cards must be put aside before eleven o'clock.

The Club, *par excellence,* is the Shakespeare Club; nobody objects to this as classical knowledge never comes amiss. To be a student of the Bard of Avon is a hall mark in the literary world. We have arranged to meet every two weeks, first at one house in the Bradford neighborhood and next and next, until the round has been made. The various housekeepers have volunteered to provide a fine supper for the Shakespeare Club at all their meetings.

Here is a secret, to be told to none, just yet; the Bezique Club will have suppers provided, too; not only on stated nights, but whenever they chance to meet. Father and Mother are the very most indulgent parents in the world.

June 17th, 1865.—We had our first riding lesson yesterday and we had quite a respectable company, fifteen young ladies and as many gentlemen. Best of all, they, the gentlemen, came dressed in our beloved gray. We are so proud of the Confederate Army and we love the gray uniform. We love and reverence our captive President; we place the name of Jefferson Davis at the head of all martyred heroes. Our hearts throb with pride when we think of General Robert E. Lee and we love every officer and every man who served under him. We love, and we admire the courage of the

Army of the West, which so stubbornly and so hopelessly, fought Sherman, inch by inch, in his hateful "March to the Sea"—and now, an insult has been offered these "heroes of the gray."

These men have given their parole and a Southerner's word of honor means everything to him and yet, afraid of men they have conquered; afraid of the men whose sworn promise they hold, an order comes from headquarters, that Confederate soldiers, both officers and privates, must remove from their uniforms all brass buttons and every insignia of rank.

At first, I have been told, it was the intention of the military to order the gray uniform to be discarded, but realizing that many of these men had nothing else to wear, this present order was issued. The cowards! They ought to be ashamed of themselves!

This piece of news quite spoiled the riding for me. I wonder if the time will ever come when I can take insults coolly?

Cousin Henry's uniform, which he wore this afternoon, is right new, uncle Tom having ordered it by a blockade-runner, when Cousin Henry was in prison at Johnson's Island. It is a magnificent suit of French broadcloth and he is so handsome in it; now he must "remove or cover all buttons and all insignia of rank." Isn't it a pity?

I have to go to town tomorrow. Father does not feel well enough to go and he has some business which needs attention. Of course Mother could do all that, but she insists that she will never go again to Tallahassee until the last Yankee soldier is gone.

June 18th, 1865.—I went to town today, arranged the business for which I went and also saw something that made my blood boil. As Sister Mart and I sat in the carriage in front of Uncle Arvah's store, Church Croom came to speak to us. From his uniform every button had been cut and replaced by large orange thorns. Being a private soldier, there was nothing else our conquerors found objectionable. I was perilously near tears when cousin Henry came, wearing the splendid new uniform of the day before. Over the Major's star on his collar, the thinnest of crape had been sewed; the chevrons on the sleeves were covered with the same material; the buttons, too, were wearing mourning.

Lieutenant Eppes came next. The gold lace had been ripped from collar and sleeves; the buttons were covered with black bombazine, but where the braid had been removed, the unfaded gray showed his rank as plainly as ever.

We saw many others during the day who had obeyed this order from headquarters, an order which has reflected no credit on the powers that be but has only served to make them ridiculous. This striking a man when he is down is despicable in my mind. Sister Mart is at home for a few days, she dined at Goodwood to meet General Scammon. He is the brother of our Miss Scammon whom we loved so dearly when she was our governess. He told Sister Mart that his sister would never allow a word to be said in her presence derogatory to the South.

"She is a Copper-head, regardless of the color of her hair," he said. "It is universally admitted that red hair denotes temper, and you should see her blaze whenever the Southern people were scored, as of course, they often were."

Aunt Sue had invited all the family to meet him but Father was not well enough to leave home and Mother positively refused to go. I am still hiding behind my youth, for the entire household looks upon me as a child, in spite of my nineteen years; in accordance with that belief I am excused from some things and, I am afraid, terribly spoiled in others. The advantages of being the youngest of nine sisters far out-weighs the disadvantages of the situation.

June 21st, 1865.—We held our first meeting of the Shakespeare Club last night, the play selected is, "The Merchant of Venice." The parts have been assigned and practice will begin immediately. The meeting was held here and we had a fine supper and, after much persuasion, Mother played for us to dance, the first time we have danced since that dreadful 9th of April, but we have agreed to try the cheerful role for a while. The Club will meet on the 4th of July at Greenwood.

I am reading poetry with Father now. The reading was so very dry last winter that the thought of poetry is delightful. I love it and Mother does, too. She likes me to repeat verses and I have learned nearly all of Scott's poems by heart. I can repeat Spencer's Faery Queen, Cowper's Task and nearly all of Pollock's Course of Time; but I do not like this last one. It is so horrible that I sometimes dream of the hands reaching out of the gloom and the anguished voices crying for help, while the accusing words fill the air about them: "Ye knew your duty, but ye did it not."

Last winter we read Rollins' Ancient History, the paper was yellow and the print bad, the contents was interesting but dry. I had just finished Josephus when I undertook Rollins and I really feel as if I have had a surfeit of historical lore.

I have not been allowed to even take Byron down from the top shelf, where the seven beautiful little volumes sit. Father, however, seems to know a great deal of Byron, for he sometimes repeats portions of his poems to me. What I have heard I like very much, perhaps I can read it all some day. While I have read Shakespeare it has been under protest, but Miss Damer insisted we must read it when she was governess; now we will have to re-read it in order to keep up with the other members of the club. We had a meeting of the Bezique Club last night, and played—*whist.*

June 24th, 1865.—Mid-summer day. I long to go

to the woods, down to the "Fairy Dell," where the wonderful spring is bubbling musically and little Mabel is filling her pitcher with the sparkling waters. I seem to hear my sweet sister's voice again as she pressed me to her side and repeated,

> " 'Tis good to make all duty sweet,
> To be alert and kind,
> 'Tis good, like little Mabel,
> To have a willing mind."

I cannot go to the Fairy Spring, however, it is a full half mile from the house and even our own woods are no longer safe from intrusion. The negro soldiers are everywhere. We are spied upon by our own servants at every turn and so we do not feel safe to get out of hearing of the rest of the family, unattended.

Though the war is over we have not replenished our wardrobes; this for the good and sufficient reason that we have no money, something new to us. Never before have we known the lack of it. Indeed, in the days of the Southern Confederacy we had it in such quantities that it has been said by some wag: "In days gone by, the Southerner went to town with his pocket full of money and took along a wagon to take his purchases home; in these war times, he takes a wagon load of money to town and brings back his goods in his pocket." Well, we will get used to it after a while.

But to go back to the scant wardrobe. When the Club meets we like to look as brother Junius says, "As pretty as pinks," and, with that end in view, I have been hard at work remodeling a dress. It is of white Paris muslin, trimmed with baby ribbon in a pale shade of blue. Again Sister Mag has come to the rescue and has lent me a lovely white sash, edged with picots of blue, which exactly matches my ribbon. A lucky girl, am I not? Will I look pretty in it, little Diary?

July 4th, 1865.—Never in all my life have I known

a Fourth of July, which did not mean a frolic for both white and black. Today there is no barbecue. We are not going to listen to spread-eagle oratory of the Glorious Fourth. To be sure we have not observed this ceremonial during the four years of war, but in days gone by we were most particular to observe the day.

I wonder what the negroes think of this change of program? I would like to know how they are spending the day? I haven't much time for such speculations, for Josie Evans is spending the summer with us and I love to be in her company. She is a delightful companion and a veritable star in all social gatherings. She has a marvellously beautiful, sweet and powerful voice and she has made a study of music. It was her intention to go on the stage but her mother would not permit it. I am sorry, for she would be wonderful on the stage, she has just the pose of an actress and her fine figure and graceful bearing would make for success. Isn't it strange that appearance means so much? She is a fine elocutionist and her reading tonight will be well worth listening to.

July 5th, 1865.—We had a grand time at Greenwood last night. The Shakespeare Club is the most entertaining mode of amusement I ever tried. I had a sore throat and could not read so my part was given to one of the other girls, Nora Holland, it was. That being the case I had a better opportunity of judging the rest. Most of the readers did remarkably well; all were educated and all were more of less accomplished, and well-read. The readers made a pretty picture as they sat around the big kerosene lamps which were a new acquisition in the Holland household, for four years we have had lights of domestic manufacture only, so these looked quite grand.

I sat in an open window and listened and looked, but I fear my attention was somewhat distracted from the subject in hand, because, just outside, on the porch, some one was kneeling, talking of far different matters. Having heard that the next meeting would be held at Uncle Tom's we adjourned for supper. Cousin Peggy is a famous housekeeper and this was a fair sample of her skill. It has been a long time since the southern housekeeper felt that she could be spared from the camp and the hospital for entertainments, but our soldiers are at home now and we must give them the very best we have.

July 6th, 1865.—Something disagreeable happened today. The Riding class was to meet at Hattie's and we were going around Lake Iamonia, and as the distance was longer than our rides usually are, we had to make an earlier start.

At four o'clock Cousin Lizzie and I were leaving the grove by the big front gate, which opens on the Thomasville road. "Rebel," the pony I was riding, has an ugly trick of backing and kicking, if a noise alarms him, and just as we were riding through the gate Lieutenant Zachendorf and a squad of his men came riding past. Their accoutrements made a jingling noise, which offended "Rebel's" ears and he immediately backed toward the soldiers, kicking with all his might, his heels fairly flying. I could do nothing with him; he paid no attention to either rein or whip and orders were of no avail. I was in despair. Lieutenant Zachendorf halted his squad and ordered me to "Stop that Devil." I explained that I could not manage him and they rode away, after telling me if it ever happened again he would have me arrested and tried before his court. We went on to Captain Lester's house, where we joined the party but I did not enjoy the afternoon. I think I shall have to stay at home hereafter.

July 8th, 1865.—Things go from bad to worse. Father has been sick for several days; not very sick at first, but he grew worse and yesterday and today we have felt uneasy about him and our doctor brother has been with him until this morning. Mother's room never looked cleaner or cooler, or daintier than it did today. Father's room opens into hers and everything, in both rooms, except the mahogany furniture was white. These apartments were always clothed in the crispest, snowiest of draperies during the summer months; even the cushioned chairs wore white dresses in summer.

Father was sleeping, Mother sat reading her Bible by the west window. Into this pure and peaceful atmosphere walked Peggy, unkempt, unwashed, dirty and disgusting beyond description.

Mother looked up from her Bible and asked, "What can I do for you Peggy?" I was arranging a bowl of roses out in the hall and hearing voices, came into the room.

"I is jis' kum fur a visit Miss Patsey," and, with that, she came forward and seated herself in one of the large, white-cushioned rockers.

"Get up Peggy," said Mother, but Peggy tossed her knotty head.

"I ain't agwine ter git up. De ladies what kums here sets in dese cheers an' I is jis' as good as dey is."

What a picture she made, leaning back, her dirty head making dirty prints on the chair cover, her scaley feet stuck straight out before her and the most impudent expression on her black face that you ever saw.

My diary, I was so angry I could scarcely see. I fear I am not of much use in an emergency but Sister Mart is and she rose quickly to the occasion. Calling Bill and Fannie to help her, she forced Peggy to leave the house.

We thought the incident was disposed of, but no, Peggy went straightway to Centreville and reported to the military authorities that "Miss Patsey done gie me a insult."

Finding that she really had been forcibly ejected from the house, they sent an orderly with a note saying

Mother must apologize at once to Peggy or she would be arrested at twelve o'clock on the following day and tried before the court presided over by Lieutenant Zachendorf. These may not be the words he used but I am giving the gist of the note.

Father was too ill to tell him of it, and Mother does not think anything will be done but we are terribly anxious. Sister Mart has made a plan, which I hope will prove to be the right thing. She has bound me over to secrecy and she and Jordan and Fannie have had a confidential talk. Early in the morning Jordan is to have the carriage at the door and Fannie will be in readiness to accompany Sister Mart to Tallahassee to interview General Foster. She will get Uncle Arvah to go with her to call on the general. She will hurry back and I must keep mother in good heart until she gets home.

July 9th, 1865.—Our troubles are over, hurrah for Genera Foster! Sister Mart and Uncle Arvah made General Foster an early visit. She went in much trepidation, for she had not been quite civil when she met him at Goodwood. He had offered her his hand in greeting and she had drawn back, putting her hands behind her and saying, "Please excuse me."

She told him what had happened; she described Peggy; she told of our indignation, of Father's serious illness and of the constant difficulty of life on the plantation.

General Foster listened attentively as she talked; then he said, "I will give you a guard for your premises, Miss Bradford; a sergeant and one man, will, I think, be sufficient. I shall also give you an order to Lieutenant Zachendorf and this order Sergeant Cornell will deliver in person.

"Your guard will be instructed to attend to all plantation affairs and all I ask of you is that they be fed and housed and that they be given the freedom of the premises."

Sister Mart was delighted. She is very impulsive and extended her hand to General Foster.

"General," she said, "the last time we met I refused to shake hands with you, now I ask the privilege."

It is a piece of merciful consideration for us and we cannot thank him enough. I have not seen him for I stay rather close at home.

When Sister Mart got back from town, we had not yet left the breakfast table. She entered the room, followed by two soldiers in blue uniforms. I thought they had come to arrest Mother and my heart stood still. What a relief it was when the situation was explained. Sergeant Cornell took the order to Centreville and we have heard nothing more of the arrest for "impertinence to Peggy." We will sleep better tonight.

July 10th, 1865.—We have always had a late breakfast; early this morning Adeline, who usually has a second nap before she comes to the kitchen to get breakfast, woke us all to tell us she had orders from "dem sojers" to have breakfast ready in ten minutes. There was some hurrying, you may be sure, but even so we were not in time, Mother being the only member of the family to put in an appearance. We'll do better tomorrow.

Ever "sence freedom drapped," we have had trouble with the milkers. The cows would be left standing for hours, and we would not have fresh milk for the morning's meal. The poor little calves would call mournfully for their mothers, until some one of the household would turn them together. Of course, at such times we had no milk. Today Pat elected to leave the cows and calves to shift for themselves, but it did not work. Cornell and Hibell came in, each with a foaming pail of milk and, not even looking towards us, said in a gruff voice, "Strain it, and put it up." This is something I know all about for "Granny Vi'let's" spotless dairy was ever an attractive place to me. I suppose we are to obey the guard also. Pat got her deserts, but I am a wee bit sorry for her.

Father has found out that we have two Union soldiers on the plantation and he is glad they are here. He is too ill to manage the negroes himself.

August 5th, 1865.—I have very little time for writing these days; not that there is so much work to do, our hands seem almost empty now that the war is over. We must try to make up to our soldiers for the years of hardship and privation. We have company nearly all the time and Mother makes ready for them as cheerfully as ever. Aunt Morea and Adeline have orders to serve a bountiful supper every night.

The way this order came about was very amusing. In the neighborhood, about seven miles away, a youthful uncle, with six nephews, were keeping bachelor's hall; they were frequent callers and often spent the evening. One night they were announced while we were at supper. Mother went into the parlor and invited them to join us.

"Thank you, Mrs. Bradford," spoke up six of them, almost simultaneously, "we have had our supper."

The seventh one, who was really better acquainted than the others, said, "Mrs. Bradford, they may have eaten supper but I am a guest in the house and they did not give me any, so if I may, I will gladly accept your invitation."

It was a laughing crowd Mother ushered into the dining room and, on leaving, they were given to understand that supper waited their pleasure any, or every night.

It is not the fault of these boys that they are idle. After four years of war, they came home to find an absolutely demoralized business world and until conditions change, they cannot hope to find positions. Of course those who have homes can find employment of a sort, but some, like these boys of whom I write, are far from home.

There is another family only two miles distant. Dr. Burroughs was a surgeon in the army and when his family fled before the enemy, who were bombarding their home in Savannah, he rented this place for his wife and babies. Under such conditions they did not have much of comfort around them and, when Dr. Burroughs came after the surrender, he brought with him four young soldier brothers, who brought with them only the clothes they wore and these very much the worse for the wear.

They were very cheerful over it and the doctor kindly shared his scant wardrobe with them, but unfortunately, the youngest one was tall and large, while the doctor was equally small. The clothes just would not either stretch or grow and poor Charley was disconsolate until a kind friend stepped in to the rescue, with a full-sized suit. These boys are also frequent visitors and one and all were made welcome at Pine Hill; so, little Diary, you see why it is necessary to have plentiful suppers. Mother says, "Boys love good things to eat," and I am sure she is right. Let them have a good time while they can, there is work, hard work before us all if the South is to be salvaged.

These are serious days and there is much food for thought; but we cannot always be sad and wear a long face. We must cheer these soldiers of the Confederacy who have so many battles ahead of them. A hand to hand fight with poverty is no joke and that is what is staring us Southerners starkly in the face in the near future. Even so we will be merry while we may.

October 31st, 1865.—All this time I have dressed as a school girl. In the time of war we did not make any effort to follow fashion, just so we had a dress, it really mattered very little to what age it properly belonged. If it was suitable and becoming, so much the better, but no one offered criticism of another's dress; we simply wore what we could get. Now it seems to be different;

I am actually grown up, though they say I do not look it, and now that Sister Mart is to be married in December, I shall be "Miss Bradford" and must dress accordingly.

Father ordered some things from New York and Mother has had some dresses with trains made for me, and Uncle Arvah will select a cloak and bring with him, when he comes, bringing his winter stock of goods. Of course I felt somewhat elated over these new possessions but I do not know if I like the idea of giving up my free and happy childhood.

November 7th, 1865.—Boxes from Smallwood & Earle have arrived in Tallahassee. Uncle Arvah, too, has gotten back home and I am on the *qui vive* for a sight of my new belongings. The wagon went to town this morning to bring the boxes out. Sister Mart is more excited over this event than I am, for some of her wedding clothes, her *trousseau,* or a part of it, is contained therein.

November 8th, 1865.—Well, the contents of the various boxes have been inspected and proven to be satisfactory. Sister Mart has a lovely dress of Marie Louise silk, beautifully made and the filmy laces look just like a bride. All my things are beautiful, I have congress gaiters to match every dress, laces of various kinds and I am the proud possessor of a dozen pairs of "Jouvains" kid gloves. I just love kid gloves! Mother took each pair from the box and put my initials inside and when I asked what that was for, she said it was to keep me from giving them away. Miss Stevenson has made me a hat, which she sent out on the wagon. It is pretty and the next time I go to town I shall wear what Brother Amos calls my "young lady togs."

November 15th, 1865.—Of course, I have always known that it is the custom in the South for girls, when they put up their hair and put on long dresses, to be addressed by gentlemen, not related, by the title of

"Miss." I knew this but I never thought of this formality coming *my* way. This morning, when I appeared on the street, in a sweeping train, etc., etc., and met my dear old friend, Mr. Mariano Papy, I was really shocked to have him bow formally and address little me as "Miss Susie." He then went on to pay some graceful compliments, which is just a way he has, but I could not help protesting against the change. Mr. Papy was Grandpa's private secretary and was living at Live Oak, when I was born. He has carried me in his arms in baby days and sung me to sleep. I meet him nearly every time I am in town and he has never called me anything but "Susie."

I called on Mrs. Papy before leaving town and confided my hurt feelings to her, this is what she said:

"Our little girl should not have grown up if she feels this way; there is nothing else to be done; you have and always will have, a warm corner, all your own, in Mr. Papy's heart, but, my dear child, conventionalities must be observed as the good of society demands it."

Perhaps she is right but I do hope Mr. Blake will not feel called upon to follow suit. When I told Father and Mother about Mr. Papy, Mother said it was all as it should be and father laughed and said, "We must all pay the penalty of mature age."

I do not believe my family will ever think of me as anything but a *baby*.

THE OLD SOUTH DIED HARD

When General Lee surrendered at Appomattox, the Southern people were crushed by the unexpected blow. Pampered children of luxury, they were; never had they been accustomed to poverty or labor and now both stared them in the face. But the days rolled by and the negroes remained, for the most part, on the plantations, which they had known as "home." So long as these stayed in their accustomed places, they did the work which had hitherto fallen to them. It is true they were free, but perhaps it was not so bad after all.

The domestic machinery moved smoothly. Generally speaking, the negro, except in a few instances, had not changed perceptibly in his manner to the white folks. While he took his time on all his jobs, he had also been slow in slavery days. The master sat on the porch and gave his orders as of yore; the mistress of the household still left much to her cook, her housekeeper and her maids.

The whole country was under martial law and some men were arrested and tried by this court and punished more or less severely; but these men had offended in some way; it was easy to see why they fell under the ban. But gradually the eyes of this Old South were opened; changes showed up. No longer was a cheerful, smiling obedience rendered—the "carpetbaggers" swarmed like a flock of vultures to feast on the little the war had left. Their influence upon the negro was very bad; had he been left to map out for himself the new life of freedom, much of evil would have been averted, but it was the ultimate intention of these carpetbaggers to pit the two races against each other.

So long as the negro of slavery days loved his former master; while the ex-master loved the ex-slave, nothing could be done by this dirty rabble that had swooped down upon us, "seeking whom they may devour." This love and confidence must be destroyed ere they could work their will.

We chanced to be on a visit to friends in Georgia, hospitable folks they were and in palmy days their wealth had equaled their hospitality. At this time, the summer of eighteen-hundred and sixty-five, they had not realized the change, which had come to the Southland, and money continued to flow like water. In nothing else was this lavish expenditure shown more plainly than in the gifts, which were continually showered upon their servants, who were never slow in asking for what they wanted. The cook, Penny, was especially gifted as a beggar and we never knew her to be refused.

One morning the party planned a trip for the following day to the famous Blue Spring, near Albany. To spend the day there, it would be necessary to make an early start, so the cook was called in and, after some directions had been given her as to the provision to be made for a picnic dinner, she was told to have breakfast on the table at seven o'clock, sharp. She said nothing and looked anything but amiable but no notice was taken of this. We rose early next morning, eager to be on our way in the cool hours of the morning, but there was no breakfast, no cook, no lunch. The carriages stood ready at the gate, the other servants had done their parts. The head of the house was furious; he had yet to become accustomed to insolent disobedience. He called the cook and we heard for the first time, what a friend calls "A flow of Sunday School talk." We had been carefully reared and we were shocked. Recalled to his senses by his wife's hand upon his arm, our host apologized.

Falling, unconsciously, into plantation vernacular, he exclaimed, "I beg your pardon, but free niggers would make an angel cuss." Our expedition was postponed for another time and the cook departed for an adjoining state in search of "greener fields and pastures new."

We Southern people have yet to learn the dignity of labor. The remark made by the little son of our host, as we rode along through a stretch of "piney woods," where but few negroes could be seen, indicates this. He is only four years old, this little boy, and in his short life he had never seen a white man ploughing. Passing a clearing in the pines, where corn was growing and being ploughed he cried out excitedly, "Look, look, see de marster working in de field."

Do not think, however, that we were slow in learning, on the contrary we took a genuine pride in doing well these tasks to which we had hitherto been unaccustomed. No complimentary notice, no acquired accomplishment, no anything in life ever inspired in our breast the pride and the pleasure that was ours, when, after many failures, (carefully hidden) we could, at last, prepare a delicious meal, to partake of which we could feel satisfied to invite our family.

Yes, there is no denying the fact that,

> "We can live without poetry, music and art,
> We can live without love, we can live without heart,
> We can live without learning, live without books,
> But civilized man cannot live without cooks."

It requires time and patience, it requires thought but success in the culinary and gastronomical field is worth the effort. As the year wore on, instances such as we have related grew more and more frequent; the negroes enjoyed hugely the taking of some grievance, (sometimes real but oftener imaginary) to the military authorities at Centreville. After we found the "open sesame" to Lieutenant Zachendorf's judgment, we had but little trouble at his hands. "Money makes the mare go," it is said and money certainly appealed to Lieutenant Zachendorf. In the household at Pine Hill, nothing of this nature occurred, while the guard remained on duty, they were faithful to the trust reposed in them and we were careful to treat them with the same polite consideration which was shown to any stranger guest. To say we were made more comfortable by their presence is to put it mildly, so smoothly did out-of-doors life move on, that we hardly missed the power to command, which had once been ours.

In December there was a wedding at Pine Hill, Martha, next to the youngest daughter and Captain Patrick Houstoun, ex-Confederate, married and left the old home. The bride was beautiful. In her dress and veil of "illusion" she looked like "the Snow Maiden" of fairy lore, as she came slowly forth, to meet the waiting groom. Her veil was not falling from the traditional orange blossoms but was held in place by a double white japonica, on one side, and a magnificent cross of diamonds on the other.

As Bishop Rutledge pronounced the solemn words, which made them man and wife, the silence was absolute, then pandemonium broke loose in the yard around the house. Howls of rage, shrieks of derisive laughter; hoarse exclamations. "Hell broke loose," said one of the guards. For days previous, it had been whispered among the negroes that on the night of the wedding, they would force an entrance and mingle with the guests on terms of equality and but for General Foster's kindness, they would have succeeded and the result would have been bloodshed.

If the whole Army of Occupation had been like General Foster and his "regulars" it would have been far better. In command of the guard was Lieutenant Coolidge, a slender stripling he was, straight as an arrow in his blue uniform, but in his young face were the marks which, wherever seen, betoken manliness and courage. Nay, more, Dame Nature had set her own seal upon him that all might see: "There is a gentleman."

This sign manual of Nature is a singular thing, and looking back, you find in almost every instance, *"une raison d'etre."* We found out after a while the *why* in this case. The young officer bore himself with such composure and dignity, in what must have been a very trying position, that he won the respect of all.

Protected by crossed bayonets, in the hands of blue-coated soldiers stationed at every entrance, the festivities went on as usual and we still feel grateful.

As the year neared its close the Freedman's Bureau sent representatives to every plantation and farm throughout the country to divide the crops and settle accounts. The plan by which these settlements were made originated with our conquerors. We have never known just how it was done but we could not influence the division and we were greatly surprised to find the planters really received more than they had expected. The negroes were not satisfied; many of them complained bitterly.

During these months that Zachendorf had reigned at Centreville, the negroes had a habit of digging up all kinds of grievances. We have mentioned this before, but we must tell of something which this procedure on the part of the negro brought about.

In the Bradford neighborhood, in fact in the adjoining neighborhood known as the Pisgah neighborhood, the only people who could possibly have been looked upon as objects of charity were the Kane and the McPherson families. Mrs. Kane was a widow with "three sets of twins and several singles," as she would tell you. Mrs. McPherson was her mother and she had two sisters and they lived in cottages built by the neighbors, very near each other. They did little or no work, and the neighbors vied with one another in supplying their wants. Captain Lester was one of the wealthiest planters in the community; he was a giant in stature, with a heart as large as his body. For years he had made it a part of his week's work to send to this family a quarter of beef. Now the beef which came from Captain Lester's was famous throughout the neighborhood for its fine condition and its size; the captain did not butcher veal.

The surrender did not cut off Mrs. Kane's supply of fresh meat and regularly each Tuesday the quarter of beef found its way to her door. She had watched with envy the constant stream of darkies coming and going from the camp; her cottage was on this road and it was not far to the camp; digging and delving in her scant brain she finally rose triumphant; she would go to Lieutenant Zachendorf and complain of Captain Lester. Just what her complaint should be she had not yet decided but it must be something about the beef.

Dressed in black calico, with a slatted bonnet of the same material, she went bright and early to camp; she was taken before the reigning monarch and questioned by him as to the cause of her visit.

"I cum ter tell you Mister Sackadog," said she, "what a stingy man Cappen Lester is."

"How's that?" asked the monarch.

"You see, Mister Sackadog, I got three sets er twins an seven singles an' my Ma an' my two sisters an' we all gotter eat, an' dat man sont beef ter my house dis morning an' it ain't enuf ter go 'round."

"How much is it?" asked Zachendorf.

"Hit ain't but jis' one quarter."

"Do you mean a whole quarter of beef or is it veal?" asked the lieutenant.

"No, I ain't a-meanin' calf meat, hits a cow," she replied.

"Well," said the officer, "you take that quarter of beef back to Captain Lester and tell him from me never to waste his kindness on you again." She stood still and then realizing dimly what he meant, she began to whimper.

"Shut up," he said. "Begone out of my sight and don't you ever come here with any of your d——n nonsense again."

She retraced her steps and, if it had been left to her, it possibly might not have gotten out, but the negroes all hate "po white trash" and it was a fine joke to them.

A feeling of deep-seated unrest pervaded the whole South, none knew what was in store for us. President Davis, whom we loved so dearly, had been imprisoned in Fortress Monroe and we were kept in distress all the time because of the cruel treatment he had to undergo. A sufferer for years from neuralgia, which had settled in his eyes, his captors conceived the idea of adding to his suffering by having a sentry pass his open door every half hour during the night and throw into his face at each passing, the rays of a strong lantern, thus torturing his poor eyes by flashing the light into them and also waking him, if perchance he slept. Mrs. Davis writes that when she hung her shawl upon a chair and placed it between the President and the door, she was ordered to take it down. Dr. Craven tried to get General Miles to show some mercy but he would not listen. We were sad over this and such inhumanity kept alive the hatred engendered by the four years of warfare.

How can we love our enemies, when they continually torment us? It was a sad, sad Christmas in the South. So many vacant chairs, so many cruel changes and yet, there was never so much "marrying and giving in marriage" as now. What will the New Year bring us?

LEAVES FROM THE DIARY

December 18th, 1865.—I thought I would be lonely beyond description when Sister Mart got married. It happened five days ago and I have not had time even to think. Weddings, like funerals, call together kindred and friends.

There was a big wedding; the bride was beautiful; friends flocked from far and near to Pine Hill; the supper was all a supper should be and champagne flowed like water. Again I say, at my wedding there shall be nothing but "Adam's ale" to drink.

The next night Sallie Ward was married and I was a bridesmaid at her wedding too. It was a church affair, the bridal party, that is the attendants, went to the church in an omnibus. Did you ever hear of such a thing? The bride and the groom went in a carriage but I am sure we had the most fun.

I have been to a big entertainment of some kind every night since Sister Mart was married except the 17th, which was Sunday. Doesn't the Bible tell us we must rest on Sunday?

Tonight Aunt Sue is giving a large party; "the gem of the season," we say, for everybody knows the entertainments at Goodwood are not quite equalled anywhere else. There is one thing about this particular party that I dread; uncle Arvah has invited General Foster and his family and the officers in his command. I see Uncle Arvah's side and he is right, but it will be painful to meet our conquerors. So far I have met only one and I cannot hope they will all be like him. To meet these blue-coats socially! Will I have the strength of mind to do it? Not much time for you my diary.

It is not difficult to get a dress now, but there are a thousand and one things to get through before tonight. Aunt Sue likes to have help in arranging flowers in the different rooms and the table in the dining room, which she has already dressed, is a dream of beauty.

December 19th, 1865.—The party was splendid in spite of the —, there now, I came near writing Yankees, and I promised myself I would never say that again, after General Foster's kindness. General Foster sent his band to play for us to dance. I had so many of my old friends around, I had not a single vacant space on my card but I saw Sister Mart dancing with Major Conant.

I know I will be lonely enough after Sister Mart has really gone. I am the only one left to Father and Mother. Josie Evans is Mattie's governess this winter, so I still have company at home. I do not like to entertain young gentlemen by myself, I am afraid they will find it stupid, but Josie is very bright and entertaining. Then, too, she sings delightfully. She was here tonight. She was one of the bridesmaids so she just had to be present, school or no school.

Father is nearly well again and he gave the bride away. We had been afraid he would not be well enough and he looked so handsome in his new dress suit ordered from New York for the occasion. Mother had a new silk, too, and the New York dressmaker fitted her beautifully. She had not made a dress for Mother for more than four years yet she had not forgotten how.

December 27th, 1865.—Christmas has passed and gone. I shall not try to tell of it; there is too much of pain and sorrow; too much of loss and change to wish to place it on record. No matter how hard we try to be cheerful, the heavy heart is there just the same. We did not invite company for Christmas; of course, our own family were here. Buddy and his wife and children, Brother Junius and Sister Mag and Brother Amos and the dear little ones. They were the only ones who enjoyed Christmas, though all tried to enter into the spirit of the day.

January 1st, 1866.—A New Year but a Happy New Year? No, indeed. We got up this morning to find ourselves the only occupants of Pine Hill plantation. It was a clean sweep, all were gone. Nobody to get breakfast; nobody to clean up the house; no maids to look after the wants of "milady;" no butler to serve the meals; no carriage-driver if we should care to ride. Not a servant, not one and we unused to work.

It is night now. Aunt Robinson taught me to make up beds long ago, when she took me to sleep in her room, so we have each of us a neat bed to rest in. Mother said she could mix muffins if somebody would bake them. Father offered to make the coffee, that being his specialty and Mattie said she would eat some when it was done and John Branch, who had spent the night here, stretched himself and said, "I'll saddle the pony and go to town." We did not ask him to stay, though I thought he might have brought in some wood as it was low in the wood-boxes.

I am tired—tired tonight, will all the days of the year be like this one? What are we going to do without the negroes? Will we have to do these manifold duties for ourselves? Or can we hire white servants as they do at the North? I wonder where the negroes have gone, and why did they not tell us they were going? Life is a puzzle sometimes.

January 2nd, 1866.—I have slept well and I feel decidedly better. I am not going to fret because the negroes are gone, nor will I bother my brains as to their whereabouts. I am going to learn to do all these things that need doing and bye and bye I shall do them well. I baked some corn bread for breakfast; batter bread, it was, with eggs and milk. We had plenty of butter to eat with it, then I boiled some eggs and father made the coffee, drip coffee is very little trouble to make when you have boiling water and I put a kettle on the fire the first thing when the fire was made.

This, I find is my stumbling block, I am the poorest hand at making a fire. "Make a note of that and improve," said I to myself. I cannot milk a cow, neither can anyone else in the house. I think I shall have to hunt me a good milker and get married. Father just lives on milk. Boiled eggs for dinner again and more batter bread. The menu in this house seems to know no change. Supper is yet to come. What shall it be?

January 8th, 1866.—This is Aunt Sue's birthday and she has invited us to spend it with her. We accepted with pleasure. It is the first time I can remember that she did not spend her birthday with us, but we have no servants. Mrs. James sends milk for Father every night and morning. She, (fortunate woman) can milk her own cow. I fear I could never learn to do that. You see I am so terribly afraid of Bossy. She looks like a dreadful monster to me. I must stop now and dress for Goodwood.

January 9th, 1866.—Aunt Sue's servants left, too,

that is, all but Aunt Susan and Aunt Emily. They are both fine cooks and Aunt Emily's husband, who has been free all his life, stays at Goodwood and he is "doing the chores," as Charley says. Uncle Arvah has engaged a cook for her, as Aunt Susan cannot stand the fire long at a time. He says he can find a cook for us in the wilds of Wakulla County where Aunt Sue's came from. They are white women and sisters, not entirely unencumbered as each has a child four or five years of age, but Mother is glad to get any help she can. A letter from Brother Amos this morning, says he and Sister Mag and the children are coming back to Florida to live. I am so glad, it has been hard to have her so far away, especially since her health has been so bad. Cousin Sallie Bradford sent Father such a fine loaf of bread; it is a kind he is particularly fond of, "salt rising" she calls it. They must have

"Heard her cry in the land of pie."

for cousin Peggy sent a beautiful sponge cake this afternoon, and Hattie sent a leg of mutton beautifully browned all ready to be eaten. Aren't they just too good?

January 29th, 1866.—Sister Mag and her family are living with us now, Brother Amos has broken up his plantation in Georgia. He can do nothing there without labor and all the negroes have left that section of country.

We have a pretty good cook and last night Brother Amos brought in a servant he had hired. It seems that some of the colored troops have been disbanded and this one was the drum major (whatever that may be). He is very small, black and wiry and active as a cat. He says he belonged to a maiden lady in Virginia and she trained him for dining room work, so we have put him at the same thing and so far he is acquitting himself very well. Josie and I clean up the house and it is a little easier every day. It is funny to ask a little darky in blue uniform to go to the kitchen for hot biscuits.

January 28th, 1866.—Aunt Sue spent yesterday with us. She is going to have a house-party and says she must have me. I told her I could not be spared but my vanity received a blow, for all at the table insisted that I must go. I love aunt Sue and it is always a pleasure to be with her and then, too, I feel flattered that she should think I am capable of helping her to entertain.

Mother says I need not trouble about clothes, Father has given aunt Sue *carte blanche,* where I am concerned and Mrs. Brookes lives on Goodwood plantation and she can do any sewing I may need. Isn't it delightful to be cared for in that manner?

The house-party will consist of two daughters of General Sprague of the U. S. A. It seems he is an old friend of the family; Mrs. Harrison Reed, Mrs. Miller and her invalid son, Charles, who is a lieutenant in this same U. S. A., also Eliza Meginniss and Josie Evans. Mother is so kind as to give Josie two weeks holiday that she may make one of the party. We will have a delightful time, I am sure.

February 17th, 1866.—The house party is a thing of the past and will be long remembered. The Sprague girls, Maggie and Mary, (Tudie seems to be her name to her intimates), are such nice, pleasant young ladies. When I had known them a few days I said I would not have imagined they were from the North. They laughed and said they had been almost raised in the South. I like them very much.

Mrs. Reed, to quote from my black mammy, "Ain't my sort," and I have never been thrown with one of her kind before. Mrs. Miller is a sweet old lady, a South Carolinian by birth, who married a Northern man. Her invalid son, Lieutenant Charles Miller, excited my pity to such an extent that I have tried to forget his blue uniform and remember only that he suffers. I think the almost constant contact with the sick and wounded soldiers in our own army has automatically made me tender of those who are ill. His mother watches over him day and night. Aunt Sue is just as good to them both as if they were kinsfolk and, though Uncle Arvah is such a busy man, he does all he can to lighten her burden. She was very glad to have a little help in filling in his lonely hours.

I look at it in this way; I am trying to be of some assistance to dear aunt Sue and if she wants me to read to and talk to, this poor, sick boy, it is my duty to do it. So, for a while, each morning, after his breakfast tray has been brought down stairs, I relieve his mother and, while I read some entertaining book, or glean the freshest news from the papers, she walks out among the flowers, or chats with the other guests.

Our own boys tease me about my "sick Yankee," but I think it is right or I would not do it. He, poor fellow, is grateful; I told him doctors did not know everything, even the wisest of them. I told him I was supposed to have consumption, of which Drs. Clark and Geddings were quite positive, but I would not listen to them. My doctor Brother did not agree with them and he says, "help yourself to get well; do not think of the disease but fill your mind with bright thoughts and, if possible find something for your hands to do; live in the open and hope, Hope, HOPE."

He was much interested in this and, the next day, instead of lying on the couch in his mother's room, as he had done, he came down stairs, with Frank and Jack assisting him, and sat in the large cushioned rocker in the hall.

The young people in the house came about his chair and Aunt Sue said he was holding a reception. He enjoyed it until he got tired, and his mother was delighted that he had made the effort. Poor boy! He has hemorrhages but I used to have them, too, and I have quite made up my mind to live to be a hundred; if I can.

One of Aunt Sue's friends among the younger officers of General Foster's command, brought a set of croquet and offered to teach us to play. We have a lovely croquet ground and we play a part of every day. Of course we are thrown together a great deal and in this way I have become better acquainted with the guests who are continually coming in and out. There are several young lieutenants among aunt Sue's blue-coated friends but I notice they are called plain "mister," by their own people, so in future I shall drop the title.

Mr. Bumford is probably the eldest of them; he has thin, "kitty kat" whiskers and his comrades make all manner of fun at his expense, but he is good nature personified and bears his yoke easily. Mr. Wessels is quite different, he seems to have been fed on green persimmons in babyhood and contracted a habit of puckering his countenance. He is also disagreeable in his manner to me. Mr. Coolidge I have already told you of; he is the nicest one of all. There are a lot of others, too, but I have nothing special to say about them.

One day when we had played croquet a long time Mr. Bumford and I went back to the house to rest a while. On the sides of the broad steps leading up on the piazza were two immense bronze lions, their heads resting on their paws; these made comfortable seats and we proceeded to occupy them.

Sitting thus Mr. Bumford said, "Do you know what this space between us typifies to my mind?" Of course I did not. "I'll tell you then, it is the gulf which seems to lie between the North and the South and I asked myself will it ever be bridged?"

I was surprised for I had not credited him with any depth. I parried the thrust. "Why do you think there is a gulf?"

"I do not think it," he said, "I know it, just take

you and myself for instance. I come in filled with the milk of human kindness, at peace with all the world, then I catch sight of you and I immediately congeal, and in your icy atmosphere, I continually grow colder."

At first I felt angry but his manner was much pleasanter than these words sound written down, so I concluded to meet him on his own ground.

"It is a pity you are so susceptible to cold. What has become of the "hot-blooded Southerner?" said I.

"Gone where the woodbine twineth, I guess," he replied. "You Johnnie Rebs keep your tempers pretty well."

"Are you trying to make us angry when you call us Rebels?" I asked. "If you are you are missing the mark for we are proud of the name, General Washington was a Rebel, so was Thomas Jefferson and all the men who fought under Washington, and all the men who signed the Declaration of Independence were Rebels, too. In the middle of the Seventeenth Century an ancestor of mine said 'Rebellion to tyrants is obedience to God,' and today England owes to him many of her liberties; I am glad to be called a Rebel."

"The ice is beginning to melt when we can get up a quarrel," he said. "As long as you already think me impertinent, I would like to ask a few questions."

I waited but he seemed to have forgotten I was there. Breaking a twig from a japonica close at hand, he took his knife from his pocket and whittled away for dear life.

"I did not wish to make you angry when I called you a Johnnie Reb. I suppose I called you that in the same spirit which inspires you to call us Yankees. We do not love that name, of course you know it was given to the Revolutionary troops in derision?"

"Yes, I have heard that," said I. "It was a pity to foist such a name upon them. I had three great-grand fathers and one grandfather at Yorktown, when Cornwallis surrendered and I am proud of it—I hope you bear in mind that this brave army were ALL REBELS."

"Suppose we let history alone and come down to every-day facts," he said. "You are Mrs. Hopkins' name-child and a favorite niece; she is a most delightful hostess and if you would be a little less chilling you could be 'the belle of the regiment.' "

I laughed; I could not help it, for that was the least desirable position in the world to me, but, as Mammy says, "I 'membered my manners," and answered politely.

Wasn't it funny though?

The Regimental Band comes out to Goodwood often to play for us to dance, it makes fine music and we enjoy it. One night the band serenaded us and Aunt Eue sent a large tray of refreshments for their delectation. Uncle Arvah went out and thanked them and Aunt Sue hurried Sallie upstairs with flowers for us to throw down to them, but I let Sallie, herself, throw the flowers from my window.

Aunt Sue is strictly impartial and she invites the young people from both sections and we manage to enjoy it all. I am telling you this foolishness, little Diary, that when my great-great-grandchildren shall read these pages they will see for themselves that great-grandmamma stood fast by the colors of her country.

I am going home tomorrow and it will be good to get back though it really is delightful at Goodwood. The Millers say they are "heart-broken" to have me go. Charley wanted me to kiss him goodbye but I explained that Mother did not approve of kissing. I do not either, if the truth must be told.

I am going home to breakfast and will take the home-folks by surprise, so have to bid adieu to all tonight. I have met some very pleasant ladies from the North. Mrs. Major Foster is lovely; she was a school-mate of my sweet sister who died. They were in Georgetown at Miss English's school for girls and she recognized me while we were dancing the lancers and asked if my name was Bradford? She says she never saw such a likeness, it was as if she was facing her old schoolmate again.

The Spragues have gone to St. Augustine and I suppose I will not see them again. I was sorry to tell them goodbye.

I was so amused at something that happened a few minutes ago, Lucy, the up-stairs maid, came in my room and said, "Miss Sue, is you busy?"

"No, Lucy," I answered, "not too busy to listen to you."

"Well, den, I jis' want ter tell you 'bout Mrs. Reed. She telled me when she fust cum,' Miss Lucy, 'wait on me good while I am here an' when I goes I gwine do suppen hansum fer you.' I done all I knowed how fer her an' now you jis' look what she gin me."

Lucy spread out on her knee a handkerchief which had once upon a time been a useful, if not a beautiful article, but now too ragged for any self-respecting person to use.

"Ain't dat mean, Miss Sue?"

"What did you expect?" I asked.

"I dun kno', but I is wurked lak a nigger fur her an' I ain't got no use fur dis." With that she laid it on the burning coals and left the room.

February 18th, 1866.—Home again and I have talked myself hoarse telling the events of the three weeks I have been away. I am glad to get back. All say they have missed me, which is pleasant to hear. Eddie does not like to hear of the Union officers, he resents every mention of them. I told him of the Confederate uniform I made for Arvah; the brass buttons, the gold lace, for it was a captain's uniform.

Arvah was so proud of it until the Yankees, who

came to the house, made fun of him, calling him "Johnnie Reb." He cried then and said, "Me don't want to be a Donnie Web."

Mrs. Reed told him to ask his mother for a piece of blue broadcloth and she would make him a Yankee uniform. She is a neat hand at work and by night the little suit was finished and Arvah was the centre of an admiring group. I took no notice of him but the little fellow is very fond of me and when he felt tired he tried to crawl up in my lap. I did not encourage this and he said, "Me wants to love 'ou."

"No," I said. "I can't love a Yankee."

He burst into tears and could not be quieted.

"Take off dis 'Ankee." he cried, "I'se doin' to be a Donnie Web."

After that Mrs. Reed and I were rivals where Arvah was concerned. I took to slipping a piece of money in his hand when it was time to dress for the evening and then, in spite of Mrs. Reed's pleading, he would wear the suit of gray; but just let me forget to have the bit of silver on time and Arvah appears in the parlor, a tiny figure in blue, where he is surrounded by his brother officers and, listens with willing ears to the many complimentary speeches made for his benefit.

Eddie thinks this is terrible. "I wouldn't be a turncoat," says this staunch young Southerner.

MY SOLDIER IN GRAY

So young and so handsome,
So brave and so neat,
From the crown of his head
To the soles of his feet.

He's the light of my eyes,
As he marches away
To a place at the FRONT
With his comrades in gray.

LIEUTENANT NICHOLAS WARE EPPES
Confederate States Army

Four years he has battled
  For his Country's rights,
Yet the bullets have spared him
  In the fiercest of fights.

Some day he'll come home,
  I hope and I pray,
For 'tis Heaven on earth,
  With My Soldier in Gray.

March 1st, 1866.—Little Diary, I have tried hard to tell you my secret but there are some things too sacred to write about. My Soldier in Gray has held by promise for many months and, before the year is out, we expect to be married. Father and Mother are willing, for they, too, like My Soldier in Gray but they insisted he should promise them never to take me away. I am the last one left at home and they cannot give me up. I love them so well and I am glad they want me to live with them always.

When the war was over, so many soldiers did not have anything to do, some even did not have a home to go to, but my soldier went immediately to work. His father has a large plantation and the overseer left as soon as the South surrendered; this Lake Lafayette plantation is five miles from Tallahassee, where the Eppes family live and his father is an old man and feeble; so he took right hold. He lives on the plantation and is managing splendidly, they say. I often hear his praises and I feel a glow of pride; but, not even to you little friend, can I tell *all* My Soldier in Gray means to me. We met just after the Battle of Gettysburg and he has loved me ever since. Let me fasten this page down securely that none may see.

March 5th, 1866.—Aunt Sue had the Italian harpers and the little grandchild to play tonight and I am here at Goodwood. These old, white-haired men are totally blind and the grandchild leads them around, but they make the sweetest music on their harps and the boy plays the violin. I heard them last week at the capitol but we cannot hear good music too often.

March 11th, 1866.—Again I am at Goodwood. Uncle Arvah is having a card party and I was sent for; you see, he taught me to play whist and he says he is proud of his pupil. I have not played at a regular card party before but often Judge Love comes to Goodwood and we play, Aunt Sue and the Judge against Uncle Arvah and myself.

This, however, is a large party. General and Mrs. Foster are coming and many others; we have put three tables in the library and in the double parlors several more are placed. We have dressed the whole of the first floor, and the dining room is a dream. The chandelier is an immense shell of bronze, in it are water-lilies of mother-of-pearl. Six arms of bronze curve upward from this shell with its fluted edges, lighting the room beautifully and bringing out the pearly, pink tints of the lilies. The chandelier is supported by a figure of Neptune holding his tripod. It is the handsomest I ever saw and Mr. Croom, the former owner, brought it from Italy. He also brought over an artist from Rome who frescoed the ceilings of this lovely home. The mantel-pieces are of Italian marble, and all this is not in the downstairs rooms, for show, but each room is fitted up in the same way. Uncle Arvah and Aunt Sue are the very ones to have this spacious mansion for they love to entertain and indulge in a princely hospitality, which all enjoy.

March 12th, 1866.—Last night Aunt Sue asked me to dress early and take charge of her little boys until the company arrived. She likes them to appear in the parlor and it is an easy matter to amuse them and keep them "spick and span." It was cold and windy last night and I proposed to them to sit beside the fire and listen to some fairy tales. This they were ready to do and we were sitting there, deep in the thrilling story of "Beauty and the Beast," when Jack opened the door and announced the first arrivals.

In came Mr. Bumford, Mr. Wessels and Mr. Coolidge, I do not know if they came together but there they were. I looked up and spoke and the children clamored for the rest of the story.

It was soon finished and then Mr. Wessels stood before me and said, "I have something here Miss Bradford, which may be of interest to you."

As he spoke he laid across my lap a Harper's Weekly, opened to its fullest extent. I am a trifle near-sighted and I did not at first take it in, but presently I saw what it was. A caricature of our beloved President Jefferson Davis, dressed in woman's clothes, a large hoopskirt had tripped him up and a huge, booted leg was showing through the hoops. The face was unmistakable and I gazed as if fascinated.

It was hard to realize that such an insult should be offered to me. I cannot speak when I am angry. I can only cry and there I sat, the tears rolling down my face. I do not believe either of the others had an idea of what he was doing, for Mr. Coolidge came and looked over my shoulder. Seizing the paper, he crushed it in his hands and throwing it in the fire, he grasped the poker and pushed it down until only ashes remained; then turning to the perpetrator of this sorry joke, he exclaimed, "Wessels, you are no gentleman."

Little Diary, you should have seen him. He was splendid. I looked to see Mr. Wessels resent it, but he only laughed and just then other guests came and the episode was ended; but I shall always feel grateful to my champion and never will *he* rank with "the Yankees" in my mind.

It was a gay scene; the bright dresses of the ladies, the brilliant uniforms of the officers, the plentiful sprinkling of civilians, the long mirrors reflecting it all, but I did not enjoy one minute of the evening. I did not enjoy it although My Soldier in Gray was there and usually that insures a happy evening for me. I could not sleep for hours; the insult cut deep.

March 13th, 1866.—We had some errands in town this morning, so we stopped on the way home. Miss Flint told me Mr. Coolidge is related to the Eppes family here in Tallahassee. I shall find out all about that when I see My Soldier again.

I got home a little before sun-set and, in a few minutes, Charley and Lodie Austin and Cousin John Nash came to spend the evening. Mother just loves to have the Confederate Soldiers to a meal, she gets the very best of everything to put before them and they appreciate it; also they appreciate her and her music. I would like to be as charming as she is, and when I said this to Father he said, "You will never be, and this is why, you speak out too plainly. The world has a grudge against plain-speakers."

I got "a slam" from Sister Mag tonight, too. She says I am "a coquette" but that is not true. The boys like me, but I like them, too, and they like me because they feel safe in my company. I talk about the things I think will interest them, I am a good listener—I do not encourage love-making. I do not allow caresses nor do I accept presents from young men. Even if I am young I have learned one piece of wisdom, "It is the unattainable that men sigh for."

No, most assuredly, I am not a coquette and the only time I ever approached it was Aunt Sue's fault and not mine; it was three years ago, I was nothing but a child, a brave Confederate captain "came a-wooing," he was highly educated, wealthy and blue-blooded. He bore a character above reproach and I found him pleasant company. One night he persuaded me to let him put upon my finger a ring, which had been the betrothal ring for four generations. I wore that ring till morning; then I wrote a note and sent Jordan to take it back to him.

I was sorry but I simply could not stand the feeling of the ring and the thought of what it meant. That was not flirting; it was only putting things right.

I am wearing another ring now and I shall never send this one back. This is a plain gold ring while the other blazed with diamonds but the owner of the plain little ring is My Soldier in Gray, and no words can tell what he means to me.

March 14th, 1866.—Riding horse-back with My Soldier this afternoon I told him the incident at Goodwood and how gallantly Mr. Coolidge came to the rescue. I told him I had heard Mr. Coolidge was related to him and if that was so I wanted to know why he did not make friends with him? He looked very serious and I was beginning to fear I had hurt him in some unknown way.

At last he spoke, "I have never mentioned my cousin. Sidney Coolidge to you; he came to Florida to visit our family prior to the war. I, a school boy, just at the age to give the warmest admiration to a man of charm and ability such as he was. I loved my cousin Sidney and looked forward to the visit, which he had promised us at some future time.

"The war came on and during the whole four years of war, I was in the thickest of the fighting. After Gettysburg I was promoted and assigned to the Army of the West. One day I was sent to carry a dispatch for my general. Crossing the field of Chickamauga, I was hit by a bullet; (the only time in all the years) it ploughed its way through hat and hair scorching as it went. I was stunned but soon recovered, delivered the dispatch and turned to go. An officer who knew me, laid his hand on my arm and said:

" 'Your cousin, Colonel Coolidge, lies dead in that tent, don't you want to go and look at him?'

"I was still faint from the shock of the bullet and I turned quickly away that he might not see my horror and distress. I did not see him, I could not bear it, but always, I have thanked a kind Providence that on *this day* I had not fired a single shot but had been on courier duty all day.

"Now, this young lieutenant you like so much, is probably a relative, indeed I am sure he is, but this is the way I feel about it; if the Confederates had been the victorious army and I had been occupying the conquered country, if, in fact, our positions could be reversed, I should look him up, claim the tie of blood and proffer the hand of friendship. As things stand, he is the conqueror, I am the conquered and if any advances are made they must come from him."

"I am sorry," I said when he closed. "Even if he does wear the blue, he is a kinsman worth claiming and I am sure you two would be congenial." With that the subject was dropped, never to be resumed. He is a man of deep feeling, quiet and reticent, sincere and truthful but too proud to expose himself to a possible slight. The Southern Confederacy had no braver soldier than he. My brave Soldier in Gray!

April 3rd, 1866.—As soon as they could pull themselves together after the war, the women of the South organized The Southern Woman's Memorial Association. We all belong to it and a call has been made on the members to get to work and prepare for a fair, to be held in Tallahassee. This Fair is to raise money to erect a monument to our heroes. The plan is for each section of the State to have in readiness the best of the productions of that section, and in December we will have the Fair and the call is for as many as possible to be present.

It was made so far ahead that the housekeepers and those who embroider might have time enough to prepare their wares. Only in this way can we erect a monument. Our people are ruined by the war; few have enough left to provide for daily needs. Some wealthy ones still have a little left but I fear they, too, will come to want, as they do not realize the conditions which confront us. It is so natural to spend when you can get the money, with no thought for the future. Anyway, we must have that monument.

April 22nd, 1866.—I have had a trying time today. Soon after breakfast this morning my friend, the captain was announced. He came alone and he was in no hurry to go. Again he offered for my acceptance the splendid, sparkling French Marquise ring. He has made all his arrangements to go to Brazil and there make his home and he wants me to go with him, but that, I cannot do. Even if there was no other reason I would not be willing to leave our poor, conquered country to her fate. This is the time for every true-hearted, loyal son and daughter of the South to bend every energy to restore and upbuild the ruin the war has wrought. We can do this and with God's help we will. But there is another reason still and I had to tell the captain this before he could be convinced that his case was a hopeless one. He described in glowing colors the ease and luxury of the life in Brazil; the wealth to be acquired in that favored land; he painted sad pictures of the trials which awaited those who elected to cast in their fortunes with a country devastated and ruined as this is; he said Southern women were totally unfit for hardship. Perhaps so, but like my Scotch ancestress, "I am minded to try it" and, though I forbore to tell him so.

"I had rather wed Jamie, wi' bonnet in han', than to wed Saundie wi' housen and lan'."

April 23rd, 1866.—Father is looking better than he has for a year past. After the negroes left us in January, he concluded not to plant a crop of any kind but simply use his broad acres for pasture. He has a very large herd of cattle and a vast number of hogs, and these continue to increase. Though the number is often cut down by the freedmen, who lose no opportunity to help themselves, there are enough left to make quite a show. When the year 1865 ended Sergeant Cornell and Private Hibell were recalled by General Foster and I rather dreaded for Father, in his state of health, to have to struggle with plantation life. I see now I need not have feared for him.

Once having made up his mind as to the best course to pursue he is perfectly content; he has always been a student and he finds great pleasure in study. He also likes us to listen, in his leisure hours, while he tells us of his researches. This is very improving and, what I like even better, are the arguments carried on in his library. When men of bright minds get together it is a treat to listen. We go to ride every morning in Father's big, old-fashioned buggy. He taught me to drive long ago and I enjoy it.

Colonel Wyatt Aiken was here a few days ago and he drove over all three plantations with Father. He is preparing to bring out a new farming magazine, "The Rural Carolinian," and is gathering all available material. I wish he had been here when Dr. Caldwell spent the night with us. I learned from hearing him talking to Father what causes the difference between the white and the black races. Father, being a physician, knew it but he had not thought best to tell me. I am no longer a child, however, and while I have not exactly "laid aside childish things," I take a deep interest in scientific investigation. I came near going to sleep over some statistics Colonel Wyatt gave us relating to soils and fertilizers.

April 24th, 1866.—William Henry Harrison bade us goodbye this morning. Long since he has discarded the Yankee uniform he wore when he first came, and looks well in his suit of white and the cap, which he insisted on wearing, though we told him it belonged to a *chef*.

"Never mind" he said, "when I gets back to ole Virginny to my ole mistis, the fust thing she is gwine to ask me is, 'William, are your dining room suits clean?' "

He said the cap was considered a part of this equipment. We are sorry to give him up, his "ole mistis" certainly knew how he ought to be trained. Many of the negro soldiers, who were disbanded here at Centreville, have hired out on the plantations in the vicinity and some have invested their pay in small farms. Land sells for almost nothing now.

Brother Amos says we are all "land poor," and we truly have but little else. I had a crowd of girls to stay a few days and we had a delightful time. In the evenings the boys of our acquaintance came and we danced or played cards.

I do not let anyone but Father see my diary and sometimes he criticises. He only reads selected portions but he asked, "Why is it you say so little of your girl friends, when you are so fond of them and take such pleasure in their company?"

I told him that from my earliest recollection of such matters, Mother has impressed upon me the importance of speaking well of other girls. She says nothing sounds worse than to hear one girl speak ill of her companions, and that a woman should always take sides with her sister woman. This is why I do not write or speak of any faults I see and with this thought continually following me I have fallen into the habit of saying nothing, in that way I cast no reflections.

May 1st, 1866.—Now that Sister Mart is feeling better, she is beginning to talk of going back to Marion County. Captain Houstoun says he has been keeping "bachelor's hall" quite long enough. She has invited Cousin Martha, Nina Houstoun and me to go back with her and will also invite other guests and have a merry "House Party." Captain promises us "all the beaux in Marion and some besides."

We are going and doubtless will enjoy it, but I hate

to leave home when our domestic affairs are in such shape. We never know when, as uncle Arvah says, "servants will turn up missing." I am gradually learning how to do the needful things and am really a help in the house but Father and Mother think it best for me to go. Sister Mart has had a long and serious illness and has but little strength.

I am going to leave you at home, my Diary. I will have to share a room with the other girls and it is best for you to be out of the way.

May 2nd, 1866.—All is ready and we leave as soon as breakfast is over. Goodbye little Diary. "Sleep tight and wake bright," for I will need you when I return.

May 15th, 1866.—We did not stay as long as we expected and Sister Mart came home with us. Night before last we were sitting in the parlor and Captain Houstoun was sitting outside, on the porch talking to the doctor, who attends the plantation. The Captain has a low voice but the doctor has a loud, rasping voice, which carries far. We could not avoid hearing him if we had wished to do so.

"Yes, Captain," he said, "this case is the worst case of confluent small-pox I ever saw in my life. You can hardly tell he is a human being; he is just a mass of corruption."

When Captain Houstoun returned to the room I asked where this case of small-pox was? He made light of it and called the doctor "a calamity howler," but before I slept I had looked up Fannie, Sister Mart's black mammy, and found out from her that the sick negro was in a cabin very near the house in which we were staying.

That was enough. No rest for the Captain until he made arrangements for us to leave the next morning. Bright and early we went to Gainesville, where we waited for the train to take us home.

Last spring a battle was fought in the streets of

Gainesville between General Dickinson's men and the Yankees. The doors and windows of the dwellings are still full of holes from the musket balls and splintered wood-work showed where the artillery had showered shot and shell. The citizens showed us where the branches had been cut from the trees by these same balls. The hotel where we waited had been the centre of the attack and was sadly in need of repairs, both to wood-work and glass.

Leaving Gainesville behind us, we gladly welcomed the "iron horse" which would take us back to Tallahassee. There was a stop at every little station and at one of these a stout young man in farmer's clothes almost lifted into the car, a feeble old woman. She was dressed in black calico, with a bonnet of the same, and she was weeping bitterly.

As the man turned away, after kissing her goodbye, he said, "He'll meet you at the depot, Mother, I writ him you was comin'."

Again we were on our way, the poor old woman continued to sob. When lunch time came, I fixed as tempting a lunch as I could and, pouring a glass of port wine, I took it to the end of the car, where she was sitting and asked if she would not have some dinner?

Her poor old face was red and swollen and her voice trembled as she said, "Thank you, but I don't feel like I ever want enything to eat no more."

Are you sick? I asked.

"No, I ain't sick in the body, it's my heart is sick," she replied.

"Try to eat just a little bite," I begged, "and drink this wine, it is not strong and it will do you good."

"Jis to please you chile," she said, but appetite was lacking and her efforts to eat were soon over.

"Suppose you tell me what is troubling you, maybe I can help," said I.

"No, no," she sobbed. "You nur nobody can help,

they is hanged my baby, my dear baby, what never done nothing to nobody."

I was shocked beyond measure and my first thought was that I had found a lunatic, but her next words told the whole dreadful story.

"Chile, ain't you read the papers?" she cried. "Don't you know how them devils hung poor Mrs. Surratt and my boy, my baby boy? The papers call him Lewis Payne, but that warn't his name, he tuken that name so he couldn't be caught up with. When Conscription fust come and my oldest son went in the army and wore the gray clothes, I mourned and cried but pretty soon he deserted and after he hid around a while, he went to the Union men and he tole 'em he couldn't noways fight but he would work for them if he could get a safe place. Them men sent him up North somewhere and he done pretty well.

"All this time my baby boy was growing bigger and bigger and I knowed soon the conscriptors would be a takin' him, so I writ a letter to the Yankee general an' tole him he could have my baby son if he would let him work in a shop. Soon some of the blue-coats come and got him an' they said I must remember his name was Lewis Payne and his home would be Washington City and he hadn't ever been in Florida. I promised all this and I was so satisfied because I had kept him out of the Confederate Army. I thought it was such a smart thing to do, and now, they have killed my chile—they hung him with a rope. They said he had plotted to murder President Lincoln. My baby chile, who never had the heart to hurt nothing."

I found myself crying with this poor mother, she was old and ignorant, she had tried to cheat her country and this was her reward.

The train slowed up, another man closely resembling the first, boarded the train. He took the weeping woman in his arms, kissing her wrinkled face and murmuring words of comfort, but is there any comfort for such self-reproach as hers? I will probably never see her again but I shall not forget.

I did not write of these happenings in my diary because it was heart-rending and such a blot on the history of any country. Some day when reason resumes her sway, even the perpetrators of these cruel and useless murders will blush with shame for their own ignominy. The reckoning will not come here on this earth, but what will be the verdict when they stand before the bar of God? I am sorry I saw this broken woman but I wish I could remember the real name of her murdered son. She told me but I cannot recall it. All the way home I thought of her and I am debating whether to tell Father and Mother of her or not. It has made me feel dreadfully. I wept, for Anna Surratt was refused even the scant comfort of bidding her mother goodbye.

June 5th, 1866.—I will have to do some shopping and I am such a very indifferent shopper, but Mother positively will not go to Tallahassee, while the bluecoats have possession and Sister Mart is not here. Sister Mag is not well enough to trouble her with such things and Aunt Sue has gone away for the remainder of the summer. Father says make a list and give it to him and he will write to Smallwood, Earle & Co., to buy in New York and ship to him. Mrs. Smallwood is a friend of the family and will select what I describe.

Captain Bernard is going to Europe and will get the silk dresses I need, in France. There is a first-class dressmaker in Tallahassee, so I hope we will not have too much trouble with my trousseau.

I wish they were willing for me to have only simple clothes for I am marrying a poor man and I do not ever intend to live beyond his means. Father would be willing but Mother and the sisters think, because they had these clothes I must have them, too. One thing certain, Father shall not get me any expensive jewelry, he shall not get any at all; I would not see him worried for the most costly gems in the world.

July 4th, 1866.—We do not keep the Glorious Fourth; we feel no thrills of patriotism when the stars and stripes float on the breeze. That is, we are not thrilled with love of country. Our flag has been immortalized by Father Ryan in the "Conquered Banner" and in its furled folds all our love of country, all our patriotism is enfolded.

"Furl that banner, it is gory,
Yet 'tis wreathed around with Glory,
And 'twill live in song and story
Though its folds are in the dust.
For though conquered, we adore it
Low the cold dead hands that bore it
And wildly we deplore it
Furl its folds though now we must."

There are hard things in life; we cannot see why and faith must be our guide along this uncertain road. Some day, perhaps, we will understand and in time we may even forgive but never can we forget.

July 21st, 1866.—This is the anniversary of the Battle of Manassas. How hopeful we were then and it seems ages ago, so much has been crowded into life in these last years. The weather is intensely warm, clouds are gathering and a storm is evidently brewing. That will cool us off. Uncle Randal died today and Father feels it very much. He was so good to his slaves and really fond of them.

August 1st, 1866.—There is a new member of the family tonight, Richard McPherson Whitehead. He is named for his uncle Mac, who was killed at Winchester. His father and mother are delighted beyond measure and I believe it is the name more than the baby, as they loved that brother so dearly and mourned him so deeply.

In the New York Metropolitan is an answer to "The

Conquered Banner." It is written by Lord Houghton and is fine, but I wish the English people had discovered their real sentiments while there was yet time to help us; still I must admit it is a beautiful poem.

August 20th, 1866.—This is a quiet neighborhood just now, so many of our number are away for the summer. Uncle Richard and Father do not feel the need of other company, they are so devoted to each other but I am sure Mother feels a little lonely sometimes.

Jordan has gone long ago and she has no regular carriage driver. She misses her drives around the country and the visits to the neighbors. She misses the large force of servants she used to manage so skilfully. Like the rich man in the Bible, she could "say to one go and he goeth and to another come, and he cometh," and now all is different. The few servants we have are no longer cheerful and willing, they are given to grumpy spells, when they go around muttering to themselves and looking as cross as two sticks. Then, too, we never know at night if we will find any servants at all the next morning; all this is very trying to a housekeeper of the ancient regime.

August 25th, 1866.—This is Father's birthday and Mother always makes a "Red-letter Day" of it, with the delicacies of which he is most fond. Each of us had a present, selected with reference to his taste. He is sixty-eight today and so handsome.

August 4th, 1866.—I have not made a success of training Frances. She was taught the Ten Commandments. She committed them to memory, each one was carefully explained, but in spite of this I do believe she has broken them all save the sixth, she has not yet been guilty of murder, though I am afraid the will to do it is not lacking.

Mother keeps in her wardrobe a bottle of chloroform, she is very careful of this dangerous medicine and it is used for Mattie when she is suffering with the toothache. Mother locks the door of the wardrobe and usually puts the key under her pillow, but we have not yet become accustomed to the need for a lock and a key and sometimes it is forgotten.

This morning, just before day, Mother was awakened by the strong and penetrating fumes of chloroform. She opened her eyes and there stood Frances pouring the drug out on her pillow. Mother was so drowsy she could not move but by a mighty effort she screamed, this aroused Father and Frances ran, but he was too quick for her and locked the door by which she had entered the house.

She fell on her knees and implored forgiveness; said she was looking for money; said she did not intend to hurt "Miss Patsy," but when daylight came her mother and her grandparents were summoned and the case laid before them. The result is that they have sent her to an uncle who lives in Tallahassee, with orders never to come here again. I am sure I would be glad to be rid of her, for she has given me more trouble than words can tell.

August 26th, 1866.—We have to look ahead and plan for the fall wedding which My Soldier pleads for. He was born on All Saints' Day and he is asking for a birthday gift. It is almost two months off and I have been talking with Mother this morning. I do not want a grand wedding such as my sisters had; circumstances are so different now. Father's fortune has been swept away by the results of the war. It is true, he still has his land but that is almost valueless at present and it may never bring in anything again as land without labor is a poor proposition.

Father has aged since the surrender and he will never be able to recoup his losses. All this show and expense is wholly unnecessary. What I would like would be a pretty wedding dress, every girl wants that, but I want a quiet wedding with my family and his family present and some of his friends and some of my friends for attendants. Beautiful flowers from Mother's garden, some of Hattie's lovely japonicas, simple refreshments and NO WINE.

The Rev. William Esten Eppes, whom both families love, is our choice of a minister. Mother listened to all I had to say and then she said, "I will talk to Mag and Martha about it," and I knew my cause was lost. Even so it was and I can do no more. Something less grand would suit us better for we are beginning life with "stout hearts an' willin' hands but nae siller."

August 27th, 1866.—The grapes are a little late in ripening this year, they are at their best now and today we have had a couple of dozen friends to feast on them. They brought baskets and took home a goodly share. It is very pleasant to share what we have.

When we were children Mother used to read us stories from "A Father's Tales to His Daughter," a lovely little book, now out of print. It was printed in the last century and my copy is worn and old. What I remember best is this, "The Bunch of Cherries," and the lesson taught (every story in those days had a moral) was "what you possess becomes doubly valuable when you are so fortunate as to share it with another." A kindly thought, is it not?

September 25th, 1866.—Nearly a month since I have opened my diary, but I am busy these fall days. There are so many stitches to take, so many plans to make and remake; visitors coming and going; rides with my Soldier in Gray; long talks with Father in the twilight and helping Mother with the housekeeping, for she has not felt quite well of late. All this keeps me busy but I am happy. One of Father's favorite sayings is "Happiness is a road-side flower growing on the highway of usefulness."

Mrs. Kinnebrough is making some dresses for me. She is a good dressmaker and a pleasant lady; a real lady, the daughter of an English clergyman, she is quite pretty, too. It is time to be deciding just what my wedding dress is to be. Sister Mart will soon come home from Tennessee and she will help me to plan.

October 5th, 1866.—My dress has been bought and Mrs. Kinnebrough says she will have all my things ready; the dress is of plain white silk, to be trimmed with pearl bandings and illusion. With it I am to wear Sister Mag's lovely set of pearls. I like time-honored customs, so have ordered a wreath and corsage bouquet of orange blossoms from Paris. They will come on the next steamer. There is one time-honored custom, however, which will not be observed. There is to be nothing intoxicating served to the guests at my wedding. No wife nor mother shall look back with mortification to my wedding night. Another custom also has been prohibited by Mother's orders: She has let all our friends know that "no wedding presents must be sent." She says the South is impoverished, there are few who can afford to give a handsome gift and yet almost every one will spend that which they can ill-afford, rather than be outdone in generous giving. I am well satisfied with this arrangement. I would not like to think our friends had deprived themselves to give to us. Mother is quite right.

We have company most of the time these days, coming and going, day by day. Sometimes I think I would like the quiet home life just now.

October 16th, 1866.—Father has given me a beautiful little book to read, "The Ribbon of Blue." It tells of the necessity of love and forbearance in the married state and is full of selections from poets, who have written on that subject. And yet, after all, there is no advice better than was given to us by an old negro preacher, when we met him on the road.

He stopped us and said, "I done hear dat you chilluns is gwine ter git marri'd."

"That is so," said my Soldier. "What do you think of it, Uncle Caesar?"

"I thinks well of it, but I got suppin' fur ter tell de bofe of you, Trus' in de Lord, dat is needful, but dere's anurer thing: don't you nebber, de two er you, git mad at de same time."

Now, if that is not matrimonial wisdom I cannot see where you will find it.

October 28th, 1866.—It has been said "the course of true love never does run smooth," but our marriage seems to have met with the approval of all concerned. I am glad it is so. Both families are perfectly satisfied, no one comes to the front with *objections* as is often the case. We will live here with Father and Mother and I fail to see what more I could ask of life.

November 1st, 1866.—My dear little friend, my confidential friend of many years, I am telling you goodbye. Whatever the future may bring me of weal or woe will not be recorded. This is MY DAY, my wedding day.

"Happy is the bride that the sun shines on" and from dawn until the evening hour the sun has shone forth in all his splendor. Soon the man of God will come and with him will come "My Soldier in Gray," and

> "I'll love him more, more,
> Than wife e'er did before
> Be the days dark or bright."

THE EPPES COAT OF ARMS

we learned it; all superfluities were given up; we almost forgot there were such things as amusements. New books and a variety of magazines and newspapers, which had once been considered necessaries, were dropped from the list and, in most households, *The Savannah News* was our only communication with foreign affairs or with distant parts of our own country.

An occasional *New York Metropolitan,* was passed around and almost read to pieces. Had not the hands been so busily employed the minds might have suffered, but labor, done intelligently, gives mental stimulus as well as bodily strength.

These large families of sturdy boys and girls grew apace, soon they were big enough to help and, all the time they were growing, they were imbibing a love for Dixie and all it represented. They listened with delight to the stirring tales of warfare told by their sires and proudly hailed the stars and bars as "OUR FLAG."

But this came afterward, or rather, it came so gradually that we did not know it had happened. Changes came with lightning-like rapidity and we dared not look the future in the face.

CHAPTER II

THE BIRTH OF THE NEW SOUTH

WHEN General Lee surrendered the Army of Northern Virginia at Appomattox, the Old South received a death blow but life was not yet extinct. The suffering brought about for this proud people by the many insults they received at the hands of the conquering foe cannot be told in words. Oftentimes these were of such a petty nature that one wonders that they were not passed unnoticed, but the lightest touch smarts and burns on a raw surface, and our wounds were fresh.

First came an order from headquarters to the clergy of Tallahassee; the President of the Confederacy must not be prayed for, but every minister in the city must pray for the President of the United States. We were in church when the venerable Bishop Rutledge was trying to obey this order. His long white hair, like spun silk, was gently stirred by the Spring breeze, from the window at his back, his surplice falling about his aged and shrunken figure gave him an almost unearthly appearance. He was a Southerner of Southerners, and for four years his whole heart had gone up in prayer for Jefferson Davis, the South's adored President. Now with trembling lips and unsteady voice he began his prayer: "Oh, Lord, Our Heavenly Father, the High and Mighty Ruler of the Universe, Who doth from Thy Throne behold all the dwellers upon earth; most heartily we beseech Thee with Thy favor to behold and bless Thy servant The President of the Confederate States." Realizing his mistake, the poor old head fell low on his breast as he retrieved himself, and in a faltering voice repeated: "Thy servant the President of the United States and all others in authority."

That was all, but even pin-pricks hurt. The next

Sunday, wishing to know how the Methodist Church met the difficulty, we attended divine service in that church and listened to the Reverend Orson Branch, one of the South's ablest divines. Slender and graceful, intellect shining forth from his fine eyes, not yet attained to middle age, he stood in the pulpit of Trinity Church and a crowded congregation waited patiently for him to begin service. With one delicate hand upraised, he invoked God's blessing on his flock. In the Methodist Church there are no set forms of prayer and on our bended knees we listened while he continued: "Almighty God, Our Father, in Whom we have all faith and Whose mercy we do not doubt, for whom the Lord loveth He chasteneth, and scourgeth every son whom He would receive, we most humbly beseech Thee to look down upon Thy servant, the President of the United States and so endue him with Thy wisdom and Thy loving kindness, that he may realize his responsibility and the difficulties of his position. Open his eyes to *the truth* and, seeing, give him of Thy grace, that he may walk in the paths of truth and justice."

Thus did the Reverend Orson Branch comply with the order.

This prayer for the President of the United States was a part of the morning service in all the churches, so the following Sunday we betook ourselves to the Presbyterian church, to listen to Dr. John E. DuBose, a man who differed in many ways from Bishop Rutledge and from the young minister of the Methodist church. Dr. DuBose was tall and well proportioned, with the easy movements of an athlete, the strength of half a dozen ordinary men, and, (whisper it low) a temper to match his strong arm.

We were a little late, the invocation had been spoken and the choir was singing "Rock of Ages." We stole quietly in and when the hymn was ended we rose with the congregation for prayer. We have not told you that this Presbyterian pastor was a gifted man; one whom it was a pleasure to hear. Now, as his deep voice was raised in supplication, we did not wish to miss a single word. In eloquent, well-chosen language, he prayed for many things, but that we had come to hear came not. A slight pause and then the clear, distinct voice went on, "Father of Mercies, we most earnestly beseech Thee to bless and comfort Thy servant, Jefferson Davis, give him of Thy grace, that he may bear patiently the trials of captivity for he, even as Thyself, Oh, Lord, is bearing the cross for his people. We most earnestly pray that Thou wilt take under Thy care and guidance Thy servant, the President of these United States of America, open his eyes that he may see aright, open his heart that he may do Thy will, set his feet in the paths of righteousness and give him strength, that he may walk therein. This we ask in the name of the Father, the Son and the Holy Ghost."

With tear dimmed eyes his congregation gathered about Dr. DuBose as he left the church, a grasp of the hand, a sudden turning away, the silent passing of the church-goers to their homes, spoke more eloquently than words. All hearts echoed his prayer for the prisoner who was to us so dear.

Relations between the conqueror and the conquered could have been made less bitter if these annoyances had been avoided. The young men, aye, and the old ones, too, returning from the army had only the gray uniform to wear. An order was first issued that no man should appear in public in Confederate uniform. When Mr. Hopkins and some others, represented to the Federal authorities that these men had nothing else to wear, the order was changed to read that "all brass buttons, all insignia of rank, must be removed, or covered." A wave of indignation followed this piece of petty spite.

So it went on; continually something was done that

hurt the Southerner's pride. Constant dropping wears away stone, we are told, and the patience of our people was sorely tried. The incessant haling of our men and our women as well, before a military tribunal, to be tried and condemned, without the slightest pretense of justice, aroused intense bitterness. We did not know when morning dawned what might befall us ere the sun went down. Insolence from the negroes became more and more frequent. Much of this friction could have been prevented, but feeling ran high on both sides.

Then the Freedman's Bureau was established and the carpetbaggers came like unto an army of locusts, seeking what they could devour. If life for the Southerner was hard before, it became almost unendurable under these conditions. Yes, the Old South was slowly but surely dying; that is to say, the Old South was dying politically, financially and socially, but the spirit of the Old South can never die. So long as a loyal son or daughter of the Old South remains, they will recall with pride the glorious deeds of the armies of the Southern Confederacy; they will speak with tenderness of the war work of Southern women; they will

"Tell it to the last of times,
No Nation rose so fair and white
Nor fell so free of crimes."

The traditions, the principles, the customs of bygone days will be forever cherished and we hug to our hearts these comforting lines,

"Truth crushed to earth will rise again,
The eternal years of God are hers,
While error, wounded, writhes in pain
And dies amid her worshipers."

Now we will tell of this New South, which the year of our Lord Eighteen-hundred and Sixty-six brought forth. Up to this time few among us had realized the extent of our misfortunes.

While the South was gifted with brains, intelligence, accomplishments, and imagination, not many had as yet awakened to the fact that each one of us had been given two hands with which to labor, but now we were to learn. Like some child learning to walk, making slow progress yet growing stronger with every effort, the New South was building better than she knew.

In January, 1866, the negroes left the old plantations and sought other homes. At first they went into camp near some department of the Freedman's Bureau and demanded to be fed. This demand was complied with. Then the request was made for the "Forty acres and a mule," which had been promised them by their Northern friends. When these were not forthcoming, a howl of rage filled the land. Disgusted at this, provisions ceased to be rationed out and the negroes were told to hunt work.

Throughout the year 1866, they were trying to adjust themselves to some form of employment, which would give them food and shelter without work. Failing in this, the year 1867 would have been hard on them but for the fact that cotton rose to such an attractive price that the planters thought they saw a future, both for themselves and for the negroes. Enthusiastic men, imbued with the idea of making anew, fortunes from the fleecy staple, hired the negroes under the impression that they were still reliable farm hands, who could be trusted to make now, as they had done in slavery times, a heavy crop of cotton. "King Cotton" ruled once more and we had hope, if nothing else.

The homes of the South, even in those parts where the enemy had not had the opportunity to strip them, had been shorn of almost everything in the effort to help our soldiers. Men, women and children lacked the clothing needful for comfort and there was no money with which to purchase these necessaries. The whole country began to have a shabby appearance and this cotton crop was looked forward to with delight.

In the Spring of 1866, Dr. Bradford, like many others, thought of going to Brazil. He offered his Horse-shoe Plantation for sale and the first person to make an offer was Major Hancock, of the Army of Occupation. One cool bright Sunday morning in January he came and requested to be shown over the plantation, as he did not care to purchase until he had satisfied himself that it was worth the price asked.

Dr. Bradford could not accompany him so requested Captain Taylor, his son-in-law, to do so. Major Hancock wore over his blue suit an overcoat of white fur, it fitted rather loosely and he rode his horse *a la Yankee*. Captain Taylor had on a Confederate uniform, which came via Nassau, just previous to the surrender, consequently it was quite new and the gold lace and brass buttons had neither been removed nor covered. He rode a splendid horse, one he had used in Virginia and, though it was thin enough when it first came home, it was now in fine condition. He was a skillful horseman and rode his steed with all ease and grace. As the two men left the grove all remarked upon the difference in appearance.

They were gone for hours and dinner was on the table when they returned. Of course Major Hancock was invited to stay to dinner, which he did. After dinner he sat long with Dr. Bradford in the library, ostensibly making arrangements to buy the plantation. The young ladies of the family did not appear at dinner, but the parlor was near enough for sounds of merry voices to be heard by those in the library and Major Hancock listened with much dissatisfaction.

Late in the afternoon, hearing the front door open, he bade the doctor a hasty adieu and reached the door just as Lieutenant Eppes, also dressed in Confederate uniform, was descending the steps.

A formal bow passed between them and, as they mounted their horses, the Major said: "If you do not object I shall ride along with you."

No objection was made and they rode in silence for a time; then the Major said, "Why do you continue to wear that uniform? Don't you know the war is over?"

"Yes, I know that but you fellows haven't left us anything to buy with and there is a law against dispensing with one's clothing."

"Is that a fact?" questioned he, then growing confidential, he went on to say he had been at Pine Hill the greater part of the day, he had fooled the doctor into thinking he wanted his plantation, when what he really wanted was to get acquainted with the doctor's daughter.

"Perhaps if I could get to know her I might be able to kill two birds with one stone," he said. The vanity of man!

But the Doctor had now given up all thought of going to Brazil and once more he undertook the growing of cotton. The New South owes its re-habilitation to the Old South and her friends. But for the commission merchants of New York, there would have been only failure for these war-worn veterans. They had dealt with Southern planters for years before the outbreak of the war; they had tested them out; they had proved their honesty; they were well aware of the fact that a Southerner's word was his bond and they did not hesitate to trust them in this fresh adventure in the financial world. God be praised that always, everywhere, are found some men with hearts!

In this way the rebuilding of our fortunes was begun, but we had many other difficulties other than the lack of money. The negroes had learned much of evil from their carpetbagger friends, and it became dangerous for women and children unattended, to go abroad, even in sight of their homes.

In the past they could have exclaimed, with Moore's heroine,

"Sir Knight, I feel not the least alarm,
No son of Erin would offer me harm."

But fear, and terror, had taken the place of confidence and, for safety, a large enclosure of some thirty acres had been made adjoining the backyard at Pine Hill. It had a high "stake and rider" fence, no entrance from the Thomasville and Tallahassee road and a thick growth of native viburnum, prickley ash, red oak and pine screened it completely from the eyes of the passers-by. A short distance from the road a pretty pond was surrounded by willows and the ground was thickly carpeted with flowers, such as grow near the waters-edge. It was a truly delightful play-ground and here the horses were turned out to graze and the boys to amuse themselves. The only convenient way to leave the enclosure was to come through the yard and we had tried to impress it upon our youngsters that they must never climb the fence, or indeed go near enough to the road to be seen.

There always comes a day, however, when forbidden fruit seems the fairest and one afternoon as we sat sewing, feeling that the boys were safe, we heard several shots in quick succession and a child's scream. A party of negroes, returning from Tallahassee and drinking heavily, had stopped by the branch to quench their thirst. It so happened that at the same time the boys had resolved to climb the fence and go home by the road. It was most unfortunate this should have occurred, for, no sooner did the drunken negroes spy the three little boys, (the eldest was only nine) than they began to fire, round after round, at the little fellows. If they could have aimed true, no doubt they would all have been killed. Though the shot cut the shrubbery from the road-side, the boys were not hurt. It is needless to say they came through the yard after that.

"Festivals" were of frequent occurrence. We had

a good cook whose services (out of hours) were much in request among the negroes giving the festivals. Sometimes she gave one herself. These frolics were disorderly in the extreme and, as they were countenanced by the carpetbaggers, it was difficult to do anything about it. Often murder resulted but it was hushed up and, as there was no law save military law, unless the authorities saw fit to investigate, it went by the board.

It was night at Pine Hill Plantation, and after a hard day's work, we were so tired that every bone ached. Two small children, one a baby in arms, had to have attention and, after bathing and dressing the tiny tots for the night, we lay down beside the oldest one, on his little trundle bed, and, with the baby clasped in loving arms, began to tell a bed-time story. Soon all three were fast asleep. Tired as we were an unusual odor intruded itself, a smell which never fails to bring recognition, the sickening odor of fresh blood. We had dogs and we thought it might be that they had been out for game and had carried it under the house. Too sleepy to carry the thought further, we were soon lost to the world. The familiar and welcome step of our liege lord, on the long piazza, roused us and we hastened to let him in at the door. Both babies slept soundly and we left them for the supper room. Here broiled chicken, fragrant coffee, hot biscuit and fresh butter were in waiting and, as all was quiet in the nursery, no haste was made. Supper disposed of, the news of the day was discussed and the day's happenings were duly chronicled for our benefit. Returning, at last, to the nursery, a frightful apparition met our eyes; a negro man stood there. From two terrible gashes, one in the face and a longer one on the scalp, the blood oozed slowly.

No need to wonder now whence had come the loathsome smell. His shirt was torn almost off of him and from head to foot his clothing was soaked in blood.

Repressing a scream, lest we wake the babies, we clung to our dear protector and he, after a searching look said: "Spencer Davis, what are you doing in this room?"

Not until he said this did we recognize the creature before us. He was a carpenter employed on the place and well liked by all. Respectful, obliging, rather more faithful about his work than most of the free negroes, he rarely had trouble with anyone. Now we listened for his story. He opened his mouth, tried to speak and fell full length at our feet.

"We must not let him die," said the man he served. "Get some old linen and some sticking plaster, while I get hot water."

Both of us knew how to dress wounds, having learned in the war-times, and soon the fainting ngero was revived, the blood stanched and, after a stiff drink of Bourbon, he told us how it happened.

We will spare you the lingo and tell it in our own words.

He had been to a festival and there was a large crowd with plenty to eat and far more than enough to drink. He got into an altercation with another man and struck him in the face, knocking him over backward. His head hit the grindstone and Spencer was sure he had killed him. The man's wife attacked him and in a minute, drunken and enraged, the whole body of frolickers had turned to vengeful demons and were trying to take "a life for a life." How he escaped he could not tell, but terror lent wings and he made his way to the white folks, who he was sure would help him.

"How did you get into my room when all the doors were locked?" we asked.

"I clum in de windo' whilst you wus a-puttin' de chillun ter bed an' I hid," he said. "I knowed dem blood-houn's wouldn't nebber look in here fur me."

While he talked we could hear wild, hoarse cries from "the quarter" and poor Spencer shuddered.

Helping him into our dressing room we locked him in and betook ourselves and the children to an upstairs apartment, where we could get away from such awful surroundings. For two or three days he remained hidden in the smoke-house and then, when we assured him the fellow he struck was well again, he ventured forth. The episode was apparently forgotten, but not by us, and barrel bolts supplemented the locks and fastenings made the windows secure. Spencer was duly grateful and remained on the plantation for years. The horror of that moment when we faced the bloody negro, will never be forgotten.

It was winter, it was also cold; the one does not always mean the other in Florida, and for nearly two weeks the rain had fallen continuously. Now, on Christmas Eve, the sun shone out and, though the wind was cutting, we felt that we must take advantage of the change in the weather to go to Tallahassee for Christmas gifts for the children. No automobiles in those days and the roads were deep in mud and the farm horses we drove had long ago lost spirit as farm horses are apt to do. We made slow progress and the clock was striking twelve as we entered town, so we had but little time to shop. We had accumulated many bundles and we had only an errand or so and then we would be ready to set out on the homeward journey. This was at a time when the carpetbagger regime was in full force and the police of Tallahassee were negroes, including the chief of police.

The town was thronged with colored people keeping "Crismus." The farm wagon, in which we had come to town, was standing in front of a newly opened store of fancy groceries and we expected to make our last purchases there. Hurrying along, lest it be black night ere we reached home, we suddenly felt ourselves pushed violently from the crowded side-walk into the middle of the muddy street. The sidewalk was some feet above the street at that point and the fall was hard and with such force that we made a deep imprint in the mud and slush. As we fell, a familiar voice exclaimed, "Tak' dat, you dirty nigger."

Quick as thought a pair of strong arms were supporting us and we felt ourselves once more upon the sidewalk and looking in the face of a tall, fine-looking young negro in the uniform of the chief of police; he was no other than Archer, Aunt Dinah's youngest son, and owned by us in the days of slavery.

"My Mistis," he said, "is dat nasty nigger hurt you? I dun showed him what'll happen to any o' dem what meddles my white folks." Sure enough there he lay in the street, apparently dead.

"Oh, Archer!" we cried, "you have killed him!"

"No, Miss Sue," he replied, "I ain't dun' him half bad enuf, dis here club kin stun, but hit don't kill."

Tenderly he tried to wipe off the filthy mud and, walking beside us, he soon found our liege lord, who waited for us at the new store; he was standing by his horses, in conversation with Senator Conover, Florida's carpetbag representative in the United States Senate. The Senator looked on with a shocked expression while Archer recounted the adventure. When he had finished his explanation, he touched his cap respectfully and turning to us he said:

"When you cums ter town you jis' 'member dat it's your own nigger is chief er perlice, an' he ain't gwine ter let nobody hurt you."

In days gone by this could not have happened, behold the leaven of the carpetbagger; surely it was working to the detriment of both white and black. The political status had changed as entirely as had the financial situation. In 1867-'8 the Black Republican Party purchased the *Florida Sentinel,* formerly a Whig organ, and published by decent men. We have forgotten if the name was changed, but the character certainly was, as evidenced by the verses which were published therein, and presented in the next chapter.

CHAPTER III

NEGRO RIGHTS

All dat de white folks got is ouren,
  We'll git it, sure's you born,
De cows, de pigs, de chickens,
  De cotton an' de corn.

Wid de ax we'll smash de smoke-house door,
  Whey de shoulders an' hams hang high,
Wid sassiges an' pigs feet
  Ready fur us ter fry.

We'll res' in de Marster's parlor,
  An' den we'll help ourselves,
Ter de cakes, de jams, de jellies
  What sets on de pantry shelves.

When we is eat all us kin hold
  An' can't tote off no more,
We'll stick a great big littud torch
  Inside de Marster's door.

We'll sing an' shout, an' dance about,
  An' watch de flames go higher,
An' de white folks dassent raise a hand
  Ter outen out de fire.

THESE incendiary lines called forth indignant protest from many sources. Had these come from the South alone it would probably have been disregarded, but we still had some friends at the North and, in England was a growing regret that they had left the South to fight her battles unaided. Lord Haughton's answer to Father Ryan's Conquered Banner expresses this feeling:

Gallant Nation, foiled by numbers,
  Say not that your hopes are dead
Keep that glorious Flag that slumbers,
  One day to avenge your dead.

Keep it, widowed, son-less mothers,
Keep it, sisters, mourning brothers,
Furl it with an iron will;
Furl it now, but—keep it, still;
  Think not that its work is done.

Keep it till your children take it,
Once again to hail and make it
All their sires have bled and fought for,
All their noble hearts have sought for,
  Bled and fought for, all alone.

All alone! Aye, shame the story,
  Millions here deplore the stain,
Shame alas! for England's glory,
  Freedom called and called in *vain.*

Furl that Banner sadly, slowly,
Treat it gently, for 'tis Holy.
Till that day—yes, furl it sadly,
Then once more un-furl it gladly—
  Conquered Banner—Keep it, still.

Finding public sentiment too strong to be ignored, the management of the paper was changed and it became much less objectionable. A man who called himself Saunders, and seemed to be able to walk unlimited miles without tiring, made incendiary speeches throughout the county. Gin-houses were fired; many bales of cotton were destroyed; dwelling houses were watched by the occupants thereof, night and day; sometimes torches were found and extinguished before it was too late and occasionally a dwelling burned to the ground. Life became a horrid night-mare.

Crimes, too vile for words became of frequent occurrence and it came to be, in what had once been considered the centre of civilization, that "every man's home was his castle" in reality. Guns and pistols were kept loaded and ready; yes, and the women and children, the larger ones, were taught to use these weapons for their personal protection.

It was as though even our Heavenly Father had deserted us. No light of promise illumined our sky but all was darkness and gloom. Only love, that greatest of blessings, kept us from utter despair. Love is strong and stimulates exertion, and we held our heads high and put a bold front in evidence wherever we could.

One Sunday we attended service at dear old Mount Zion. The minister, a middle aged man from West Virginia, had been most kindly treated in the Bradford neighborhood; he had been on the circuit for years and at every home in the neighborhood he and his family had been entertained, sometimes for weeks. In the event of a lengthy visit, a nurse was provided for the children. If the minister's wife had any sewing she wished done, the family seamstress was at her disposal; if material was lacking, Tallahassee was near at hand and there was an account at every store in town. Life was easy for the lady in question, while these visits lasted and both she and her husband expressed gratitude.

We had heard that he had made some unwelcome remarks in the pulpit at Pisgah, but we did not wish to condemn him unheard and, on this bright and beautiful Sunday morning, a large congregation had gathered at Mount Zion to hear him preach, and each had come provided for a liberal addition to "the plate," when it should be passed. The minister was a little late—tall awkward, lanky man, with pale yellow hair, which clung closely to an ill shaped head and watery blue eyes of the palest tint imaginable. He was not pleasing to the sight but the attendants at the old church had not been raised to criticise the man of God, but to be respectful and attentive.

After the preliminary services, he took for his text Mark, 10th chapter, 25th verse. "It is easier for a camel to go through the eye of a needle than for a rich man to enter the kingdom of God."

A long pause followed the reading of the text, then he proceeded to expatiate upon the danger of riches; the evil effect the holding of great possessions had upon the human heart; the ultimate damnation of the rich man and the utter impossibility of salvation for such a one.

It was a lengthy sermon, harping ever upon the text. At the last he extended his long arms and raising his voice he shouted out, "But now, thank God, we are all poor alike." His palms came together with a resounding clap.

Again extending the black-sleeved arms, he cried out in a still louder voice, "Yes, we are all poor alike, thank God we are all poor alike. No high, no low, the Great Leveller has swept the earth and we are all poor alike. Thank God! Thank God!!

It is needless to say that the Reverend —— ——— never preached again for the Bradford neighborhood and the doors of Mount Zion closed upon him forever.

To rejoice in the misfortunes of others is not commendable at any time, but, it was doubly contemptible, when the sufferers had once been his benefactors. He still continued in the Florida Conference but we have never forgotten the almost demoniacical expression on his sallow face as he exulted in our reverses.

CHAPTER IV

THE KU KLUX KLAN

WITH the advent of the year 1866, the situation grew worse and worse. Carpetbaggers swarmed down upon the land, sowing the seeds of hate and discord between the whites and blacks. So successful were they in this nefarious work, that but little else was known and there were secret meetings held by the blacks, presided over by these aforesaid carpetbaggers.

Incendiary speeches were made and the torch was openly advocated by these demons in human form. Something clearly, must be done, but *what?*

Near Washington, Georgia, lived some scions of the old families of the South and these men had, for the most part, been first school boys together, then they had been college mates and then comrades in arms. This last tie was strongest of all and now, that a common danger confronted them all, they met to consider some plan of action.

We will not try to give you a history of the famous Ku Klux Klan. Almost in the twinkling of an eye, the country was over-run by ghostly riders, on horses, whose feet made no sound; fiery crosses, borne aloft by fleshless hands; fearful voices, which struck terror to the souls of their hearers. Here one minute and gone the next, riding like mad through groups of frightened negroes; caring not who was stricken down by the noiseless hoofs of these mighty steeds.

Where, heretofore, it had been the custom to hold the meetings we have described, several times a week, now some secluded spot was sought by the leading carpet knights and only now and then could a crowd be collected, the fear of the Fiery Cross and the ghostly riders was so great.

When the group of men who organized the Ku Klux first engaged in it they planned a disguise, which was as simple as it was effective, being nothing more nor less than a sheet, in which some slits were made, for convenience in arranging it to suit the wearer. To strengthen these slits, bindings of black were used and, so much did the touch of black add to the frightful appearance, that still more was used and now and then a dash of red.

Of course the ladies made these robes and it often fell to their lot to hide them as well, for the military authorities spared no pains to discover the identity of the supernatural riders, who struck terror to the hearts of both the negroes and their Yankee friends.

There was no law but military law in those days, and as no search warrant was needed, the dwelling houses were entered and searched at any hour of the day or night.

Not often, however, were the robes found and woe to the men of the family if a Ku Klux robe was found on the premises. They were immediately arrested and nothing short of "The Dry Tortugas" was considered a sufficient punishment.

More than once have we known the disguise to be tightly tied in a bundle and dropped into the well, to be patiently fished out when the officers of the law were gone. One dear old grandmother sat on a cushion made of three robes belonging to her three grandsons. She was always too deaf to hear, too blind to see and yet *so polite* and *so ready* to rise from her chair to have it investigated, that the cushion was never ripped open, which would have disclosed her secret. You doubtless have read of other klans than this one we are telling you of, but these incidents came to us at first hand.

One member of this band was particularly fertile in imagination and, through him, came in the most frightful features of the Klan. Dr. William Carr came of an old Georgia family, which had come hither from the state of Virginia. Highly educated, he was practicing medicine when the War Between the States began and now, having served the four years of war, he was ready to do still more for his country. In his office hung an articulated skeleton and also a human arm, which could be moved easily by pulling on the wires. In anatomical experiments, Dr. Carr had used a large rubber bag, holding twelve gallons of liquid; these suggested possibilities to his mind, for it was necessary to keep the negroes frightened and to do that something new must be seen. For two weeks nothing had been seen or heard of the Ku Klux. On the heavily wooded side of a large pond or lake, the negro population of the entire country had gathered at the urgent call of their white exhorters. The meeting was at its height and Ichabod Crane himself could not have spoken more earnestly nor could his tones have been more painfully nasal. Groans and cries of "Yes, Lord"—"Dat's so"—"Ain't dat de trufe," and similar negro expressions from time to time interrupted the speaker. Secure in the thought that "de white folks kan't fin' us here," excitement grew greater with every sentiment from the speaker and every groan from the audience.

Suddenly a terrified scream came from the thick lips of a negro woman standing on the out-skirts and it was speedily echoed from every side. Slowly came a mighty throng of white-robed figures on horseback; in front rode the bearer of "The Cross of Fire;" behind him came, not "a Skeleton in Armor" but a skeleton clothed in nothing at all. A white robe like that worn by his companions floated from its back, fire gleamed from the empty skull and the outlines showed up in lines of fire. Closely following him, came his sheeted brothers. Slowly they came at first but as the terrified darkies took to the road, or ran pell-mell into the heavy brush, the Ku Klux speeded their horses and ran after the fleeing congregation and their not less frightened leaders.

It was a month or more before another meeting was held and this time it was in another county and a guard was set, causing a feeling of security to prevail. Far back in the woods in a large house, deserted by its owners and falling to decay, the negroes decided to meet. A well of good water was on the premises and six of the number had been told to act as guards, one being stationed at the well. Sleep is the negro's strong point. He can keep awake with the best if some noise is going on but, give him a comfortable seat and quiet, and sleep "steals on him unawares." Two hours after the speaking had begun the guards were sleeping "the sleep of the just." The night had been slightly cloudy but the moon suddenly shone forth in all her splendor, just as a lone Ku Klux drew rein at the well. The sleeping negro awoke to look straight at this awful visitant and then he yelled. Such screams might well have waked the dead and the meeting broke up in great confusion and the participants hurried in the direction of the sounds. Seeing only one Ku Klux, they thought it was a good time to show their courage so closed about him. In a loud, sepulchral voice the ghost said, "I am from HELL and I am burning up. Come to the well and draw me some water."

Afraid to disobey, the trembling negro took the windlass and, when the bucket appeared, he took the gourd which hung by the well and was about to hand it to Mr. Spook, when it was violently struck from his hand and the gentleman from Hell demanded the bucket.

"Did I not tell you I am burning up?" he cried.

Raising the bucket he drained it to the bottom and demanded another bucket to quench his thirst. Another and another were drawn and drained until ten bucketsful had been disposed of. This so staggered the crowd that none was willing to lay hands on the thirsty creature.

Raising his voice, he let forth such a stream of imprecations as had never been heard and, ere he had finished, a full two-score of his companions had silently ridden up behind the crowd and scattered them to the four winds, trampling them in the dirt, when they did not move fast enough to keep out of the way.

That put a stop to out-door meetings and in fact, to all gatherings, for a long time. Then, getting a little over their fear of the ghost who drank ten buckets of water, they held a meeting during the week, at a favorite church. Nothing disturbed the quiet of the evening save their own not inconsiderable noise. The meeting was over and the door, which had been closed and barred, was opened, when a white, gleaming, highly polished hand and arm, naked of flesh and rattling horribly, was extended into the door. This was followed by a foot, which held the door open and a voice from the grave, presumably, said:

"Dave, you and Pompey come here, your old Marster wants to shake hands with his faithful old servants."

Nobody wanted to shake hands and inside was a mighty scramble to get out. The windows were forced open and "Old Marster" was left to laugh at the success of the ruse.

That was the last meeting attempted by the negroes of the vicinity, however, the Ku Klux Klan did not disband but the organization was kept up until order was restored and then, to quote Grover Cleveland, the order "fell into innocuous desuetude," the need for its existence being past.

What we have told is but a truthful account of a small part of Georgia. What happened in Georgia happened in many other places, for the Southerners had their patience sorely tried and there was nothing they could do but "take up arms against a sea of troubles and by opposing, end them."

CHAPTER V

THE SOUTHERN WOMAN'S MEMORIAL ASSOCIATION

THIS was the first association of Southern women after the War Betwen the States. Perhaps it was the first in which the women of the land had regarded themselves in a sectional light. The War was over and in every home there was a vacant chair. In most homes there was more than one. Sick at heart and lonely beyond the telling, one impulse moved them all; if only they could erect monuments to their beloved dead.

Some, who had not been left so poverty-stricken, hastened to do this but to the women of Florida even this poor comfort was denied, for they were so poor that it was difficult to supply the daily needs of their households. Oftentimes it was impossible, for there were no extra dollars and dimes so they must wait.

We do not know when or how it became the custom for social functions, of a public nature, to be held in the Florida State Capitol, but such has been the case from the memory of the oldest inhabitant. The Tournament Balls were always held there, and in the childhood of "Ye Scribe," Professor Dusenberry had a dancing school somewhere within its walls and Blind Tom gave many concerts in the Hall of Representatives. Whenever local talent wished to disport itself, this same hall was pressed into service and after the war was over the great "Gee Festival" was held there. Fancy dress Balls, New Year Balls, Inauguration Balls, all these had a place there, but in December, in the year of our Lord eighteen hundred and sixty-six, the Capitol was staged for a very different play and a far different setting.

Making a plan, the women of the Memorial Association had worked most diligently and now, from St.

Mary's to Key West, from St. Augustine to Pensacola, from every hamlet and village the women of Florida came, laden with the work of their own hands, seeking to raise money to erect a monument to the memory of the Soldier Dead, whom they had loved so well. From St. Augustine, the Nuns, Heaven bless them, had brought Spanish work, such as they only could make; lace of cobweb fineness and embroideries, which might have been done by fairy fingers; baby dresses, which would fill every mother's heart with longing; all these and more.

From Pensacola came many beautiful things, among them some priceless Spanish relics, held by their owners as precious heirlooms, but yielded up now because of the great love they bore their dead. Key West displayed the most exquisite shell work and sets of jewelry, made of fish scales and many lovely articles besides. The women all over the state sent dainty handwork. There were paintings, too, of no low order of merit, and these paintings were framed by the same loving fingers which wielded the brush. The materials used for the frames were pine cones, from which ferns and other foliage were made with flowers, or grapes of kid, all finished with shellac. Every fruit known to Florida was represented at this fair; put up in glass, the translucent beauty of the contents attracted all eyes. Cakes, made by capable house-keepers and ornamented by skillful fingers, drew forth many expressions of wonder and admiration; home-made candies in great variety and dozens of other things, which memory does not at this moment recall.

From far and near with loving hearts they had brought their treasures and now, with soft steps, they, the black-robed figures moved around the hall of Representatives, placing their offerings to the best advantage, on table or in show-cases. Of course there were some bright dresses but nearly every woman in the gathering of the daughters of Florida, wore the heavy black, which speaks so plainly of death and bereavement. Never before or since has the old Capitol opened its doors on such a scene.

Our country was poverty-stricken and the sales were slow. The prices were small, indeed, compared with the value of the articles offered, but we did not lose heart, and for seventeen long years the women of the Memorial Association let no opportunity pass to sell something, which would add to the sum brought in by the fair.

By this time it was well understood that when a sufficient sum of money should be raised a committee, selected by the votes of the Association, from different parts of our State, should be appointed to select a design and an inscription and erect the monument in the Capitol Grounds at Tallahassee to Florida's heroic dead. These conditions were not complied with but in 1882 a few women ordered a marble shaft and, without consulting the Association, had an inscription carved upon it, which gave us the heartache and made us feel that our work had been in vain.

In the South are many monuments to the Confederate Heroes and in every town of any size, in our sister state of Georgia, the first thing you see on entering it is this memorial to "The Lost Cause." No doubt it is the same in other states, but we venture to say there is not one among the number as small and insignificant, as plain and badly executed as this one, which the women of Florida placed in the grounds of Florida's Capitol, in memory of the men who fought and died for us; men whose glory will shine forth to the end of time.

Perhaps, who knows, some day the granddaughters of these Women of the Confederacy, looking at this shabby shaft, will say, one to another, "What a bitter disappointment it must have been to our grandmothers to see the fruits of their labors dwindle down to this.

We are no longer poverty-stricken, we have plenty and to spare, let us band together and erect in Capitol Square, a monument which would gladden the eyes of those devoted women; a monument which shall be worthy of the cause it commemorates."

May this dream come true, dear grandchildren of our past.

CHAPTER VI

THE HOSPITALITY OF THE NEW SOUTH

ALL the world and his wife have heard of the boundless hospitality of the Old South but few of this present generation have realized it. For real true love of his fellow-man, the old-time Southerner has no equal. It was a genuine delight to him to gather his friends about him, to spend days and weeks in entertaining them, in spreading before them, for their delectation all luxuries that money could buy. Nor was it only his friends who were made welcome; the friends of his friends found doors and hearts open to them when they came duly recommended. This was truly necessary, for this old-time Southerner was very particular who entered his sanctum, the sacredness of home was never forgotten. He must know *who* it was he was expected to receive but, once satisfied on that score, all was well. Nor did his hospitality end there, for the stranger within his gates, however lowly he might be, received a full meed of kindness, politeness and consideration. Aristocrat, he might be, but he was certainly democratic in the polite treatment accorded to all respectable folks. For such as he did not consider respectable, there was no place. With servants galore and money to spare, there was practically no limit to this far-famed hospitality. All this was as it should have been but because of this prodigality the New South suffered. In homes where the latch-string hung on the outside in other days, these new Southerners had to entertain, whether they wished or no. Kinspeople and friends had long been accustomed to come and go as they liked, without the preliminary note or message. A carriage would roll up and the occupants would alight and a hearty welcome was, in every instance, expected.

Perhaps changes had come to their own homes but never once did they ever realize that changes had come to these relatives also.

No servants, or perhaps just one, who was simply a helper to the busy mistress of the household. On the pantry shelves, where, in former days all the goodies which could be made, found a place, now stand empty jars or no jars at all; a little of this needful food-stuff or of that. Where once nothing smaller than a barrel of flour found place, sits now a small sack and the sugar bucket is often empty. The instincts of former hospitality are not lacking but the materials for taking care of guests certainly are.

Yet to these poverty-stricken homes guests come; just as they did in the years of plenty. The worm turned at last, trodden too often under the foot of "hard times." The house-mothers of this New South used their ingenuity and devised other ways of showing affection for their relatives and friends. House-parties became more and more infrequent, spend-the-day parties were occasional events and evening entertainments were most popular. The weeks of visiting, the coming of uninvited guests, the practical turning of one's home into a hostelry, is over forever. The New South has learned its limitations. Is it to be deplored or is it not? In these latter days, when the housekeeper takes her guests to the tea-room, the country club, the many and varied resorts of this pleasure-loving world, to the "movies," the golf links or the tennis courts, anywhere but to her own home. It is hard to believe that our ancestors took such trouble to entertain.

The sanctuary of the heart, that was what HOME once meant but now, in this year of our Lord nineteen and twenty-six, it is a place to come back to when there is nothing else doing, a place in which to sleep and possibly to eat, though that depends. If you have no servants (and they are sometimes hard to get and hard to keep) then the cafe is the first thought, or if you are a little more particular, then the tea room. There is no time for the home. If you want to rest, why, there is the Cinnema, where, under the cooling breezes brought about by the ever-present electric fan, your tired nerves are soothed and your mind is filled by the thrilling scenes depicted upon the screen.

What does it matter if the old-fashioned virtues are laid aside and forgotten? 'Tis said that history repeats itself. The repetition may bring about a different situation and we may again see the old-time hospitality of the Old South, but this generation will have everything to learn if such should be the case.

> "Sitting beside the fire-side of the heart,
> Feeding its flames,"

has gone out of style.

CHAPTER VII

A NEW BEGINNING

OUTWARDLY the Old South was dead, her economic system was in ruins, her wealth had taken wings, her man-power was depleted. Heart-sick and weary the Southerner gathered up the threads of life and essayed to travel the rough and stony path before him. In this he was aided and upheld by that which has ever been to man an inspiration and a light in the dark hours of life, the unselfish *love of woman.* Heavy-hearted, she resolutely put aside all semblance of woe. Unused to labor, she performed the heaviest and most disagreeable tasks with a smile and a song. Deprived of all the little accessories to dainty housewifery she beautified her home with flowers and sunshine—and her men were well worth the effort.

Just how many backs ached beneath the unaccustomed burdens; just how many sleepless nights were passed because the tired limbs and weary brain made sleep impossible, will never be known. Some fell by the wayside, "wearied with the march of life." Some turned their faces in another direction, and sought "green fields and pastures new," but for the most part the men of the South stood as firmly by their country in these dark days of Reconstruction as they had done when fighting for her rights in battle array.

The men who worked out the redemption of the South through Reconstruction were *super-men.* Home-life in the South was changed beyond the telling. Where once wealth abounded, poverty stalked, gaunt and bare. Where once the willing service of the blacks made the household machinery move smoothly on, while conversation was carried on or company entertained, the guests must either sit alone, while the head of the house feeds and waters his horse and his wife prepares the meal, with which he would later be regaled. Or, the guest must follow the steps of his entertainers, to snatch a word here and there, or if in an accommodating humor, assist in the household tasks. There was always a baby to be cared for, sometimes, two or three, and one had only to look around to find opportunity for usefulness.

The negroes grew increasingly idle and hard to control and higher and higher wages they demanded but the work accomplished did not warrant the outlay. The cotton planter was fast going to the wall. For so long we had thought "cotton is king" that it was hard to believe otherwise, yet we found starvation staring us in the face, and every peg on which a hope could hang was eagerly sought after.

In our own state of Florida, the carpetbaggers had plunged the State into a perfect slough of despond of debt. Florida was looked upon by outsiders as the abiding place of snakes, lizards and alligators. When the natives of this reptile-infested country were not shaking with a chill they were scorching with a fever. Although Florida's acreage was large, there were no facilities for transportation. Capitol hooted when invited to invest in a land which was lovely beyond words and was possessed of a climate, which would one day draw thousands upon thousands seeking investment. Lands had but little value. Many left for foreign countries, failing to recognize the fact that Florida was really the "Paradise of the Gods." Such a struggle as it was even to exist, during those years, and the bitterest part was the *political situation.* Negroes sat in the legislative halls in our Capitol, negroes filled most of the county offices throughout the State. The few white men holding office were either "carpetbaggers" or "scalawags," and no choice between them. In our courts, justice was an unknown quantity; the

"Sword of Damocles" hung over us day in and day out.

It is always darkest just before day they say. Our God holds out a helping hand to us, though we sometimes fail to see it and so, into this political maelstrom stepped William D. Bloxham, a man of unusual ability and force of character, and a native Floridian. Young, talented, highly educated, he gave of his gifts freely to save his people. William D. Bloxham had married, early in life, Miss Mary Davis, of Virginia, a lovely woman in every sense of the word.

Born to the purple, an "F. F. V.," she proved to be just the helpmate he needed. Her gentle hand was strong as iron when it came to holding him to the straight and narrow path. In his later years he was often heard to say, "All that I am I owe to my wife." Bravely this young and attractive woman stayed at home and held together the fast diminishing farming interests of Captain Bloxham, while he fought the political battles of Florida, as earnestly as he had faced the foe, in the days of real warfare.

Traversing the State, from end to end, he had an opportunity to learn much of Florida's needs and her resources and this man of wonderful memory never forgot what he had once learned. Through defeat and disaster, through the long, weary hours of rough and uncomfortable travel, through the excitement of final triumph, he never lost sight of the decisions he had made as to the best thing to be done for the welfare of his native state. It would take volumes to tell of all he has done for Florida.

As leader of the forlorn hopes of the Democratic Party, he met, and bore cheerfully, one defeat after another. A less confident and courageous man would have laid down his arms and ceased the seemingly useless struggle; not so with William D. Bloxham. Nobly seconded by the soldiers who had worn the gray, he led his followers against the oppression of the Freedman's Bureau; the reckless spending of the State's money and the utter ruin which stared her citizens in the face. Deeper and deeper in debt with every passing month, there seemed no hope, for poor Florida seemed doomed. Individually, her citizens were growing needy; there seemed to be nothing her people could attempt, which was not absolutely ruined by the trail of this Black Republican Serpent. We grew desperate, and do you wonder?

At the polls on election day, United States troops were stationed, no fair election could be held, so how could we get out of this loathsome trap, into which our enemies had forced us? "Fight the Devil with fire," did you ever see it done? In eighteen hundred and seventy-six the people of Florida, led by our own Bloxham, put forward, as nominee for the Democratic Party, George F. Drew, a Northerner by birth but a Floridian by adoption, a man of considerable wealth, of spotless character and of business ability. With George F. Drew for governor and William D. Bloxham as lieutenant-governor, the Ship of State might succeed in weathering the storm.

As usual in every campaign, Bloxham toured the state; his matchless eloquence drew crowds of listeners, even his political opponents seemed unable to stay away. In all parts of the State, able men worked for the Democratic candidates and if we could have a fair election we were sure of success.

While this was going on in Florida, the great, big Nation was in the throes of a red-hot presidential campaign; Samuel J. Tilden against Rutherford B. Hayes. It was a crucial point in the history of the Republican Party. Everything, with them, depended on holding on to the reins of government. Fraud and corruption stalked in hideous nakedness throughout the length and breadth of the land. We had borne the burden of Reconstruction for ten long years, we were sick at heart and weary. All that human effort could do had been done and now, with bated breath, we waited the action of the "Returning Board."

There were mysterious whispers in the air, men gathered in knots on the city streets, they stood in earnest talk beneath shady trees on the roadside. Two strangers had come to town and, strange to say, though they came from Washington, their business was with our own men and not the Carpetbaggers. What it all meant we did not know but have a little patience and soon it will leak out.

More strangers came, a room was rented, a number of our representative citizens were called into consultation, a few preliminaries were settled and lo and behold a convention was in session, in the little city of Tallahassee, to decide some questions of great importance.

Day after day they sat in secret session, then one morning there was a crowd at the depot in Tallahassee. There was much of jollity and merriment, some of the Republican lights were there, notably the two Chandlers, Zack and Bill. Never friends, they were now on the same errand. Mrs. Bill Chandler accompanied her husband and being fond of a joke she had chalked on her valise, such as every man carried on his travels, in those days, "William Chandler—No Relation to Zach." This might have been a good joke but for the fact that the despised "Zach" had, in some manner, gotten hold of the inscription and he, too, was walking around with *his* valise, conspicuously placed, placarded thus, "Zach Chandler—No Kin to Bill."

These two travelers had to meet many jokes and jibes from their companions and the train moved off with much laughter and cheers from the by-standers at the station.

A tense excitement pervaded the air and we were on the *qui vive* for that which might happen next. Soon it developed that this Returning Board had carefully canvassed the vote of Florida and it was officially announced that the entire Democratic ticket had been elected but the state had gone overwhelmingly for the Republican presidential candidate, Rutherford B. Hayes.

The rejoicing was great when we knew, for a certainty, that our ticket was really elected but there was "a crumple in the rose-leaf." The Carpetbaggers had control of the government of Florida. It was rumored that they did not intend to let Drew take his seat in the gubernatorial chair.

The day of the inauguration drew near. If there had been excitement before it was doubled and trebled now. Men, with grim determination in their faces, cleaned their guns and loaded up; pistols were looked over and fired to make sure they were ready for duty. Florida women had the heart-ache that day, for they had learned to dread all things in politics. For years their men had carried the ballot boxes to the Court House at the peril of their lives and sometimes horses hoofs had to be padded to insure against a footfall betraying the carrier of the ballot box, while negroes with guns waited by the road-side for their coming, prepared to have the box at all hazards. This work of the following day was a daytime affair, in the open town, in the Capitol Square the gathering of whites and negroes would take place.

On the inaugural morning, the sun rose angry and red; a murky, yellow cloud obscured its light somewhat, the air was still, like a calm before a storm. Governor Stearns and his satellites held the fort in the Capitol; by eight o'clock the negroes began to collect in the Capitol grounds and by nine o'clock the streets were full of them. By ten o'clock they were beginning to get a little impatient, still not a white man appeared. The town clock tolled out eleven and, as though summoned by the call of the old clock, there appeared, almost simultaneously, from four different directions, large bodies of white men armed to the teeth. A look into their faces, as they rode into town, was sufficient to tell they were in dead earnest. Slowly they came and silently, as though no words were needed and, as they filed into the town and surrounded the capitol square, the negroes trembled and began to scatter. Wherever they could find a hiding place they lost no time in occupying it and there was a very noticeable decrease in the black hordes, which had paraded the streets so noisily a short time before.

Drew and Bloxham, accompanied by a few others, walked slowly up the steps of the eastern portico and took their stand. There were some angry words inside the capitol; the big doors, which had been closed, opened, disclosing Stearns and Conover with others of their ilk.

The white men had filled capitol square by this time and nearly every black face had disappeared; just how many were inside the capitol building none knew. Suddenly the air was rent with cheers and yells, coming from the direction of the depot. Louder and louder they grew, nearer and nearer they came. Some of these new-comers wearing red shirts, some waved red flags. Yelling like demons, they rushed into the square car-load after car-load of men, eager to help with the inauguration. Armed men they were, no idle threats and the Carpetbaggers and negroes recognized this fact and the inauguration proceeded quietly.

Not a sound was heard except from the solemn group on the east portico. There was not standing room in capitol square and the streets were full; the silence was intense. When all was over and these men, who for ten years had been working for this end, realized that they had succeeded, that once again they had Home Rule—the famous "Rebel Yell" went up like incense to Heaven.

Just how thankful they were none may know, but though the words were unspoken, or rather unsung, in every heart echoed that grand old "doxology:"

"Praise God from whom all blessings flow,
Praise Him all creatures here below,
Praise Him above, ye Heavenly host,
Praise Father, Son and Holy Ghost."

Our story is ended. We have carried you with us through twenty-six years of more than usual interest. We have sought to give you an insight into the domestic, the social and the political life of the South during that period. To do this we have had recourse to several sources. Carefully culling from "The Diary" such leaves as seemed to us to throw light on the subject, we have supplemented these with a more extended review of some things; it may be we have left out some domestic happenings, which might have proved interesting to the public, but we did not wish to be tiresome.

We have recorded the actual facts, the characters are genuine, even the names are real. We have shown you the Southland both in PEACE and in WAR. We have pictured for you the heart-break of her conquered people, you have gone with us through the years of "Reconstruction" and we have let you see the "bright star of hope," which rose for us, when, in return for Florida's Presidential vote she was given "Home Rule."

We leave you here. Some day another pen than ours will finish the tale. You will hear of the deep content which settled over our land after the inauguration of Governor Drew; you will be told of the terrible awakening to the fact that the "Carpetbag Administration" had plunged Florida into a quagmire of debt, which threatened to engulf us all; of the heavy taxation, made necessary by this debt and the dire poverty it entailed upon our people.

This new pen can tell of the Herculean strength, the Socratic wisdom, with which the fierce political battles were fought. You will come to know the native Floridian, who came to the front and, by his wise management, paid off this mountain-load of indebtedness and how, when this incubus was removed, the State forged straight ahead and, best of all, you will hear that in this year of our Lord Nineteen Hundred and Twenty-six, there is in all God's World no fairer land than Florida, OUR FLORIDA.

www.ingramcontent.com/pod-product-compliance
Lightning Source LLC
LaVergne TN
LVHW010130110826
845151LV00002B/315

* 9 7 8 1 4 2 5 5 4 0 3 2 6 *